W9-BBE-029

CELEBRATION: THE METROPOLITAN OPERA

CELEBRATION: THE METROPOLITAN OPERA

FRANCIS ROBINSON

Picture Editor: Gerald Fitzgerald

Doubleday & Company, Inc., Garden City, New York

Metropolitan Opera Association / Metropolitan Opera Guild

Partial Picture Credits

COLOR

© Beth Bergman 1979: *Tannhäuser* top left; *The Bartered Bride*
© Donald A. Mackay 1979: cross-section drawing of backstage area of Opera House

BLACK AND WHITE

© Beth Bergman 1979: 40 bottom, 64 right, 65, 72 bottom, 73–75, 77 top, 78–79 far left, far right and bottom, 80 bottom, 83–85, 86 bottom, 87 top, 88–89, 92–93, 94–95 center top and bottom, 97, 99, 172, 176–77, 256–57, 263 top
© Erika Davidson 1979: 59 top, 67, 81, 90, 94 top and bottom left, 95 top and bottom right, 96, 168 top, 170 top left, 171 bottom right, 173, 182 bottom, 211 top, 215 top right, 244–45, 247 top
© Lincoln Center for the Performing Arts, Inc.: 20 top, 21 top, 218
© Jack Mitchell 1979: 126 top
© Arnold Newman 1979: 18–19
© Susanne Faulkner Stevens 1979: 21 top and center, 32, 264, 268

For complete list see back of book, page 273.

The quotation from *La Perichole* © 1956, 1957 by Boosey & Hawkes, Inc. Reprinted by permission.

The quotation from *Tribute to the Ballet* by permission of The Society of Authors as the literary representative of the estate of John Masefield.
The quotations from Leonard Bernstein's *The Joy of Music* by kind permission of the author.

Design and layout by LAURENCE ALEXANDER
in collaboration with Gerald Fitzgerald
Captions by Gerald Fitzgerald
Project Co-ordinator: Leslie Carola, Publications Manager, Metropolitan Opera Guild

Library of Congress Cataloging in Publication
Robinson, Francis, 1910–
Celebration: the Metropolitan Opera.
Includes index.
1. New York. Metropolitan Opera. I. Title
ML1711.8.N3M593 782.1'09747'1
ISBN: 0-385-12975-0
Library of Congress Catalog Card Number 78-69666

PRINTED IN THE UNITED STATES OF AMERICA
FIRST EDITION

Again to Mae

CONTENTS

FOREWORD 9

THE HOUSE—OLD AND NEW 12

THOSE WHO RAN AND RUN IT 40

THE PRODUCT 60

CONDUCTORS 100

SINGERS 128

DIRECTORS AND DESIGNERS 144

ORCHESTRA, CHORUS, BALLET 174

THE UNSEEN ARMY 194

TOUR 226

ECONOMICS 244

AUDIENCE AND FUTURE 264

GENERAL MANAGERS 273

THE REPERTORY 274

PICTURE CREDITS 279

INDEX 280

FOREWORD

By Anthony A. Bliss
Executive Director of the Metropolitan Opera Association

Celebration! What single word could better describe the Metropolitan Opera, for we are ever celebrating—debuts, farewells, openings, closings, and anniversaries. Each night the very raising of the curtain is cause for celebration as artists and audiences experience the wonder of a new and unique performance.

This book celebrates ninety-five years of celebrations at the Metropolitan Opera, from our first opening night in 1883 to the welcoming of new artists and new productions this year. It is a tribute to the loving labor of generations of company members, a record of their achievements, and a testimony to the power of opera.

I have been associated with the Metropolitan for more than half its history, for as a child I first attended opera at the age of six. I learned about opera listening to Edward Johnson, Eleanor Belmont, and Lucrezia Bori discuss the Metropolitan Opera with my father during my most impressionable years. Like my late father, I served as both board member and president of the Metropolitan Opera for a number of years. This experience, my years as executive director, and countless evenings among the audience have allowed me to witness from various perspectives the fascinating spectacle of an institution in continual regeneration. No two seasons, not even any two performances, are ever alike. The Met, our lady of the chameleons, changes because she is the creation of artists and, by nature, they are individuals who cannot remain the same. Artists are the strivers of society. It is their aspirations more than their actual performances that give meaning to art.

Even in this environment of change, I find two qualities that permeate the Metropolitan and its history. The first is grandness of scale. To begin with, our art form is bigger than life in the sweep of emotions. We add to this the largest company of performers and the largest opera house in the world. Finally, we play upon a stage of immense size—the entire North American continent. Just weeks after our first New York opening, the company set out on a tour of the United States, a tradition that continues to the present. And we will soon complete our fifth decade of live radio broadcasts, which, like our more recent telecasts, bring the Metropolitan to audiences measured in the tens of millions of people each year.

The other consistent quality is an intent of greatness. Shakespeare wrote: "Be not afraid of greatness: Some are born great, some achieve greatness, and some have greatness thrust upon them." All three seem applicable to the Metropolitan. The institution was born in full bloom as one of the few major international opera companies, for that had been the intention of its founders. The Metropolitan achieved greatness by continuing to attract, in each era, the leading artists of the world. Finally, greatness was thrust upon us, or perhaps drawn from us, by our audiences, who have never demanded less than the best. We sometimes live up to those expectations, on occasion we fall short, but for almost a century the aim has been the top.

The author of this book embodies the noblest traditions and values of the Metropolitan Opera. I have known, admired, and respected Francis Robinson through the more than thirty years he has served the company. There is no more avid proselytizer for the art, nor can anyone exceed his encyclopedic knowledge of opera. He alone could have written this work, for his life itself has been a celebration of the Metropolitan Opera.

CELEBRATION: THE METROPOLITAN OPERA

THE HOUSE—
OLD AND NEW

At the heart of the cities stand the great opera houses," Franz Werfel says in his preface to Verdi's letters, about the best short history of opera ever written. "This is true not only of Milan and Naples but equally, and more significantly, of Paris and Vienna. The Metropolitan Opera," which then was at Broadway and Thirty-ninth Street, "is not exactly the geographical center of Manhattan; still, every New York child knows the glamour that has always surrounded it."

Werfel's history was more reliable than his geography. Times Square is almost square in the middle of Manhattan, but it emphatically is no longer the heart of the city, and it would be a shoddy historian indeed who didn't take note that New York, unlike its Old World sisters, has a way of shifting. It must be more than accident that for a century and a half, opera has seemed to have something to do with it.

The first home of opera in New York was the Park Theatre, which stood on Park Row, the east boundary of City Hall Park. Next came the Academy of Music at Fourteenth Street and Irving Place, where the Con Edison Building now stands. Mrs. Wharton's Gramercy Park is six blocks north. There were only nine boxes in the Academy, and they were held on to from season to season by descendants of the first families.

New York opera-lovers past and present: the audience of December 1872 watching a gala performance of Gounod's Faust *in the ornate auditorium of the historic Academy of Music at Fourteenth Street and Irving Place (below) and the public of today (right) enjoying a festive intermission at the new Metropolitan Opera House at Lincoln Center for the Performing Arts. The Academy, which opened in 1854 with Bellini's* Norma, *starring Giulia Grisi and Giovanni Mario, stood as the undisputed temple to the lyric muse for three decades. Its supremacy was only challenged in 1883 with the construction of the first Metropolitan Opera House. Though both of these old theaters are now demolished, since 1966 the Metropolitan has flourished in new surroundings, where opera of the highest quality continues and where patrons may pass an entr'acte on various tiers, a balcony overlooking Lincoln Center Plaza or the grand staircase which is illuminated by glittering chandeliers*

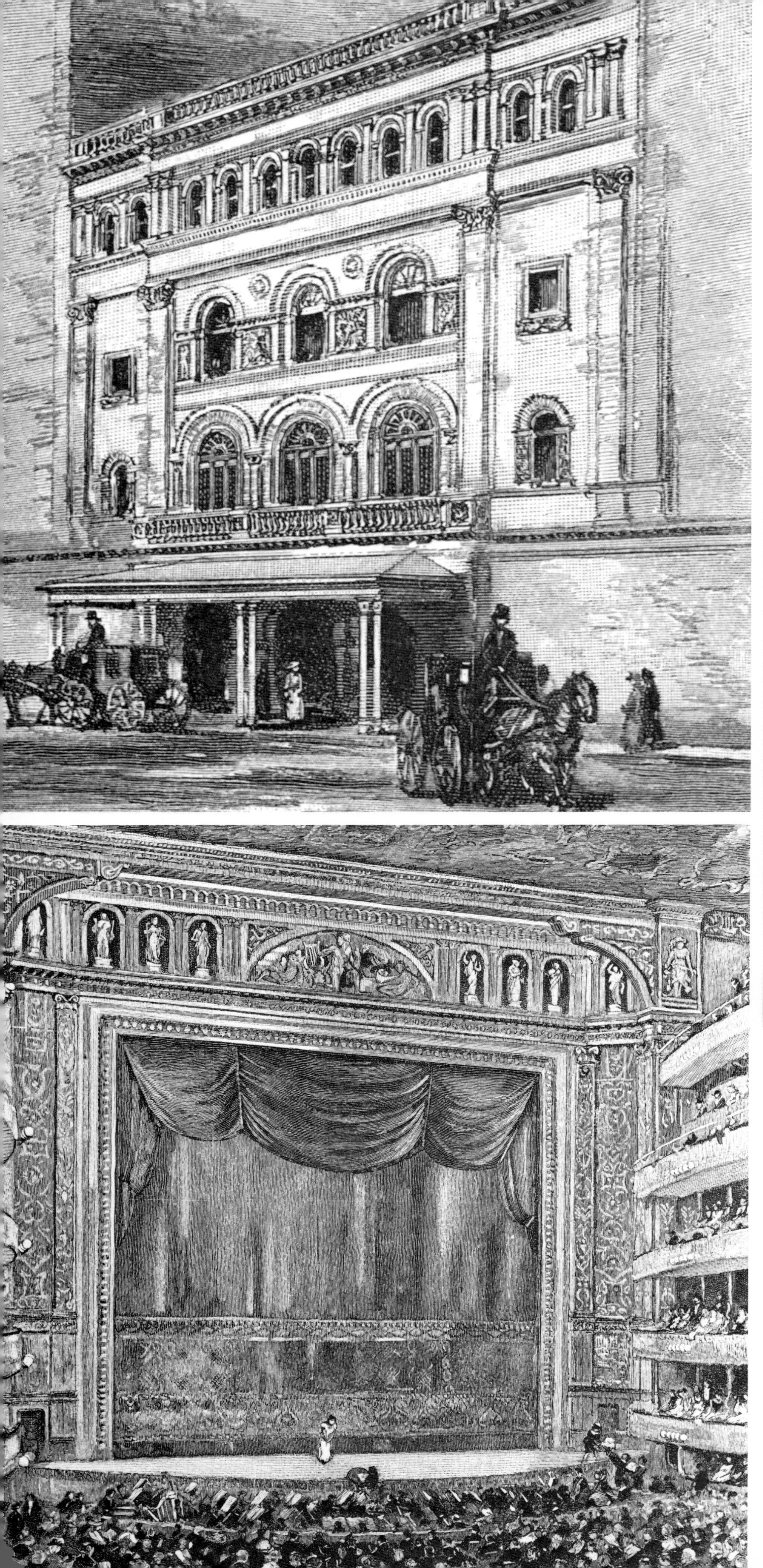

CLEMONS
CLEMONS BUILDING

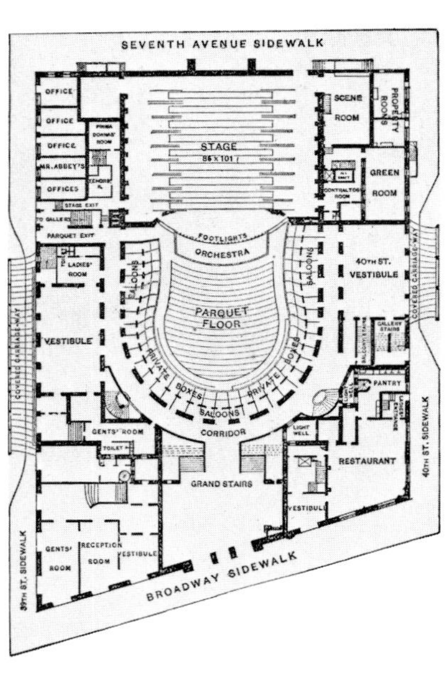

SEVENTH AVENUE SIDEWALK
OFFICE
OFFICE
OFFICE
MR. ABBEY'S
OFFICES
STAGE
SCENE ROOM
PROPERTY ROOMS
GREEN ROOM
STAGE EXIT
PARQUET EXIT
LADIES' ROOM
FOOTLIGHTS
ORCHESTRA
SALOONS
SALOONS
40TH ST. VESTIBULE
PARQUET FLOOR
VESTIBULE
PRIVATE BOXES
PRIVATE BOXES
GALLERY STAIRS
PANTRY
SALOONS
CORRIDOR
GENTS' ROOM
LIGHT WELL
LIGHT WELL
TOILET
RESTAURANT
GRAND STAIRS
VESTIBULE
GENTS' ROOM
RECEPTION ROOM
VESTIBULE
BROADWAY SIDEWALK
39TH ST. SIDEWALK
40TH ST. SIDEWALK
COVERED CARRIAGE-WAY
COVERED CARRIAGE-WAY

The old Metropolitan Opera House at Broadway and Thirty-ninth Street: an 1883 engraving of the front entrance, where carriages deposited patrons (top left), and another of the auditorium, which originally had a subdued elegance, with Apollo and the Muses gracing the proscenium (far left). The theater was referred to as the "yellow brick brewery" because of the pedestrian quality of its architecture, shown here in a photograph dated 1912 (above)

If the new millionaires of railroads and banking and real estate were vexed when they could not get box room at the opera, the resentment of their wives must have amounted to something like fury. True to form, these redoubtable go-getters banded together and built their own opera house, way uptown at Broadway and Thirty-ninth. That house had 122 boxes! Before we left, these had shrunk to thirty-five. On the parterre the present house has twenty-nine.

Opera began toward the end of the sixteenth century as a strictly court function. By 1650 the city of Venice had eleven opera houses. In a span of fifty years opera had begun coming to the people. It has been coming ever since.

"The yellow brick brewery," as the first Metropolitan Opera House was quickly dubbed, was not a theater in the terms of 1883, when it was built. Paris, Vienna, Bayreuth, La Scala all antedate the Metropolitan, the latter by more than a hundred years. All of them had adequate stages. The old Metropolitan Opera House did not.

Sightlines in the auditorium of the old Metropolitan Opera House (right) were far from ideal, with some 700 of the theater's 3,778 seats marked obstructed or side view. Many ticket holders in the upper tiers found themselves seated behind poles, having to crane their necks to see the action onstage. Others, positioned high on the sides, discovered decidedly peculiar angles in their opera glasses (top left). In addition, because of the lack of storage space backstage, scenery for each performance had to be carted from a warehouse (left) and then back again—physically ruinous to the quality of the sets, financially ruinous to the company's budget. Still, despite all its obvious flaws, the public venerated the old Opera House, which cast a spell on everyone who entered it. The Metropolitan's decision to leave it for a new home and, ultimately, to the wreckers' ball brought howls of protests from traditionalists, but time moves on

There was room on the stage for one production and one only—whatever you were performing or rehearsing. If there was a rehearsal or a matinee, the evening's scenery sat out on Seventh Avenue, whatever the weather, with only a thin tarpaulin between it and the elements, be they rain, sleet, snow, or scorching sun. Lumber can't take this, let alone canvas and gauze. After the matinee or rehearsal the scenery and properties for that production would be loaded and carted off to the warehouse. The transfer bill climbed to more than a quarter of a million dollars a year, not to mention the wear and tear on scenery once beautiful and new. This madness went on for eighty-three years.

Before the house had reached its quarter-century mark, it was obvious something had to be done. In fact the first thing to grab Giulio Gatti-Casazza

LINCOLN CEN
FOR THE PERFORMING
CHICAGO P UMATIC
DELMA
GR. CORP.

SOFIA
BROTHERS
FIREPROOF
STORAGE
WAREHOUSE

At the construction site of Lincoln Center for the Performing Arts at Broadway and Sixty-fifth Street, a sign displayed the architect's vision of the entire complex (top left), with the new Metropolitan Opera House in center position with a tall office tower at its rear, a design later discarded. The first building under construction was a new home for the New York Philharmonic (bottom left), which in 1962 abandoned Carnegie Hall for its own Philharmonic Hall, later renamed Avery Fisher Hall in honor of its generous benefactor. In 1963 the celebrated Yugoslavian diva Zinka Milanov, assisted by Thaddeus Crapster, Ray C. Daly and the Metropolitan's Anthony A. Bliss (above), installed a golden bolt into a column of the Opera House to signal the start of steel work there, a major step in its progress. By the fall of 1964, the project was so far along that the theater's auditorium could be discerned from the stage area (below), an awesome sight

when he arrived in 1908 to become general manager was that there was no rehearsal room, no storage space. Otto H. Kahn, the investment banker, who was chairman of the board, seeing Mr. Gatti's long face and sunken heart, said to him, "We have noticed these things before you. But don't worry about it, and have patience. In two or three years a new Metropolitan Opera House will be built, answering all needs." It took fifty-eight years, four months, one week, and five days for this to come to pass.

In that time there were ten new Metropolitan Opera Houses that never got off the architects' drawing boards—Washington Square, 110th Street, Columbus Circle, the East Side site of the United Nations. The RCA Building in Rockefeller Center originally was to have housed the new theater, but the Metropolitan, all but wiped out by the Great Depression, couldn't go along.

Lincoln Center grew out of the need of the Metropolitan Opera and the New York Philharmonic to have new homes. Charles M. Spofford, a brilliant young lawyer, a member and later president of the board of the Metropolitan, had gone to Mayor La Guardia to talk about the need for a new opera house. The Little Flower thought it ought to be an arts center, also taking in the Philharmonic. The idea was a good twenty years old when President Eisenhower turned the first spade of earth at the ground-breaking ceremonies of Lincoln Center on May 14, 1959.

Anthony A. Bliss, now executive director of the Metropolitan, had suggested Spofford take the idea to John D. Rockefeller 3rd, and it was Mr. Rockefeller who saw the grandiose plan through. Without his leadership and generosity, Lincoln Center would never have come into being. It is unique in the history of the world. Bounded on the east by Columbus (Ninth) Avenue, on the west by Amsterdam (Tenth) Avenue, on the south by Sixty-second Street, and on the north by Sixty-fifth Street, with Fordham University and its Law School spilling over below and the Juilliard School with Alice Tully Hall accessible by an overpass above Sixty-fifth Street, it covers fifteen acres. Other structures of Lincoln Center are Avery Fisher Hall, home of the New York Philharmonic, and the New York State Theater, which houses the New York City Opera and the New York City Ballet, the Vivian Beaumont Theater for drama, and the Library and Museum of the Performing Arts, which shelters the fabulous drama, music, and dance collections of New York Public Library.

If you saw the movie *West Side Story*, the area which the plane zeroes in on at the beginning of the picture was what is now Lincoln Center. It wasn't just going; it was gone. Already it was a slum. The land was procured under the Federal Housing Act for Slum Clearance, Title 1 of which allows a city to condemn slum property and resell it at a loss to private developers. The federal government covers two-thirds of the loss, the city one-third.

The Metropolitan at least had a roof over its head and owned its own quarters, inadequate though they were. The Philharmonic situation was different. Carnegie Hall had been condemned and was moving people out. Subsequently it was saved, but in the late 1950s the Philharmonic was looking at deserted movie houses, prize-fight arenas, anywhere to give its concerts. Philharmonic Hall, now Avery Fisher Hall, was pushed through first, opening in September 1962 in the presence of Mrs. Kennedy. The so-called "Cultural Explosion" was in full blast, and with the Kennedys in the White House it was going to be a new era for the arts.

With West Side tenements as backdrop, representatives from the various performing arts to be housed at Lincoln Center surround one of the early models for the complex. Shown clockwise, from lower left, are the priestess of modern dance, Martha Graham; the celebrated British ballerina Alicia Markova, as Giselle; the distinguished American composer William Schuman, then president of the Juilliard School; one of that institution's young students, Dorothy Pixley; Lucine Amara, soprano of the Metropolitan Opera, costumed as Donna Elvira in Don Giovanni; *Rudolf Bing, the company's general manager; Reginald Allen, at the time Executive Director of Lincoln Center, later to return to the Metropolitan Opera as special assistant to the president and general manager; the late George Judd, manager of the New York Philharmonic; the orchestra's music director, now its conductor laureate,*

Leonard Bernstein; Julie Harris, the actress; and another advocate of the theater, Robert Whitehead, head of the Repertory Company to be housed at the Vivian Beaumont Theater. In addition to Miss Amara, Mr. Allen and Mr. Bing, three of this group were to be personally associated with the new Metropolitan Opera House. Miss Graham's dance company gave its first season at the theater during the summer of 1978; Dame Alicia acted for several seasons as director of ballet for the Metropolitan's resident ballet; and Maestro Bernstein conducted new productions of Mascagni's Cavalleria Rusticana *and Bizet's* Carmen *for the company, while his* Mass *was staged there in the spring of 1972 as a guest attraction not long after its world premiere in Washington, D.C., at Kennedy Center*

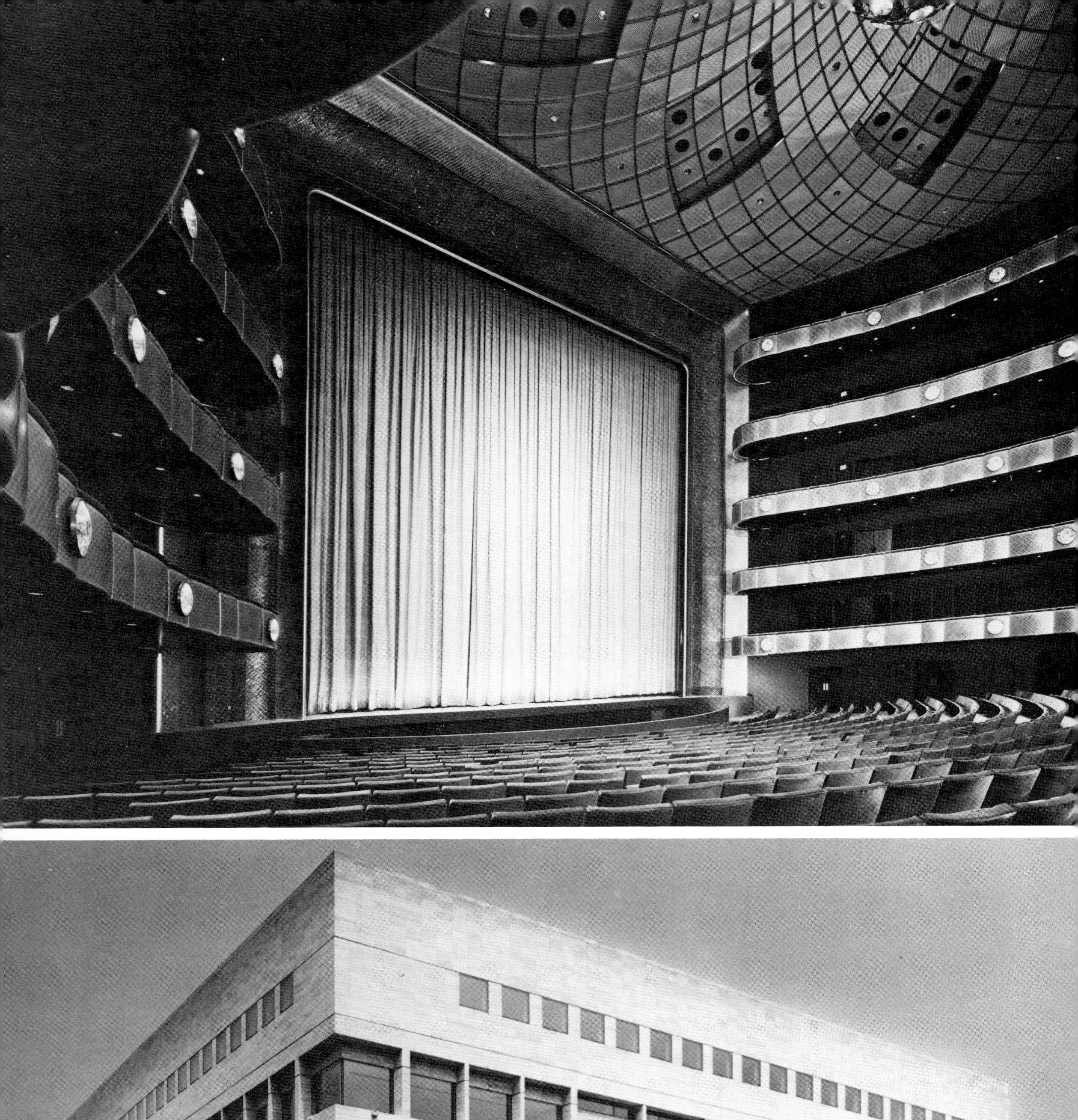

Distinguished neighbors: the New York State Theater (top left), home of the New York City Opera and the New York City Ballet. It is the creation of architect Philip Johnson, who said, "I designed it for George," meaning George Balanchine, choreographer and resident genius of City Ballet. The horseshoe-shaped auditorium, which seats 2,737, has five tiers, with continental seating—no aisles—in the Orchestra section. Architect Pietro Belluschi went through sixty-five sets of plans for the Juilliard School (bottom left). The structure, in addition to classrooms, houses four performing arts auditoriums–the handsome Juilliard Theater, accommodating 933; the Paul Recital Hall with 278 seats; a semicircular Drama Theater with a 206 capacity; and 1,096-seat Alice Tully Hall, designed by Heinrich Keilholz and home of the Chamber Music Society of Lincoln Center

Avery Fisher Hall auditorium (top right), where the New York Philharmonic resides, has undergone numerous changes since it opened in 1962. The building's height of nine stories matches that of the facing New York State Theater across the Plaza. The original architect for the 2,742-seat concert hall was Max Abramovitz, whose interior design and decor have been significantly altered over the years, most recently by Cyril Harris, to perfect its acoustical properties. The 1,089-seat Vivian Beaumont Theater's facilities (center right) were worked out by architect Eero Saarinen in collaboration with veteran set and costume designer Jo Mielziner; after Saarinen's death, John Dinkaloo supervised the final construction, which has a lobby of sparkling glass walls that looks out onto a separate plaza, with a Henry Moore sculpture, Reclining Figure, *in a reflecting pool, a vista also seen from the north lobby of the Metropolitan Opera House. The Mini-Met played at the 299-seat Forum Theater—now called the Mitzi D. Newhouse Theater—downstairs at the Beaumont. Damrosch Park (bottom right) is a 2.3-acre site directly south of the Metropolitan, with a band shell named in honor of Daniel and Florence Guggenheim. Here, on a balmy summer night, as many as 4,500 music-lovers can gather on benches to enjoy an outdoor concert*

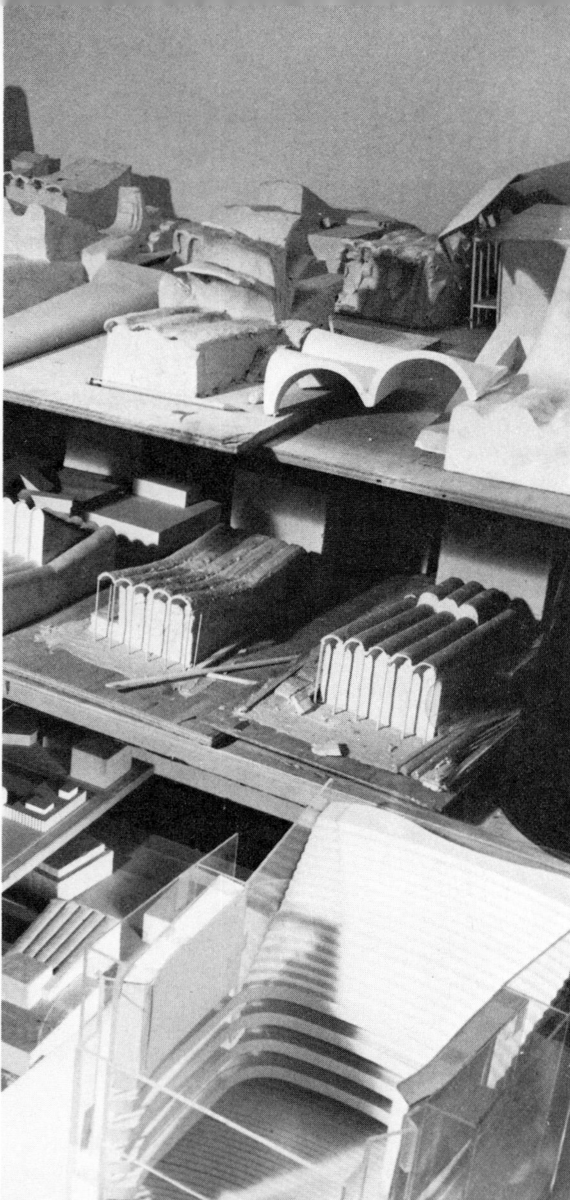

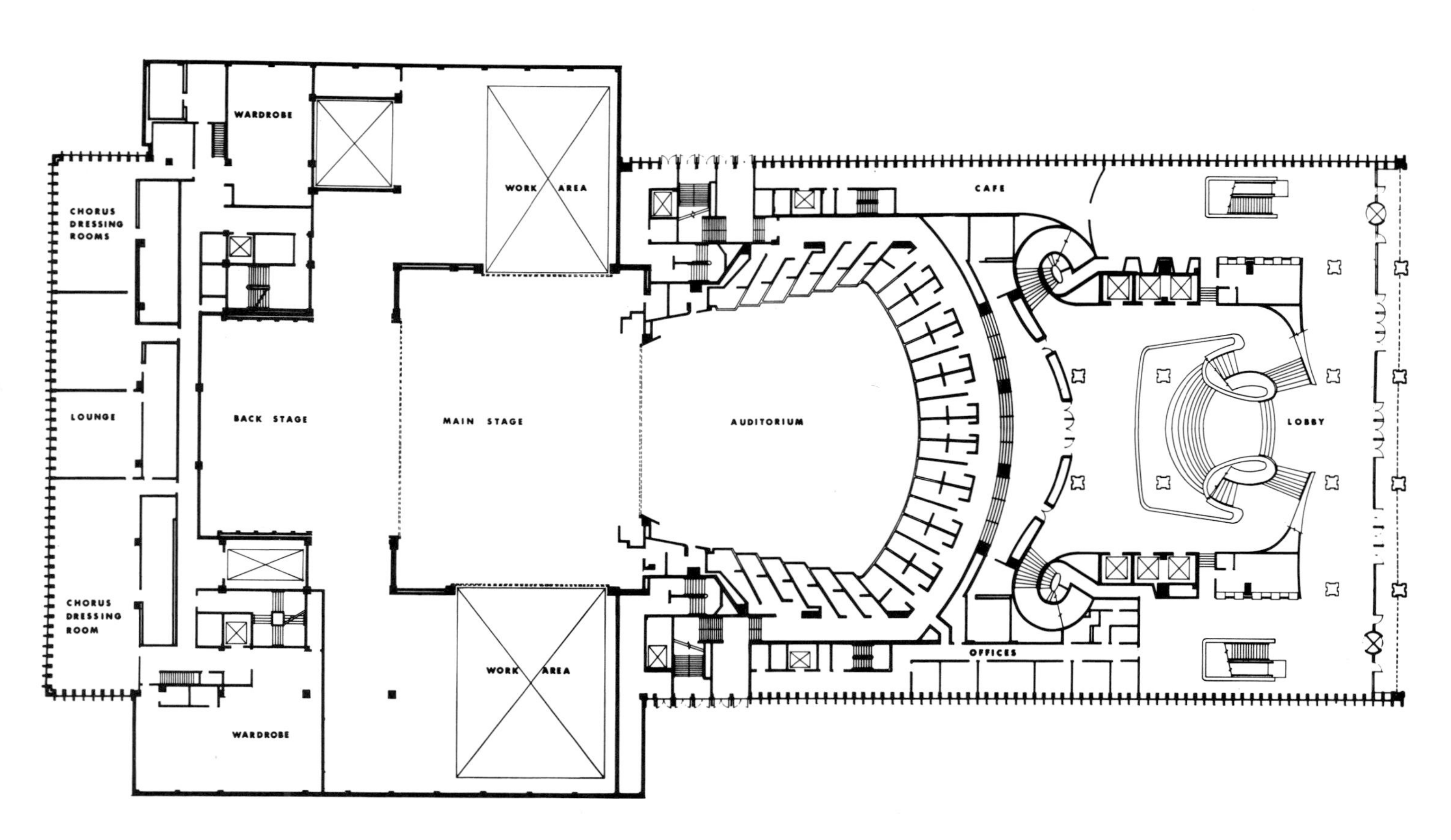
WARDROBE
WORK AREA
CAFE
CHORUS DRESSING ROOMS
LOUNGE
BACK STAGE
MAIN STAGE
AUDITORIUM
LOBBY
CHORUS DRESSING ROOM
OFFICES
WORK AREA
WARDROBE
SCALE IN FEET
0 5 10 20 30 50

The chief architect for the new Metropolitan Opera House was Wallace Kirkman Harrison (top left), who was born in Worcester, Massachusetts, in September of 1895, almost seventy-one years to the day before the theater was inaugurated. For the designer to arrive at his final version of the Metropolitan, Harrison built many alternate models (top center) and drew up countless floor plans, only to discard them and start again from scratch. The floor plan shown (bottom left) is Harrison's final version. During early 1964, with the construction of the theater nearing completion, a topping-out ceremony, which marked the completion of the roof, was attended by a trio of most interested parties—Rudolf Bing, who eschewed a construction worker's hard hat in favor of his trademark bowler, Leontyne Price and Robert Merrill (above), who were to continue as major luminaries of the Metropolitan. Harrison once wrote, "Just as Bach had to get out a new composition every week, or Mozart had to turn over new works while practically on his deathbed—the architect has to get the details out, though, at times, it seems impossible. If you want to know my idea of what an opera house built in New York for the Metropolitan Opera should look like, go and look!"

The New York State Theater came next, April 1964. The Metropolitan Opera threw open its doors to the public for the first time on September 16, 1966. It had been five years in the building at a cost of nearly $50 million. It was something of a statistic that there had been more than 700 drawings before construction started on the former opera house. For the present house there were 7,000.

As architect of Rockefeller Center, Wallace K. Harrison would have been builder of the Metropolitan Opera House thirty-five years earlier had the plan to put it there gone through. There was to be a plaza to the north, through to Fifty-third Street, where the hall for the Philharmonic would have been. He frankly confesses he got his later inspiration from St. Mark's in Venice—the square, the colonnades of the New York State Theater on the left, Avery Fisher Hall on the right, between them the five arches of the Metropolitan Opera House. Looking at them head on, you think they are taller than St. Mark's. Actually they are not. Ninety-six feet is still quite a reach, but St. Mark's is a hundred. Perhaps the famous bronze horses and other decorative details hold St. Mark's down optically.

The travertine—42,000 cubic feet of it—is from the same quarry at Bagni di Tivoli that provided the marble for the Colosseum in Rome, much of which later found its way to St. Peter's Basilica. In the pavement of the plaza the travertine has a peculiar property. At night it appears translucent, as though it were lighted from underneath, like those ground-glass dance floors on the *Île de France* and other old luxury ocean liners. Very glamorous.

Come up to Lincoln Center on a Saturday night in summer. See the people who may never want so much as a look inside any of the theaters strolling up there, drinking in the beauty—and space—of the place. Is it any wonder we are New York's No. 3 tourist attraction?

In the bronze frames of the façade are 156 glass panels, some rising to a height of eighteen feet. Before these were installed, a section was taken to an air hangar at the University of Miami and tests made under wind pressure for leakage and air-pressure variations. Opera houses are built to last.

The structure has been likened to a forty-five-story skyscraper on its side. It measures 451 feet in length, 175 feet in width at the façade and 234 at the rear. At the front it is seven stories high, six above ground level and one below, at the back thirteen. Below the stage level we go three floors right into the solid rock of Manhattan.

The effect of the main lobby is difficult to describe, the impression of it impossible to convey even with photographs. The sweep of the twin curves of the grand staircase is inviting and awe-inspiring at the same time. Few women can contemplate that staircase without seeing themselves descending in a long gown. The carpet is a rich but live red—what other color for an opera house? The ceilings are gold leaf. The beauty of the chandeliers hits you in the throat as well as the eye. These are the gift of the Austrian government—more of them inside, thirty-two in all—and their inspiration is no less than the sunburst. Some of the crystals are no bigger than marbles, and many of the rods slender as a pencil. The time to see them is just before a December matinee when the sun is almost due south. The sun has colors no light bulb ever dreamed of, and the prisms catch a red and blue and green and gold of a purity and intensity you may never have seen before.

These magic chandeliers were given in gratitude for our having rebuilt the Vienna State Opera with Marshall Plan money. Eyewitnesses tell of the Viennese standing in the Ringstrasse and weeping at the sight of their opera house bombed and burning. These chandeliers, then, are more than light.

In marble niches fifty-four feet high on either side of the grand staircase stand two sturdy bronze masterpieces by Aristide Maillol, *Venus with Arms* and *Summer.* In the center at the top of the grand staircase is Lehmbruck's lovely *Kneeling Woman*, a gift of the government of West Germany to commemorate the $2.5 million it gave specifically for stage equipment. So many visitors have caressed the left hand of the nameless lady its dark bronze color has given way to gold, "It's like loving a baby before it is born,"

The Metropolitan Opera House as it appears in the summer twilight, with some music lovers gathered in the plaza near Avery Fisher Hall at the outdoor café (above) while others cool themselves around the illuminated central fountain (right), which shoots up at intervals, a spectacle as thrilling as it is lovely. When a visitor stands by the fountain facing the Opera House, he has the New York State Theater to his left and Avery Fisher Hall to his right. At night the Metropolitan glows with warmth and light, its crystal chandeliers ablaze and the murals by Marc Chagall a festival of color. Inside the theater one can admire many works of art, at the top of the grand staircase a limpid Lehmbruck sculpture, his famous Kneeling Woman *(below). The grandeur and sweep of the staircase (next two pages) lead one to the Grand Tier level of the Opera House and a work by Aristide Maillol called* Summer

Marc Chagall, the celebrated Russian painter, the day he mounted the serpentine bar on the Grand Tier of the Opera House to pose under one of the murals he created for the Metropolitan, The Triumph of Music *(left). While in this precarious position, he autographed the wall under his masterpiece. Beneath Chagall's other mural,* The Sources of Music *(above), opera-goers dine at the Grand Tier Restaurant or take intermission refreshments. This mural, cool in yellows, blues and greens, inspired a poster (below). An earlier poster in red, drawn from* The Triumph of Music, *celebrated the inauguration of the Opera House. Both have become collector's items*

Mrs. August Belmont said while the new Metropolitan Opera House was still an unknown quantity. That polished bronze hand would seem to indicate Mrs. Belmont's dream came true.

Marc Chagall's colossal paintings, thirty by thirty-six feet, on either side of the Grand Tier, are best seen from the plaza but are also glorious from the street or close up. The north side represents *The Sources of Music.* The giant central double-headed figure holding a single lyre is King David and Orpheus, symbolizing the union of Eastern and Western music. Never above playing favorites, Chagall gives his own preferences the biggest splash in *The Sources of Music*—the prisoners in *Fidelio*, the animals in *Die Zauberflöte* (Mozart is shown as an angel), but he also includes Tristan and Isolde and a homage to Verdi. In *The Triumph of Music* he pays his compliments to himself and his wife under a marvelous tree, to his friend Rudolf Bing, who thought of Chagall long before the Paris Opera got the idea to have him do its dome, to American music, and to Russian music, specifically *The Firebird.*

As characteristic as his own name on a work is Chagall's signature of locale. In the lower-right-hand corner of the south mural is a miniature St. Patrick's Cathedral. In the same position on the north mural is the New York skyline from the East River, complete with UN Building, under a crescent moon. Below that is the Tree of Life (the capitals are Chagall's), and in 1977 there was a documentary on his life and work to celebrate his ninetieth birthday. It was called *The Colors of Love.* That year he became the only living artist ever to be exhibited in the Louvre.

When the murals were unveiled, shortly before the opening of the house, the artist was on hand. Michael Rougier was on a scaffold with his camera for *Life* magazine, facing the south panel, which is above the Grand Tier serpentine bar. "Will you ask Mr. Chagall to get up on the bar as though he is pulling the cord?" he asked. At that time I had been a press agent for nearly thirty years, and before that a newspaper man for five. I still

A folio of the new Metropolitan Opera House: exterior of the theater by winter (left), by spring (right) and on midsummer's night, 1977 (next two pages), as captured atop an elevated platform stationed in the center of Lincoln Center Plaza, a view that shows the Opera House flanked by the New York State Theater and Avery Fisher Hall, with Damrosch Park illuminated to the rear left and the Vivian Beaumont Theater in the shadows to the rear right. Marc Chagall's twin murals (subsequent two pages) were executed under a generous grant of the Henry L. and Grace Doherty Charitable Foundation made to the Metropolitan Opera in memory of Grace Raroin Doherty and Helen Lee Doherty Lassen. The red one, The Triumph of Music, *contains images Chagall referred to as The Song of the People, The Musician, The Singers, The Ballet, Homage to American Music,* The Firebird, *Homage to French Music, To Rudolf Bing, Russian Music, Chagall and His Wife, and New York. The yellow mural is titled* The Sources of Music, *with allusions to Orpheus and King David, Beethoven,* Fidelio, *Bach and Sacred Music,* Romeo and Juliet, *Wagner (*Tristan and Isolde*), The Angel Mozart,* The Magic Flute, *Homage to Verdi, The Tree of Life, and New York*

MET
MET
MET
MET

THE TRIUMPH OF MUSIC Song of the People Musician Singers Ballet Homage to American Music Firebird Homage to French Music Rudolf Bing Russian Music Chagall and His Wife New York

THE SOURCES OF MUSIC   Orpheus and King David   Beethoven   Fidelio   Bach and Sacred Music   Romeo and Juliet   Wagner (Tristan und Isolde)   The Angel Mozart   The Magic Flute   Homage to Verdi   The Tree of Life   New York

had a certain hesitancy about asking a near-octogenarian to climb up on a bar. Chagall went up as though by levitation, did a sort of *Hello, Dolly!* runway act down the bar, pulled the cord, and capped it off by inscribing his name with a great flourish on the wall by the cord. That precious signature is protected today by a pink gelatin against an overzealous painter and the furious sunlight, magnified by the glass.

The times I have entered the auditorium now run into the thousands. On hundreds of those occasions I have thought of Elisabeth's rapturous outburst which opens Act II of *Tannhäuser*, "Dich, teure Halle, grüss' ich wieder, froh grüss' ich dich, geliebter Raum!" Dear hall, I greet you again; joyful I greet you, beloved room!

They tell us St. Peter's in Rome is not as good a building as it should be because it doesn't look as big as it is. By that rule the auditorium of the Metropolitan Opera House is the most successful room of our time. It doesn't look as big as it had to be. An opera house shouldn't be pygmy, but neither should it gobble up the audience. Human scale is all-important, in the theater as in life.

The first thing early visitors would say was, "It isn't as big as the old house." Obviously, it must be, since it seats 166 more people than the old house—3,778. The distance from the apron of the stage to the middle of the center loge is ninety feet, exactly the same as in the old house. The fact that Mr. Harrison could achieve this, add a number of seats, and still maintain some feeling of intimacy is a major triumph.

The garnet and gold auditorium of the Metropolitan Opera House as it looks from the vantage point of the audience when facing the proscenium (top left) and also as it looks from center stage (previous two pages); this last photograph was taken on the opening night of the 1972–73 season with Leonard Bernstein on the podium waiting to conduct the new production of Carmen. *Also shown is the brilliant central chandelier of the auditorium (bottom left) and the man who designed this and all the other starburst chandeliers in the theater, Hans Harald Rath (below) of J. & L. Lobmeyr, Vienna, as a gift of the Republic of Austria. The final view (bottom right) focuses on the façade of a Parterre box that touches the stage's gilded proscenium*

Except for the ivory facings of the boxes, everything else is red and gold. Four thousand rolls of gold leaf—more than a million two-and-a-half-inch, almost transparent squares of the precious stuff—were used here and in the lobby. Like the one in the old house, the curtain is gold damask. The chairs are covered in red velour. Wood, sound's best friend, has been used wherever possible and is exposed on the backs of the chairs. The wall around the orchestra floor and in back of the boxes is Congolese rosewood.

Just as Mr. Harrison made 7,000 drawings, he and his associates made countless trips to Europe, to opera houses new and old. At all times he carried a color postcard of the Cuvilliés Theater in Munich, that little jewel box in the Residenz in Munich, in the pocket of his jacket. He had no mandate from the board except to come up with the best. Think of it—we might have been saddled with one of those antiseptic jobs, about as inviting as a hospital operating room. The unanimous decision was that for sound alone you can't beat the old horseshoe. There is an old song, "You Can't Holler down My Rain Barrel." Maybe not, but you can certainly holler *up* one, which is what Italian sopranos and tenors have been doing for nearly four centuries now.

In the eighteenth and nineteenth centuries, with no steel for balconies across, the horseshoe was the only solution. There was also a social reason—the royal or ducal box in the center, with the other loges swinging from it toward the proscenium. It was decided there is no handsomer decoration than people, people in the boxes and hanging from the upper levels. They are also good for sound.

In the old Met, with its forest of posts in the upper levels, nearly a third of the seats were side or obstructed view. In the present house it is necessary to overprint only 170 tickets per performance as not affording full view.

Finally, there is the mood. With the bulk of our repertory nineteenth century, to put those works on in one of those antiseptic houses such as sprang up in Germany after the war would be like hanging an old master in a chromium frame.

And now that we are in the auditorium, another paean to the chandeliers. They are the work of Lobmeyr of Vienna and were designed by Hans Harald Rath, president of the firm. I found out later Lobmeyr was not only the public but private illuminator to Richard Strauss and Hugo von Hofmannsthal: Rath lighted their houses as well as their productions. All this happened from behind a small, inconspicuous door on the Kärntnerstrasse. How Viennese can you be?

The chandeliers arrived in December. New York had never seen Christmas ornaments like these. They also made you think of a piece of jewelry, magnified thousands of times, that a lady might choose for a dark gown. In fact the chandeliers were done in miniature as brooches for a lucky few.

The main chandelier measures seventeen feet in diameter. The twelve satellite clusters are on a level with the Grand Tier, and many a complaint was heard from arrivals in the early days of the house. Then, as the house lights dimmed just before the performance, the auxiliaries would swiftly glide up to the ceiling. This would touch off a burst of applause during those first months. That would have pleased the heart of Max Reinhardt, who invented the trick when he took over the Josefstadt Theatre in Vienna.

Mr. Rath personally supervised the installation of the last stem and ball. And can you believe what he did above and beyond the call of duty? There is nothing so dirty as a new house—cement, plaster, sawdust, and just dust. Mr. Rath came back and oversaw the cleaning of his fixtures before the house opened. Miles of chamois, oceans of ammonia. Incidentally, the chandeliers are lowered yearly during the summer for a going-over before the new season.

There are three restaurants offering fare as varied as their décor and mood. On the plaza level the Opera Café, all wood and little lights, limits its menu to drinks, sandwiches, and a few hot specialties for those looking for something quick before curtain or at intermission. The Grand Tier, named for its imposing locale, is the deluxe restaurant of the house. Wonders are performed nightly, getting sometimes as many as 400 diners through a full-course meal and into the auditorium on time. The Top of the Met is less formal than the Grand Tier, and it is lighted up by murals as miraculous in their way as Chagall's are in his. They are by Raoul Dufy and were originally the scenery for *Ring Around the Moon*, a play by Jean Anouilh produced by Gilbert Miller in 1950. Too valuable to be consigned to the city dump once the play closed, they were saved by Mr. Miller, who gave them to us.

If they had been conceived for their spaces they could not be better. They fit perfectly—size, scale, color, subject matter, everything—and fairly jump for joy. "A Parisian celebration," Herman E. Krawitz's official guidebook to the Metropolitan calls them, and they depict a Lucullan dinner, a lively game room, and a horse-and-carriage scene reminiscent of Constantin Guys.

On the Dress Circle level are the board room and the Opera Club, the latter done in deliberately smoky colors, with a handsome chandelier and Regency-style chairs with chinoiserie.

Before, during and after a performance at the Metropolitan Opera, patrons have a variety of agreeable environs in which they may enjoy the company of friends. Members of the Metropolitan Opera Guild have access to the elegant Eleanor Belmont Room (above) on the Grand Tier. The general public has a wide choice of attractive spots—the Grand Tier Restaurant, the nearby serpentine bar, other bars on the Balcony-Family Circle level and in Founders Hall, and the Opera Café off the north lobby

The Top of the Met, a restaurant with a sweeping view of Lincoln Center Plaza, is charmingly decorated with murals by Raoul Dufy (below). Members of the Opera Club retreat to their own private room (right) on the Dress Circle level, a glamorous setting that sometimes houses post-performance cast parties lingering into the wee hours

Opening night at the new Metropolitan Opera House, September 16, 1966, as thousands of onlookers crowded into Lincoln Center Plaza to catch a glimpse of the notables attending (top left). Among the early arrivals were heads of state and leaders in the arts, science and the humanities. Shown here (bottom left) are John D. Rockefeller 3rd, one of the more generous contributors to the building of the new Opera House; Mrs. Lyndon B. Johnson, representing the President of the United States; Mrs. and President Ferdinand Marcos of the Philippines; and Lauder Greenway, chairman of the board of the Metropolitan Opera. Just before the performance began, a crush of news photographers (above) materialized before the gold curtain to record the brilliant audience on this historic occasion (below). The total capacity is 4,077, of which 277 are standees, patrons and staff who are in the back of the Orchestra section, in the Grand Tier, Dress Circle and Family Circle. If a ticket holder arrives after a performance has begun, he may follow the performance on television sets stationed in lounges on the Orchestra level and take his seat during a pause in the music, usually during a change of scene or after the act concludes

Back to the Grand Tier, we come to the Eleanor Belmont Room, named for Mrs. August Belmont, who literally saved the Metropolitan in 1933 and two years later founded the Metropolitan Opera Guild, a tower of strength to us ever since. The Belmont Room is reserved for Guild members and their guests and has also been the scene of many lively gatherings, such as opening-night dinners, anniversary parties, press conferences, and the like.

Billy Baldwin, the decorator, took his colors from the bird figures in the Chippendale mirror Mrs. Belmont gave for the room—blue and green, with accents of vermilion. There is a handsome and lifelike portrait of the great lady herself. Under the mirror is an ornate console, and on it are the hands in bronze of the exquisite Lucrezia Bori, a leading soprano of the Metropolitan, Mrs. Belmont's ally in the campaign that saved the company and the only active artist to become a member of the board of directors of the Metropolitan.

In the Belmont Room is the finest work of art in our collection, a mask in colored wax of Anna Pavlova by Malvina Hoffman. The likeness is so eerie that many people think it is a death mask, but it was done from life. Pavlova was a member of the company at the time I was born, so I never saw her at the Metropolitan, but those of us who were around at the time she died in 1931 will never forget the universal sorrow. "Whose untimely death," *Vanity Fair* said, "has robbed the world of its most beloved ballerina," and a German newspaper ran a French poem, the last two lines of which I translate:

> O earth, rest softly above her,
> She trod lightly on thee.

Three large frames contain an incredible collection of autographs of composers. From J. S. Bach to Alban Berg, it is virtually a history of music.

Many of the portraits of former artists in Founders' Hall came from the old house. Before the journey uptown they were all carefully photographed and patterns of brown paper cut to their actual size and placed throughout the house. Mr. Harrison said nothing doing, not on his red velvet walls. Most of the lobby walls are curved, anyway. It turned out to be the best for all concerned. White walls are the best background in the world for paintings, and those oils and busts give importance to the area. There is never a performance that the ushers and doormen don't have to practically shoo out the lingerers. The public seems never to get enough of them.

Falling between the front of the house and backstage are List Hall and the press office. Open before the performance and at intermissions for the convenience of the critics, the press lounge has a black-and-white carpet by David Hicks and low red banquettes, brighter and more inviting than most cocktail rooms. List Hall is where the chorus rehearses before things begin to be pulled together onstage. Seating 144 persons, with a pitch of one row of seats to a step, it is ideal for lectures and chamber music and is the scene of the live intermission features on our broadcasts. You can almost feel the sound here.

Which brings us to the miracle of the acoustics of the auditorium. The consultants were Vilhelm L. Joardan of Copenhagen and Cyril M. Harris of New York, and the results are about as perfect as anything can be.

A talk with Cyril Harris is a revealing experience. The next time you see the great columns in the Metropolitan Opera House, consider they rest on footings of lead and asbestos anti-vibration pads, isolated from the bedrock to prevent any transmission of sound into the house through the rock. The ceiling is suspended on springs. The heavy ventilation machinery rests on concrete slabs afloat on Fiberglas with the Fiberglas around it. This takes as much imagination as a fugue. It was so far out the workmen couldn't take it in, couldn't translate it.

"Sometimes they think you have made a mistake and 'correct' it. They saw that Fiberglas sticking out at the edges and cemented over it. We had to disconnect it again," Mr. Harris tells you. As Charles Ives said, "The wrong notes are in the right places."

Cyril Harris hails from Los Angeles. The junior high school he attended was across from the sound stages of Warner Brothers. He was bitten early by the sound bug, and it took—permanently. There was a stint at Bell Laboratories, and he is professor of electrical engineering and architecture at Columbia University. He takes on only about one hall a year, and the finest in the country have had the benefit of his counsel—Avery Fisher, the homes of the St. Louis Symphony and Minnesota Orchestra, Kennedy Center.

Michaux Moody, the manager in Richmond, Virginia, decided it was time his piano tuner heard a concert and gave him a couple of tickets for Paderewski. When they next met and the tuner didn't mention the concert, Moody asked him how he had liked it. "Well," the tuner said, "it's got to be better than it sounds."

The case of Cyril Harris is just the opposite. A conductor might envy his ear. He has written the definitive work on the Highland bagpipe and is doing a similar work on the French horn. His subscription seats in the old house were under the overhang of the parterre. When his neighbors left early, he would slide over into their seats, which were clear of the overhang. He noted the sound was infinitely better. Overhangs in the new house are at a minimum.

Before the house opened, Harris heard a whistle. The ventilation system has automatic fire shutters. One was partly closed and the air was trying to get through. Heaven and earth were moved to find it.

The first performance in the new house was a student matinee of *La Fanciulla del West.* Mr. Harris was in the topmost reaches of the Family Circle. "I could hear every card go down," Harris recalled of the famous poker game when Minnie plays the sheriff for the life of Dick Johnson. "I knew we really had a winner."

That student matinee was in April 1966, before we had left the old house. It was supposed to be a great secret. The students boarded their buses in the Bronx and Connecticut and Jersey thinking they were headed for Broadway and Thirty-ninth for the last time. Instead they wound up at Lincoln Center. A few important members of the press had been tipped off. Their smiles were their verdict. On opening night, five months later, a visiting critic reported, "With the first note of the national anthem a $49 million sigh of relief went up."

A dozen years later, Wallace Harrison, recalling a test before that first student performance, said, "Three kids came out and sang *Don Giovanni* with orchestra. It was the high point in my life."

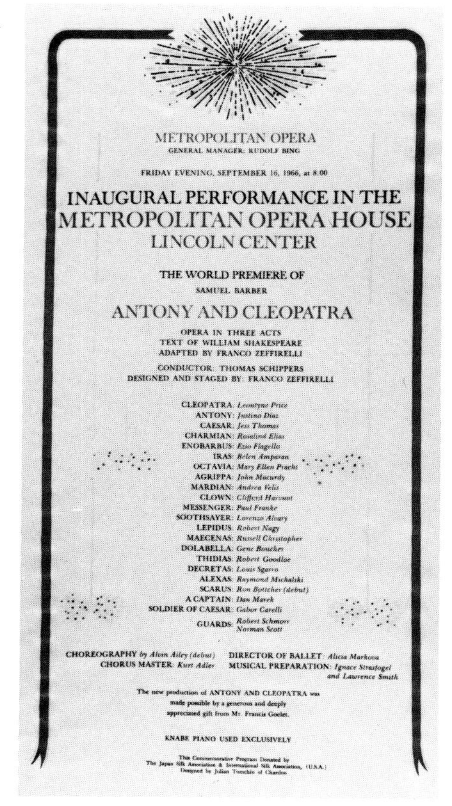

METROPOLITAN OPERA
GENERAL MANAGER: RUDOLF BING

FRIDAY EVENING, SEPTEMBER 16, 1966, at 8:00

INAUGURAL PERFORMANCE IN THE METROPOLITAN OPERA HOUSE
LINCOLN CENTER

THE WORLD PREMIERE OF
SAMUEL BARBER
ANTONY AND CLEOPATRA

OPERA IN THREE ACTS
TEXT OF WILLIAM SHAKESPEARE
ADAPTED BY FRANCO ZEFFIRELLI

CONDUCTOR: THOMAS SCHIPPERS
DESIGNED AND STAGED BY: FRANCO ZEFFIRELLI

CLEOPATRA: *Leontyne Price*
ANTONY: *Justino Diaz*
CAESAR: *Jess Thomas*
CHARMIAN: *Rosalind Elias*
ENOBARBUS: *Ezio Flagello*
IRAS: *Belen Amparan*
OCTAVIA: *Mary Ellen Pracht*
AGRIPPA: *John Macurdy*
MARDIAN: *Andrea Velis*
CLOWN: *Clifford Harvuot*
MESSENGER: *Paul Franke*
SOOTHSAYER: *Lorenzo Alvary*
LEPIDUS: *Robert Nagy*
MAECENAS: *Russell Christopher*
DOLABELLA: *Gene Boucher*
THIDIAS: *Robert Goodloe*
DECRETAS: *Louis Sgarro*
ALEXAS: *Raymond Michalski*
SCARUS: *Ron Bottcher (debut)*
A CAPTAIN: *Dan Marek*
SOLDIER OF CAESAR: *Gabor Carelli*
GUARDS: *Robert Schmorr*
Norman Scott

CHOREOGRAPHY *by Alvin Ailey (debut)*
CHORUS MASTER: *Kurt Adler*
DIRECTOR OF BALLET: *Alicia Markova*
MUSICAL PREPARATION: *Ignace Strasfogel and Lawrence Smith*

The new production of ANTONY AND CLEOPATRA was made possible by a generous and deeply appreciated gift from Mr. Francis Goelet.

KNABE PIANO USED EXCLUSIVELY

This Commemorative Program Donated by
The Japan Silk Association & International Silk Association, (U.S.A.)
Designed by Julian Tomchin of Chardon

A new opera was commissioned from the distinguished American composer Samuel Barber to inaugurate the theater, Antony and Cleopatra, *with text adapted from Shakespeare's tragedy by Franco Zeffirelli, also the production's designer and director. A souvenir silk program (above) commemorated the occasion. When the premiere ended, composer, librettist and conductor Thomas Schippers joined hands before the gold brocade curtain, warmly accepting the audience's applause (right). On the Grand Tier, at a post-performance party, Sir Rudolf, who had led his company to the promised land, was bussed on the cheek by his elated wife, Lady Bing (below). The table decoration was an Egyptian obelisk, created especially for the evening*

THOSE WHO RAN AND RUN IT

For a few, the number thirteen is as lucky as it is anathema to untold millions. Earle R. Lewis, an assistant manager of the Metropolitan Opera and the wizard of the box office for forty years, used to tell of an evening when Mrs. Lewis practically had to go out on the street and compel a stranger to dinner. Rosa Ponselle arrived to discover there would be thirteen at table. She would not so much as cross the threshold of the dining room until the surprised last-minute guest had been corralled.

Jascha Heifetz, on the other hand, persuaded his pupil and protégé Erick Friedman to alter the spelling of his name until it conformed in number of letters to his own. While Lily Pons' name did not add up to thirteen characters, she was convinced it was her lucky number, and her automobile license plate was LP-13.

The Metropolitan Opera may fall into this second category. In its ninety-six years the Metropolitan has had thirteen managements. The thirteenth, though dating only from the season 1975–76, by its extraordinary imagination and vigor—creativeness may be the word—has already realized many of its dreams. The record of accomplishment is high. Prospects for the future are big and bright.

The triumvirate that now guides the destiny of the Metropolitan Opera: Anthony A. Bliss, executive director (right), who oversees the company's business affairs, trying to keep the ledger in the black; James Levine, music director (above), who makes casting decisions and conducts the lion's share of the performances at the Opera House and on tour; and John Dexter, director of production (below), who stages many works and keeps a quality control on the dramatic values of every work in the repertory. Together with Bliss and Levine, Dexter also helps plan future seasons, with a goal of expanding the repertory and the audience

In the autumn of 1974 the board of directors came to the conclusion that the post of general manager of the Metropolitan had become too heavy for any one man to bear—too heavy and, worse, too sprawling. There has been talk of a similar move in the executive branch of the United States Government. Surely the only jobs bigger, tougher, more complex than general manager of the Metropolitan Opera had come to be are president of the United States and mayor of the city of New York.

The board decided it would set up a tripart management, with Anthony A. Bliss as executive director, James Levine, who was already principal conductor, as music director, and John Dexter as director of production. This is a long way from anything that had been tried before. A triumvirate headed the Metropolitan in the nineties, but none of the three was an artist.

Many wagged their heads and said it wouldn't work. It has. Almost immediately the shows became consistently better. Please note the modifier, consistently. Nobody is going to say anything could be better than *Turandot* on a good night in the early sixties, and there were many others, but the general level of performance lifted perceptibly. All the roles, not just the leads, were more carefully cast. Everything was better prepared and rehearsed. You don't need a computer to see the connection between this and increased box office receipts. The season of 1977–78 was 96.3 percent of capacity, more than 10 percent above the season of 1974–75.

Bliss was born to a family high in the art world. His aunt, Miss Lillie Bliss, owned the first Cézannes in this country, and her collection was one of the nuclei of the Museum of Modern Art. His father, the late Cornelius N. Bliss, came on the board of the Metropolitan in 1932 and was named chairman six years later. Following the elder Bliss' death, Anthony Bliss was elected to the board in 1950 and became president in 1956. As a boy in the family box he had heard Caruso. The Metropolitan is in his blood.

THE BIG TONE

In 1883–84, the Metropolitan Opera's maiden season, the stockholders who built the new theater engaged the well-known impresario Henry E. Abbey (above) to arrange for the artists and select the repertory. For the opening bill, on October 22, 1883, he presented Gounod's Faust *with Franco Novara—born in England Frank Nash—as Méphistophélès (top left) and the great Swedish diva Christine Nilsson as Marguerite (top right), a performance sung in Italian, as was the entire repertory that first season. Among other illustrious names that came to the fore under Abbey's aegis was the Italian contralto Sofia Scalchi (bottom left), who was the Siébel in the first-night* Faust *but is shown here as Maddalena in* Rigoletto *(bottom left), another of her many roles. Italo Campanini, whose brother Cleofonte conducted numerous performances, was the inaugural night Faust as well as the Metropolitan's first Lohengrin, Edgardo and Don José in* Carmen *(bottom right). The U.S. premiere of Ponchielli's* La Gioconda *(below) was another highlight*

STEINWAY
PIANO-FORTES.
THE STANDARD PIANOS OF THE WORLD.
Warerooms, Steinway Hall,
NEW YORK CITY.

Park & Tilford,
917 and 919 Broadway,
656-660 Sixth Avenue.
118, 120, 122 Sixth Avenue,
NEW YORK.
— AND —
39 Rue de Chateau d'Eux,
PARIS.

RUNKEL BRO'S FINE VANILLA CHOCOLATE

C. F. KLUNDER
FLORIST,
No. 907 BROADWAY, NEW YORK.

OXLEY, GIDDINGS & ENOS,
Gas Fixture Manufacturers,
CLOCKS, BRONZES, FANCY BRASS ARTICLES, SCONCES, ETC., FOR HOLIDAY PRESENTS
224-230 CANAL STREET, NEW YORK

METROPOLITAN OPERA HOUSE.
MR. HENRY E. ABBEY, Director.
Acting Manager. MR. MAURICE GRAU.
Thursday Evening, Dec. 20th, 28th Subscription Night,
"LA GIOCONDA"
LAURA (Wife of Alvise) ... Mme. FURSCH-MADI
LA CIECA (Her Blind Mother) ... Mme. SCALCHI
ENZO (A Genoese Nobleman) ... Sig. STAGNO
BARNABA (A Spy of the Inquisition) ... Sig. DEL PUENTE
ALVISE BADOERO (One of the Heads of the State Inquisition) ... Sig. NOVARA
ZUANE (A Boatman) ... Sig. AUGIER
ISEPO (A Public Letter-writer) ... Sig. GRAZZI
UN CANTORE ... Sig. CONTINI
UN PILOTA ... Sig. BARBERIS
AND
LA GIOCONDA (A Ballad Singer) ... Mme. CHRISTINE NILSSON
Monks, Senators, Sailors, Shipwrights, Ladies, Gentlemen, Populace, Masquers, etc., etc.
The action takes place in Venice in the 17th Century.
The Incidental Divertissement will be supported by
MME. CAVALAZZI AND CORPS DE BALLET
Musical Director and Conductor, SIG. VIANESI
Weber Piano and Mason & Hamlin Organ Used.
PRICES OF ADMISSION
For all Performances during Italian Opera Season.
Admission to Family Circle ... Fifty Cents
General Admission (to all parts of the House) ... Two Dollars
Doors open at 1.30 and 7.30. Performances at 2 and 8 precisely
Business Manager ... Mr. W. W. TILLOTSON
Treasurer ... Mr. CHAS. H. MATHEWS

Wm. Knabe & Co.
MANUFACTURERS OF
GRAND, UPRIGHT AND SQUARE
PIANO-FORTES.
UNEQUALLED IN
TONE, TOUCH, WORKMANSHIP AND DURABILITY.

Bacon Pianos.
FRANCIS BACON'S PIANO FACTORY,
Grand, Square and Upright Pianos
BROADWAY and 42d STREET.

RICHARD HECKSCHER, JR.
COAL.
Trinity Building, 111 Broadway
435 East 23d Street.
EAST INCE HALL
ENGLISH CANNEL COAL
A SPECIALTY.

MITCHELL, VANCE & CO.,
Gas Fixtures, Lamps, Clocks
AND BRONZES,
836 and 838 Broadway, New York.

BARRETT HOUSE,
BROADWAY AND 43D STREET, NEW YORK
Rooms, $2.00 Per Day and Upwards

James Levine was a child prodigy and began his musical studies in his native Cincinnati at the age of four. Six years later he was soloist with the Cincinnati Symphony in the Mendelssohn D-minor Piano Concerto. He came to the Juilliard School in New York and studied conducting with Jean Morel. Under the Ford Foundation's American Conductors Project he worked with Alfred Wallenstein, Max Rudolf, and Fausto Cleva. At the invitation of George Szell he became apprentice and later assistant conductor of the Cleveland Orchestra, the youngest in its history.

While in his mid-twenties he began to be known by virtue of several concert performances of opera that he conducted in Cleveland with leading Metropolitan artists. He was engaged by the San Francisco Opera in 1970 and the following year by the Metropolitan. He is music director of the Ravinia Festival, summer home of the Chicago Symphony, and formerly the Cincinnati May Festival, and he has been a guest with all the major orchestras of this country. In Europe he has conducted the London Symphony, the New Philharmonia, at the Hamburg Opera and the Salzburg Festival.

There is no more vital figure in the theater today than John Dexter. He began as an actor and turned to directing in 1957. At the Royal Court Theatre in London he staged all the plays of Arnold Wesker and some of John Osborne. In 1963 he was appointed associate director of the National Theatre, where he directed fifteen productions including Laurence Olivier in *Othello* and Peter Schaffer's *Equus*, which had the same great success in this country. Broadway has also seen his productions of *Black Comedy* and *Royal Hunt of the Sun*. *Equus* won him a Tony as the season's best director.

Always drawn to opera, he directed *Benvenuto Cellini* by Berlioz at Covent Garden. His production of *I Vespri Siciliani*, which marked his entry to the Metropolitan, has been seen in Hamburg and Paris. His Hamburg credits also include *Un Ballo in Maschera*, *Boris Godunov*, *From the House of the Dead*, and *Billy Budd*. In Paris he staged a new production of *La Forza del Destino*.

One cannot imagine more diverse challenges than his Metropolitan assignments—*Vespri*, *Aida*, *Dialogues of the Carmelites*, *Lulu*, *Rigoletto*, *Prophète*, *Billy Budd*, *The Bartered Bride*, *Don Pasquale*. He has met them all.

For the first twenty-five years the financially doubtful privilege of presenting opera at the Metropolitan was a concession let out to the highest bidder. There was no Metropolitan Opera Company as such until the regime of Gatti-Casazza. Those gentlemen who built the house were a real estate company. They owned the boxes, and they did not go out of business until 1940. In the early days they did little more than lease the house.

The first manager was Henry E. Abbey. He had been a jeweler and theater owner and manager. His only practical experience in music, according to Henry E. Krehbiel, the venerable critic and chronicler, seems to have been "as a cornet player in a brass band in Akron, Ohio, whence he came." Nevertheless, he gave New York grand opera, so grand that Lilli Lehmann in her autobiography found cause to marvel at the lavishness of it. The Metropolitan's first Norma and Isolde, whose frugality dictated she take the horse cars instead of a hack through the slush to the opera house, records that "every costume, every shoe and stocking" came from Worth in Paris. Abbey also served up the greatest singers the world could provide, establishing the Metropolitan's position from the start. The loss on his first season amounted to almost $600,000. George S. Moore, who was president of the

board at the time he held the same position with the First National City Bank, was asked to translate that figure into today's money. For once he was silent, throwing his hands up in dismay.

Needless to say, Mr. Abbey's contract was not renewed. As we shall see later, he took on the Metropolitan again as part of the first triumvirate, but—*Grove's Dictionary* puts it briefly and sadly—he "died in the effort." He was only fifty years old.

Under Abbey everything had been sung in Italian, even *Faust* the opening night and *Lohengrin* two weeks later. For the next seven years everything was in German. The first Aida at the Metropolitan was a lady of formidable name and girth, Therese Herbert-Förster. The first half of the last name was her husband's. Prima donnas to this day sometimes do that. When Maria Callas first sang at the Metropolitan, she was billed as Maria Meneghini Callas, no hyphen. Mr. Herbert was first cellist in the Metropolitan Opera orchestra. The first name was Victor—yes, he of *Naughty Marietta*, *Mlle. Modiste*, and *Babes in Toyland.*

Leopold Damrosch was a friend of Liszt and Wagner and brought some of the greats of Bayreuth with him—Amalia Materna, who had been Kundry in the world premiere of *Parsifal*, and Marianne Brandt, who sang the role at the second performance. Richard Wagner had died only the year before, but America heard the entire *Ring des Nibelungen*, *Tristan und Isolde*, and *Meistersinger von Nürnberg* before the Metropolitan had concluded its fifth season.

Running the Metropolitan, we have noted before and will see again, can be a killing job. Leopold Damrosch died less than three months after taking office. He had conducted every performance until six days before his death. His son Walter, a handsome young man of twenty-three, shared the podium with another conductor and should have been made general manager, but the directors thought he was too young. In view of this, it is one of those ironies that Dr. Damrosch became the paterfamilias of serious music in this country.

For seven seasons, 1884–91, all operas were sung in German at the Metropolitan, which provoked a battle between the Teutonic forces of the conductor Anton Seidl and the Italian camp headed by Luigi Arditi (above). Luminaries of the period included Amalia Materna as Brünnhilde (below), Lilli Lehmann and Albert Niemann as Isolde and Tristan (top left and right), the conductor Leopold Damrosch (bottom left), Max Alvary as the young Siegfried (center right) and Emil Fischer as Hans Sachs (bottom right)—the singers all participants in the U.S. premieres of the operas in which they are shown

19
copyright
by
A. Dupont

Instead of giving the nod to Walter Damrosch, the stockholders retained their secretary, Edmond C. Stanton. A great-uncle of Louis Auchincloss, Stanton might himself be the subject of a novel. With an eye on a German decoration, he produced *Diana von Solange*, a little number by a Teutonic princeling, Ernest II, Duke of Saxe-Coburg, and some other disastrous novelties, but he did leave a lesson in how to deal with recalcitrant tenors. It was the dress rehearsal of the Metropolitan's first *Siegfried.* Max Alvary wouldn't sing. Stanton was sent for. "I cannot sing both today and tomorrow," Alvary said. "Choose—I'll sing either today or tomorrow." "Sing today!" Stanton replied curtly, and went back to his office. The tenor sang—both days. Stanton knew Alvary wasn't about to lose that important premiere.

Abbey was given another chance with John B. Schoeffel, a silent partner from Boston, and Maurice Grau, the impresario of Covent Garden, who initiated the negotiations that were later to bring Caruso here. Their wheeler-dealer methods quickly inspired some wag to substitute for Abbey, Schoeffel, and Grau the nicknames "Ante, Shuffle, and Grab."

Edmund C. Stanton (above), general manager of the Metropolitan, 1885–91, and Golden Age stars who followed his regime—Emma Calvé as Ophélie in Thomas' Hamlet *(below left) and Jean de Reszke as Gounod's Roméo (below)*

Maurice Grau (above), who with Henry E. Abbey and John B. Schoeffel was Stanton's successor, stayed until 1903. Among the stars he offered were Emma Eames as Juliette (below) and Victor Maurel as Falstaff (below right)

There was no opera at the Metropolitan the season of 1892–93. A disastrous fire had gutted the theater during the summer. The death of Abbey broke up the triumvirate, but the season of 1896 carried the three names. After that, Grau went his way alone.

Even more lavish than the entertainments he used to put together for Queen Victoria at Windsor Castle were Grau's "Nights of the Seven Stars". Any evening he did *Les Huguenots*, these were the rule. Imagine *Tristan* with both De Reszkes, Nordica, and Schumann-Heink; *Don Giovanni* with Scotti, Nordica, Gadski, Fritzi Scheff, Édouard de Reszke, and Journet; the first Metropolitan performance of *La Bohème*, with Melba as Mimi.

To assemble and hold together such casts is a back-breaking task, and it told on Grau's health. At the gala in his honor on the closing night of his last season, 1902–3, many of these great people sang. If the man responsible for it all was in the house, no one knew it: Mrs. Grau accepted the tribute in his name. He retired to Paris and died in 1907. He had not reached sixty.

On the opening night of Heinrich Conried's first season as manager of the Metropolitan, a thirty-year-old Italian tenor with an atomic B-flat made

his North American debut. To Enrico Caruso went the honor of every opening night thereafter until his death, except one. The season of 1906–7 he deferred to Geraldine Farrar, who was returning to her homeland to make her Metropolitan debut after five years of European triumphs.

Conried had been an actor in the Burg Theater in Vienna. When the directors of the Metropolitan tapped him, he was manager of the Irving Place Theater, which stood opposite the Academy of Music. The outline of the building is still there—the fly loft, the fire escapes from the balconies—but its last days as a theater came in the thirties, when it had turned into a burlesque house and was the scene of the early triumphs of Gypsy Rose Lee. At the beginning of the century, however, it was the home of the classic theater of New York's sizable German population. Conried gave the plays of Goethe, Schiller, Lessing, and Shakespeare. Germans claim the Bard of Avon as their own and piously tell you the Schlegel translations are better than the originals. The juvenile at the Irving Place was Rudolf Christians, father of the beautiful Mady Christians.

Man of the theater that he was, Conried overhauled the stage of the Metropolitan extensively and almost lost his lease by giving the first American performance of *Salome.* The scandalized directors, including J. P. Morgan, who held the center box, served notice on Conried that *Salome* was "objectionable and detrimental to the best interests of the Metropolitan Opera House" and there would be no further performances of the work. The banishment of Herodias' exigent daughter lasted twenty-seven years. *Salome* did not return until 1934.

Olive Fremstad was Salome in that single performance. In preparation for the role she had gone down to the city morgue and asked to be allowed to pick up a human head to determine its weight. Without going so far, her successors might take a lesson here. Some of them throw the silver charger around as though their grisly trophy were only the papier-mâché that it is.

Conried brought down the undying wrath of the Wagner family by defying international copyright and giving the first staged performance of *Parsifal* outside Bayreuth. The master never intended his last work to be given beyond the sacred confines of his own festival theater. Puccini came over for the first Metropolitan performances of *Madama Butterfly* and

During his five-season reign as general manager of the Metropolitan Opera, 1903–8, Heinrich Conreid (below) introduced a number of significant works into the company's repertory. Puccini himself was present for the Opera House premieres of his Manon Lescaut *and* Madama Butterfly, *the latter starring the young American soprano Geraldine Farrar as Cio-Cio-San (above left). Strauss'* Salome, *its title role graphically portrayed by Olive Fremstad (above), created a furor among the bluenoses and was forthwith banned as indecent. The Conreid era also brought forth a singer among singers, one who for eighteen seasons, starting in 1903, would be the pillar of the roster—a tenor from Naples named Enrico Caruso (right), shown in what was perhaps his signature part, Canio in Leoncavallo's* Pagliacci. *Caruso was to sing thirty-seven roles with the Metropolitan, with 626 performances in the Opera House and another 235 on tour*

Caro M° Ziegler: eccovi la mia im

gine di quando ci siamo conosciuti

1908 - Con affetto G Gatti Cas

Giulio Gatti-Casazza (left) became general manager of the Metropolitan Opera in 1908, having already served with distinction in a similar post in Italy, as director of the Teatro alla Scala in Milan. He was to head the Metropolitan for a record twenty-seven seasons, not retiring until the end of 1934–35. His first two years in New York were clouded by a rival faction, headed by his co-manager, Andreas Dippel (above), formerly a leading tenor on the roster, 1890–1908, and with Gatti's arrival, charged with administration of the German wing. In time Gatti prevailed in the power struggle with Dippel, an able man who left for a managerial post at the Chicago Opera. There were other clouds during the Gatti era at the Metropolitan—matrimonial. One of his prima donnas was his wife, the temperamental Frances Alda, who lost him to the lovely prima ballerina and later ballet mistress Rosina Galli. A consummate diplomat, Gatti managed to keep both ladies on the roster, with Alda finally retiring in 1929 as Manon Lescaut

Manon Lescaut, and it must have swelled Conried's Austrian heart in what turned out to be his last season that he was able to lure Gustav Mahler to the podium of the Metropolitan. Mahler made his Metropolitan Opera debut on New Year's Day 1908, with Olive Fremstad as Isolde.

Mahler did not long survive the coming of Arturo Toscanini. Although it was the next season, it was the same calendar year. A timpanist in the Metropolitan Opera Orchestra, who had played under Mahler, not at the Metropolitan but in the Philharmonic, told a wonderful story about him. On one tour the orchestra had a layover in Buffalo, and a group went out to see "the Falls," as they call Niagara up there. Mahler stood silent for a moment before this seventh wonder of nature and then muttered, "*Endlich,* finally, *ein Fortissimo!*"

The length of the regime of Giulio Gatti-Casazza, 1908–35, is unlikely ever to be surpassed by the general manager of any major opera house. It is as remarkable in the annals of opera as the reigns of Louis XIV, Queen Victoria, and Emperor Franz Joseph are in history, and it was as brilliant as it was long. Mr. Gatti had got La Scala before he was thirty. He had the Metropolitan before he was forty, and he ruled the place with an iron hand.

He brought with him his leading conductor, Toscanini. In their inaugural opening night *Aida* they had Emmy Destinn, making her American debut, Caruso, Louise Homer, and Antonio Scotti. Toscanini lost no time helping himself to *Götterdämmerung* and *Tristan*, and Mahler's days were numbered.

The Gatti-Toscanini honeymoon here lasted seven years. In view of the temperaments of the two men, that was perhaps a long time. Toscanini left under circumstances never fully explained, but the grievance must have been fierce and deep. In spite of overtures from two of Mr. Gatti's successors and a long tenure in New York with the Philharmonic and later the NBC Symphony, he never returned. "I will conduct," he said, "on the ashes of the Metropolitan." The schism was patched up sufficiently, however, for Toscanini to attend the farewell luncheon for Mr. Gatti in the opera house twenty years later.

You often hear the charge leveled against the Metropolitan that it is indifferent to works by American composers. Nothing could be more incorrect or unfair. True, Mr. Gatti ran an Italian house. He didn't know how to run any other kind. The correspondence, even the "No Smoking" signs backstage, was in Italian, but almost his first act here was to inaugurate a competition for native works. In his twenty-seven years he produced sixteen operas by Americans—better than one every other year. Most of them were terrible, but no one can say he didn't try.

The same accusation used to be made as regards American artists—that they had to have the seal of European approval before they were welcome at the Metropolitan. Two of Mr. Gatti's brightest stars, Rosa Ponselle and Lawrence Tibbett, had never set foot on foreign soil prior to their triumphs here. He also introduced Grace Moore after his chief conductor, Artur Bodanzky, had told her, "No matter how hard you work, you will never be an opera singer."

Unlike his successors, Mr. Gatti was unplagued by financial worries for twenty-five years. Otto Kahn considered it his personal, private, and particular privilege to pick up the tab. With his help Mr. Gatti had built up a considerable reserve, which was wiped out by the crash of 1929 and the

Great Depression that followed. It looked as though the house would not open the autumn of 1933; in fact the board announced it was "without sufficient funds to assure another season." Our world was wrapped in gloom. That is when Mrs. Belmont went into action. That story comes in another chapter.

During Giulio Gatti-Casazza's years many American singers were given the opportunity to realize their potential, none more brilliantly than Rosa Ponselle, who had never sung in an opera when Gatti signed her, but who developed her natural gifts and triumphed in such challenges as Norma (above). Gatti also engaged a gifted young Canadian tenor who had been making a name for himself in Italy, Edward Johnson. He made his debut as Avito in L'Amore dei Tre Re, *was a poetic Pelléas and created the title role in Deems Taylor's* Peter Ibbetson *(below). In 1935, when Gatti's successor, Herbert Witherspoon, suddenly died, Johnson, who had been engaged as assistant manager, inherited the top job*

The season of 1932–33 was cut by a third, from twenty-four to sixteen weeks. All the artists except one took a 10 percent cut in pay. There was also a 10 percent cut in the roster, resulting in some interesting casting elisions. Singers found themselves undertaking roles they had never studied before, sometimes not even in their vocal categories. A high baritone might be asked to take on a tenor part. The beloved George Cehanovsky acquitted himself admirably as the tenor Knight of the Grail in *Parsifal.*

The scheme was working out so smoothly that Mr. Gatti was tempted by the thought of a second 10 percent cut. He decided he would send up the trial balloon on his friend Cehanovsky—no more loyal or cooperative colleague in the history of the Metropolitan. George went white. "*Signor direttore,*" he replied in his flawless Italian, "you cut me once and made me a tenor. If you cut me again, I'll be no more use to you!" Gatti wept with laughter. The subject was not brought up again.

The old man's last season was brightened by the debut of Kirsten Flagstad. Her unheralded coming in the midst of the darkest days the company had ever known was, in the words of Mrs. Belmont, "a golden ray of light." She and Melchior, in company with their colleagues of the glorious German wing of that time—Thorborg, Schorr, Rethberg, Lehmann, Lawrence, Branzell—put the Metropolitan back on the gold standard.

By now there was strong feeling that it was time the Metropolitan had an American at its head. To that contingency was tied a sizable chunk of the estate of A. D. Juilliard, a late member of the board, which incidentally we never got. It found its way to the school that bears his name. It was announced that Herbert Witherspoon, a leading bass with the company for nine seasons and more recently director of the Chicago Opera, would succeed Mr. Gatti. A native of Buffalo and a graduate of Yale, Mr. Witherspoon couldn't have been more American.

After six arduous weeks of preparation, not only for the new season but a new administration, Mr. Witherspoon died of a heart attack in his office in the opera house. Brave hopes and plans were dashed, but he did bequeath a valuable legacy in the person of his wife. Blanche Witherspoon was the first director of the Metropolitan Opera Guild and filled the post ably.

Knowing his singing days couldn't last forever, Edward Johnson, a leading tenor at the Metropolitan for thirteen years, before that in Chicago and before that in Italy, decided, in his phrase, "to give away his purple tights" and turn his knowledge, experience, and charm to management. His own personal management turned him down, but the board of the Metropolitan was delighted to get him as Witherspoon's assistant, to organize a spring season at popular prices with young American artists. It was Johnson's meat. He would also make speeches, kiss matronly hands, and raise money, at all of which he was highly adept. As a speaker he came only slightly after Winston Churchill and Mrs. Belmont.

Five days after Mr. Witherspoon's death, Mr. Johnson was singing *Peter Ibbetson* in Detroit. It was there he got the telegram telling him he was it. Pelléas, Roméo, the first Italian Parsifal? His own misgivings must have

Edward Ziegler (above), a music critic for various New York newspapers between 1902 and 1917, served for many years as Gatti-Casazza's right hand. In 1935, when Edward Johnson (below) became the Metropolitan Opera's commander-in-chief, Ziegler continued as the power next to the throne, holding the title assistant general manager. Johnson weathered the great depression and World War II, bringing a record number of native-born artists to the roster. His final season was 1949–50, when he was feted at a gala farewell performance of Tosca *starring Ljuba Welitsch, after which a pageant with artists of the company past and present paraded in costume to pay homage to a manager as loved as he was respected*

been greater than anybody's, but in the best British tradition—everyone thought he was American, but he never renounced his Canadian citizenship—he seized the wheel and righted the ship.

Thrown into a job for which he had no training and at the beginning almost as little taste, Johnson never got credit for being as good a manager as he was. Eight of his fifteen seasons were in the black. The most biased report cannot give him all the credit for this. The country was still struggling to its knees from the worst depression the world had ever known, and World War II was soon to break over our heads. There was neither money nor material for new productions, and the supply of singers from Europe was cut off. Johnson made a virtue of necessity. Some of the stable of young Americans he discovered and developed are still around—Kirsten, Steber, Stevens, Resnik, Peerce, Merrill. Tucker and Warren are, alas, gone.

He made welcome at the Metropolitan some of the greatest conductors of the day—Bruno Walter, Sir Thomas Beecham, George Szell, and the three Fritzes, Busch, Reiner, and Stiedry. In Prague he had engaged a young Yugoslav soprano at a ridiculously low fee on condition that she lose seventy-five pounds and learn in Italian the roles she had just transferred from Croatian to German. She became the foremost Verdi soprano of her time, Zinka Milanov.

Edward Johnson had that thing the great generals have. I can think of only one or two of us who wouldn't have gone out and died for him. He never asked the company to undergo any hardship he himself was not prepared to take, and he set us an example. In the days when we still traveled by rail, our trains, though "special," had a way of arriving and departing at 8 A.M. We were leaving Bloomington, Indiana, one spring morning. Now, Bloomington is the site of Indiana University, one of the great universities of the country, but the town had only two railroad tracks through it and almost no station platform. Three or four cars would fill, and the train would pull up to accommodate the next. It was pouring rain. We finally got loaded. It was one of those moments when the tempter asks you why you ever went into show business in the first place. Edward Johnson went through the cars singing "Oh, What a Beautiful Morning." Never did soggy spirits lift so fast.

Anyone who was around the latter half of Mr. Gatti's time will tell you it was Edward Ziegler who really ran the Metropolitan. James Gibbons Huneker, the critic, used to say Ziegler was a young man who dyed his hair white. He and Lewis stayed on with Mr. Johnson as assistant managers, and Frank St. Leger was the boss musically. St. Leger had come to know Johnson in Chicago, where he was a conductor and Johnson a leading tenor.

Rudolf Bing was the darkest of dark horses when he was announced to succeed Johnson the season of 1950–51. Margaret Carson, the Metropolitan's press representative, cabled the music editor of *Newsweek*, who happened to be in Vienna, "RUDOLF BING NEXT GENERAL MANAGER." Emily Coleman thought "Bing" was cablese for an exclamation point and that Max Rudolf, a conductor who stayed on as Bing's right hand musically, was the choice. The appointment had been as closely kept a secret as the atom bomb, and when Bing went for photographs to accompany the story, it was under another name.

Actually, Bing had an impressive background as general manager of the Glyndebourne Festival and founder of the Edinburgh Festival. With the war over only two years, he had to think about such details as soap and linen in the Edinburgh hotels. Claudia Cassidy of the Chicago *Tribune* said in all her experience she never attended a festival so well organized.

It was as though his whole life had been pointed toward this. He was hardly out of his teens when he went to work for a bookstore in Vienna that had a concert agency attached to it. Here he came in contact with a number of big personalities in the music world, some of whom he was associated with later—Bruno Walter, Maria Jeritza, Lotte Lehmann, Eugene Ormandy. In Berlin he ran a government agency for the placement of artists.

Sir Rudolf's reign (he was knighted at the beginning of his last Metropolitan season) is second in length only to Mr. Gatti's, twenty-two years. In many ways it is equally memorable. He broke the color barrier at the Metropolitan, first in the chorus and ballet, then by engaging Marian Anderson in 1954, opening the way to leading roles for other black artists. Guided by Anthony A. Bliss and Reginald Allen, an assistant manager who had come in under Johnson, he instituted pension and health benefits for the company and year-round employment for the chorus and ballet, an offer the orchestra declined. Robert Herman and Herman Krawitz were deeply involved in instituting these programs, working out the endless and complicated details. "I am not prepared to sign death warrants," Bing said his first year here when time came to superannuate certain choristers without a sign of pension.

When Bing arrived, the New York season was eighteen weeks. By the time he left, it was thirty-one. His first act was to increase it to twenty-two and split the subscription, offering more and shorter series. When he came there were six; when he left there were twenty-two, more than quadrupling the number of subscribers, from 5,000 to 21,000.

His outstanding artistic innovation was his insistence that opera is drama as well as music. He engaged the finest directors on Broadway and the West End to stage his productions, and the foremost painters and designers to mount them.

Controversial from the start, he did not reengage Lauritz Melchior but opened the door for the return of Kirsten Flagstad. The great Norwegian soprano had gone back to her homeland while it was under German occupation, and there were those who refused to be reconciled to that. "I am listening to God," Bing said at a recital of Flagstad before her reentry. In his first statement to the press he had said, "I will attempt to run this house on the principle of quality alone."

He found himself the center of almost as violent a storm when he fired Maria Callas. The biggest star of her time had made her Metropolitan debut with us the opening night of the 1956–57 season. She was signed to return the next season, and the first Metropolitan Opera production of Verdi's *Macbeth* was planned for 1958–59, as much for her as for Leonard Warren in the title role.

The Metropolitan believes in sharing the wealth. Each season it takes as many of its new productions as possible on tour, and *Macbeth* was scheduled to go the spring of 1959. Callas had agreed to make that tour, but in the autumn of 1957 we knew she was giving us the softening-up bombing for canceling it. She didn't ask for a release from that part of the agreement, but she asked to be allowed to return to Italy toward the end of the New York season. Enough had been said for us to know she would not return.

Rudolf Bing (right), who in 1971 was knighted by Queen Elizabeth II of England, took over as general manager of the Metropolitan Opera in 1950, steering the company on an ever expanding course through the 1971–72 season, a twenty-two-year record exceeded only by that of Giulio Gatti-Casazza. It was Bing who insisted that opera be good theater as well as good music, demanding an annual series of new productions. Among his other credits, he engaged the first blacks to perform with the company and he led the Metropolitan to its new home at Lincoln Center. Bing proved an autocratic ruler, equally willing to accept blame and praise. In running so large a theater, one in which he claimed responsibility for every decision, he developed a capable string of assistants whom he trusted, relied upon and, when the occasion warranted, defended. Among those on his staff were his artistic administrator Robert Herman (above) and his business and technical administrator Herman E. Krawitz (below). Since leaving the Metropolitan, Sir Rudolf has lectured, taught at Brooklyn College and held a high post in concert management

"I would rather tell Atlanta and Minneapolis and Toronto now [October] they are not going to have her than to tell them in the spring," Bing said. So when he found her in breach of contract on another matter, he announced to her—and the world—that Maria Callas and the Metropolitan Opera were parting company. All hell broke loose.

Her claim was she couldn't sing *Tosca* on a Tuesday and *La Traviata* on a Friday: "My voice is not an elevator." But all this had been agreed upon months before and a schedule attached to the formal contract. He got her on a technicality. It was a little like getting Al Capone for income tax. Those dates could have been patched up. Bing's real reason was her nondelivery of the tour, which he couldn't prove—but he was quite right.

The telegram of dismissal reached her in Dallas the day of a Cherubini *Medea.* Those who witnessed the performance said there had never been anything like it. Very likely there never will be again. Hell hath no fury . . . That night it wasn't Jason and his new young bride she was consigning to the nether regions, it was Rudolf Bing. He never swayed in his admiration of her as an artist, however. He brought her back for two performances of *Tosca* in 1965, and they were friends again.

The company was heard beyond the shores of North America for the first time in fifty-six years when it played a return engagement in Paris in 1966. That same summer and the following year it gave festivals in Newport, opera in concert form similar to the free performances it now gives in the parks of New York during June, also initiated by Bing.

For two seasons the Metropolitan Opera National Company, with Risë Stevens and Michael Manuel as general managers, toured the length and breadth of the land offering new and old repertory with great style and verve, not to mention affording opportunities to a fine roster of young Americans. A financial crisis in the wake of the move to the new house was the death knell of the National Company. The Metropolitan Opera Studio under the direction of John Gutman also gave the chance for many a gifted young singer to be heard. Quite a number graduated to the big troupe.

Gutman had been a journalist in Berlin and had known Bing first when he was artistic administrator in Darmstadt, later when he was at the Charlottenburg Opera in Berlin. An accomplished linguist, Gutman had served as an announcer for the OWI during World War II. Among his admirable translations for the Metropolitan were *Boris Godunov* and *Arabella*, and his *Meistersinger* has been performed by the New York City Opera.

Reginald Allen and Max Rudolf had held responsible posts in the Johnson administration before they became assistant managers under Bing. Allen, who had been manager of the Philadelphia Orchestra, went to Hollywood about the same time Stokowski did, and after service in the Navy during World War II he returned to head the J. Arthur Rank organization on the West Coast. For a time he was chief executive officer of Lincoln Center but returned to the Metropolitan as special assistant to Mr. Bliss, who was then president of the board.

Max Rudolf brought vast operatic knowledge and experience, not to mention skill as conductor and administrator, when he came to the Metropolitan. He had been a colleague of Bing at Darmstadt and later was at the German Theater in Prague. He left us to become conductor of the Cincinnati Symphony, carrying that illustrious orchestra to new heights. After that he was head of the opera department at Curtis Institute for three years.

The Bing era made news, none more sensational than the prolonged war between the general manager and the tempestuous soprano Maria Callas, who was fired by Bing in 1958 but who finally made up with him, returning to the old Opera House in 1965 for a historic performance of Tosca *costarring Franco Corelli as Mario Cavaradossi (left). Among the aides who helped Bing most during moments of stress, as when Callas was overly demanding, were his chief musical advisor, the conductor Max Rudolf (above), and his assistant manager, John Gutman, a friend from the old days in Germany (below). At his desk or on the podium, Maestro Rudolf could be counted on to give Bing exactly the solid sort of collaboration he required. Gutman served in the capacity of dramaturge—a man of letters and knowledge, with his ear tuned in to all that was happening around the musical world and with a special knack for spotting outstanding young talent*

Robert Herman and Herman Krawitz were each only twenty-eight when they came to the Metropolitan. Son of the legendary Babe Herman of Brooklyn Dodgers fame, Bob Herman had studied under Carl Ebert at the University of Southern California and had been a super in our performances when we went to the West Coast in the late forties. He began as an assistant stage manager and advanced to assistant manager in charge of the artistic side of the administration. Since 1973 he has had spectacular success as general manager of the Greater Miami Opera.

Wallace Harrison said of Krawitz, "Herman had an instinct. It was in his fingers." From summer theaters and tent musicals on Cape Cod, Mr. Bliss brought him in in 1953 to boost the efficiency of our stage operation. Two years later, when it was certain a new Metropolitan Opera House would be rising, Bliss sent him to Europe to study the other great opera houses of the world. Next to Harrison himself, Krawitz was the man most responsible for the creation of the new house, at the same time serving as the assistant manager in charge of business and technical matters. He went on to become president of New World Records, which began as a Bicentennial project of the Rockefeller Foundation to record the best of American music on one hundred discs. He is also a successful independent television producer and executive producer of American Ballet Theatre.

The demand for tickets for the gala honoring Sir Rudolf on his retirement was the greatest in the history of the company up to that time. Forty leading artists, some of them the greatest singers in the world, and the chorus, orchestra, and ballet went through twenty-nine numbers. It was one of those nights only the Metropolitan Opera can produce.

An automobile crash in Sardinia in July 1972 took the lives of Bing's successor, Goeran Gentele, and his two younger daughters. He had been general manager of the Metropolitan Opera only eighteen days. It was a crushing blow. Gentele had been named Bing's successor in December 1970 and had spent a season and a half in the house observing and making plans. Hopes were high. When asked in one of his first interviews what he thought an opera house should be, his answer was one word—"Alive."

His first three major innovations completed according to his designs were enormous successes—a stunning, highly original new production of *Carmen*, the Look-ins to give young audiences their first taste of opera ("I believe in poisoning them young," Gentele said), which he had personally staged with great success in Stockholm and which Danny Kaye carried on here, and the Mini-Met over which his gifted and beautiful wife, Marit, presided, giving attention to old and modern offbeat works in the Mitzi E. Newhouse Theater of the Beaumont Theater across the way.

Turning his back on the army, the diplomatic, the law, all the careers of his distinguished family, Gentele attended Sweden's Royal Academy of Dramatic Art. He emerged as actor, writer, director, producer, and had made films with his wife when he was offered the post of intendant of the Royal Opera, Stockholm. A stellar attraction of Expo 67 in Montreal, his company was to have come to New York two years later, but the Lincoln Center Festival, which was to have been his showcase, had succumbed.

Negotiations for the New York visit were being handled by Schuyler G. Chapin, a vice-president of Lincoln Center, whom Gentele later invited to become his chief assistant manager. After the fearful accident, Chapin was made acting general manager for a season, then general manager.

Starting as did many another notable as a page boy at NBC, Chapin was hardly out of that uniform when he donned another, that of the Air Force. He flew ninety-five missions in the China-Burma-India theater.

Back in civilian life he was Jascha Heifetz' representative and later a salesman for Columbia Artists Management. From that he went to Columbia Records where he rose to vice-president. As producer of Leonard Bernstein's films for television, Amberson Productions, he won an Emmy for the documentary on the 200th anniversary of Beethoven.

During his tenure he not only saw many of Gentele's admirable projects realized, among them the first staged performance in New York of Berlioz' epic *Les Troyens* and the American premiere of Benjamin Britten's *Death in Venice*; he also made innovations of his own. Under him the company paid its historic visit to Japan.

Gentele's production of *Un Ballo in Maschera*, based on the life of Gustav III of Sweden, was world famous. It had been cheered at the Edinburgh Festival and in Montreal at Expo 67. Without him there was no point in going on with plans to produce it here. Chapin substituted another Verdi work, *I Vespri Siciliani*, which had never been produced at the Metropolitan, though the company had sung it in concert form at Newport, and which had been a great success under John Dexter's direction at Hamburg. The two had known each other when Dexter came to Lincoln

Goeran Gentele (top left) of Stockholm's Royal Opera was named to replace Sir Rudolf Bing in the general manager's chair. A director of note, he announced plans for the 1972–73 season, to open with a new Carmen *he himself would stage. A car crash in Sardinia, only days after he took office, ended his life. Gentele had engaged the Czech-born conductor Rafael Kubelik (bottom left) as the first music director in the company's history. After Gentele's death the Metropolitan carried on under the guidance of Schuyler G. Chapin (above, at far right), another Gentele appointee, who was named general manager until 1975, when the board of directors abolished this post in favor of a tri-part form of leadership divided between Anthony A. Bliss, executive director; James Levine, music director; and John Dexter, director of production. Shown above with Chapin are three men who have served the Metropolitan Opera in many valuable capacities—Charles Riecker of the artistic administration (at far left); Francis Robinson, now tour director and consultant; and Michael Bronson, the business director*

Joan Ingpen (above), the Metropolitan Opera's artistic administration director

Center with the Royal Shakespeare Theatre. Chapin invited him back. *Vespri*, all black and white and its set mainly a wide staircase that all but filled the stage, wasn't everybody's dish, but nobody could deny it carried quite a wallop. It was the first collaboration of James Levine and John Dexter, and it socked the audience right in the eye and ear. Josef Svoboda designed and lighted the stark production. Montserrat Caballé and Nicolai Gedda sang the leads, later Renata Scotto and Placido Domingo. There were many revelations in the score, particularly the duet in the last act. What went on in the orchestra underneath was marvelous. Justino Díaz majestically saluted the "adored earth" of Palermo.

Gentele's first step had been to appoint a music director. In the entire history of the Metropolitan, Rafael Kubelik was the first to hold that title. After his resignation, Levine, who had been named principal conductor by Gentele, later succeeded to the post.

Soon after leaving the Metropolitan, Mr. Chapin was named dean of the School of the Arts at Columbia University.

Two of Gentele's other key appointments were Charles Riecker as artistic administrator and Michael Bronson as business and technical administrator. In their mid-thirties, both were already at the Metropolitan. An accomplished pianist and linguist, Riecker brought to a largely diplomatic post his considerable powers of persuasion, and anyone who had seen Michael Bronson when he was driving the station wagon for the Metropolitan Opera Studio and then running the show knew he wouldn't be doing that for long. Bronson's job is as vast as his title, as you will see when we go backstage in a subsequent chapter. It was his department that realized the dream of the company's visit to Japan.

Much of the enormous burden of dealing with the fourteen unions represented in the Metropolitan Opera House is borne by Bronson. Bronson is also producer of the live telecasts of the Metropolitan, beginning with *La Bohème* on March 15, 1977—the first telecast of a complete opera from the new opera house. His family owned Green Mansions, a well-known resort hotel and theater in upstate New York, so he got his start in the theater young, which is the best way.

The latest addition to the artistic administration is Joan Ingpen as director of the artistic administration. She was controller of planning at the Royal Opera House, Covent Garden, from 1962 to 1971. After that she joined the Paris Opera, where she had planned the seasons through 1980 before coming to the Metropolitan.

David M. Reuben (below), press and public relations director for the company

The latest addition to the Metropolitan's masthead is David M. Reuben, who became director of press and public relations with the 1978–79 season. A native of New York City, Reuben joined the Metropolitan's press department in 1963 and worked there for two summers while attending the University of Pennsylvania. He received his B.A. degree in 1964, and after army service in Vietnam he returned to the Metropolitan in 1966. He served as assistant house manager for two years before rejoining the press department. For three years he was the Metropolitan's press representative. Johanna Fiedler, the beautiful daughter of the legendary conductor of the Boston Pops, succeeded to the post.

James V. Forrestal, who went from Wall Street to Washington to become Secretary of the Navy, said business is 90 percent getting people to work together, government 95. Any artistic endeavor must be about 98, and the present management of the Metropolitan Opera is a team.

THE PRODUCT

Tradition is a word that has become suspect since Toscanini's withering observation that it may be only the memory of the last bad performance. He was speaking of one kind of tradition. We are talking about another when we say that in the very beginning a Metropolitan tradition was established, that of big and varied repertory with the finest artists the world can produce.

In the first season, when everything was sung in Italian, there was still variety, and French and German works were to be heard. In the ensuing seven years there was again French and Italian repertory aplenty, though offered in German. Immediately thereafter the custom of performance in the original language was established. Variation from this was rare, and usually for good reason.

It may seem ridiculous that the first *Boris Godunov* and the initial *Eugene Onegin* at the Metropolitan should have been in Italian, but remember the principals in that first *Onegin*—Muzio, Martinelli, and De Luca. Later we went to English, which made infinitely more sense. Now we do *Boris* and *Onegin* in Russian, which makes the most sense of all.

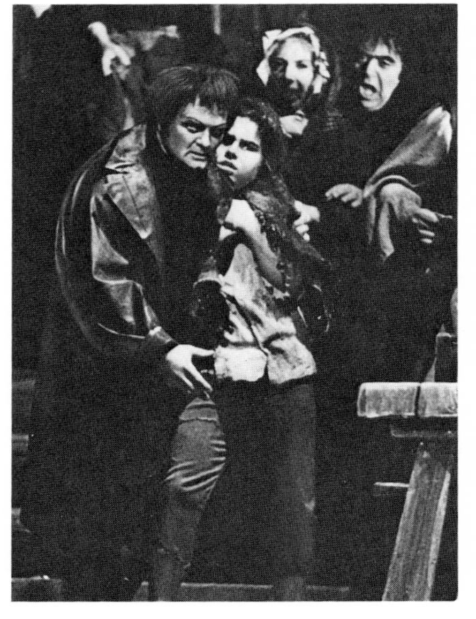

Contemporary works added much interest in the Metropolitan Opera's first season at Lincoln Center, 1966–67. A new production of Britten's Peter Grimes *for Jon Vickers (above) established this twentieth-century masterpiece in the permanent repertory*

Before we left the old house, there had been 11,078 performances of 212 different works. For a like period no other company in the world can boast such a record.

What determines the repertory of the Metropolitan? In an operation where a sold-out house pays only about half the cost of raising the curtain, you can never let your eye stray too far from the box office. You simply can't get too far out. Casting also has a large say in the decision. Obviously you can't perform certain works unless you have the right singers. Conversely, when you have Marilyn Horne, James McCracken, and Renata Scotto you can think about *Le Prophète*, which hadn't been done at the Metropolitan for nearly half a century and which was a smash hit of the 1976–77 season.

Season in and season out, however, it seems to be the works themselves. Based on number of performances, the top three at the Metropolitan for as long as anybody can remember are A, B, C, in that order—*Aida*, *La Bohème*, *Carmen*. There is no foreseeable sign of a breakup in this triad. "The public," Rudolf Bing used to say, "is interested in masterpieces."

In the first dozen years in the new house, up through the 1977–78 season, there have been 2,628 performances of eighty-six different works. This is almost a fourth of the total output in the old house, twelve years against eighty-three years! There have been fifty-five new productions. Forty-one, nearly three-quarters of them, have been successes, again an amazing count by anybody's standard.

There were also two world premieres staged—Marvin David Levy's Mourning Becomes Electra *with Evelyn Lear making her debut in the title role (below) and Samuel Barber's* Antony and Cleopatra, *which starred Leontyne Price as the Queen of the Nile, Rosalind Elias and Belén Amparán as her handmaidens, Charmian and Iras (right), faithful unto death*

Nine new productions were announced for the opening season. Well, it was Goethe who said, "I love him who yearns for the impossible." They all got on, but among the tolls was the rebellious turntable. Franco Zeffirelli's ambulatory sphinx in *Antony and Cleopatra* had to be pushed around by stagehands. Samuel Barber's massive work based on Shakespeare's tragedy had been commissioned to open the new house.

Shifting as it does between three worlds, *Die Frau ohne Schatten* in Nathaniel Merrill and Robert O'Hearn's production depended heavily on that turntable and practically had to be redirected. By consent of everybody in the house, Richard Strauss' ambitious allegory is the biggest, most com-

plicated production in the repertory. It proved to be the sleeper of the inaugural season in the new house and became the prototype of the production in Paris with the same superb cast, headed by a beautiful and appealing pair, Leonie Rysanek and James King, as the Empress and Emperor, Walter Berry and Christa Ludwig as the Dyer and his wife, and Karl Böhm again on the podium. It came back to the Metropolitan two seasons later with the same artists—and the turntable working this time.

Another triumph of the first season in the new house was *Peter Grimes.* We had mounted Benjamin Britten's masterpiece in the old house but, despite a splendid cast, had not done it justice. This time we did it with Colin Davis conducting, Tyrone Guthrie directing, Tanya Moiseiwitsch designing the scenery and costumes, and Jon Vickers in the title role, a part he has made his own. What Caruso was to *Pagliacci* and Chaliapin was to *Boris*, Vickers is to *Peter Grimes.*

Alfred Lunt and Cecil Beaton's production of *La Traviata* replaced *Faust* as fourth in the Metropolitan's repertory based on number of performances, and *Die Zauberflöte* took its mood from Marc Chagall's joyous scenery and costumes, inspired by his own mural—a blessed relief after Bruno Walter, who had almost killed it with too much love. The late conductor had choked it with incense and drowned it in holy water.

This magical *Magic Flute* is unsurpassable. Twice it has gone on tour, and Mrs. Jouett Shouse, the Lady Bountiful of Wolf Trap wanted to make it an annual celebration there.

From that first season, there are those of us who would welcome a return of Marvin David Levy's *Mourning Becomes Electra*, particularly since all but one of the original cast are still around. Boris Aronson made his Metropolitan Opera debut with this work. The patriarchal designer had the powerful collaboration of the young Greek director Michael Cacoyannis, who brought a background in the originals of the tragedies on which Eugene O'Neill based his play.

Roméo et Juliette the second season in the new house had Franco Corelli and Mirella Freni, in a later season Placido Domingo and Judith Blegen, as the star-crossed lovers to the life. *Luisa Miller*, absent from the Metropolitan for nearly forty years, was a knockout at home and on tour. The first production of the work at the Metropolitan since Ponselle and Lauri-Volpi, it was ravishingly sung by Montserrat Caballé, Richard Tucker, Sherrill Milnes, Giorgio Tozzi, and Ezio Flagello, with Thomas Schippers conducting.

Luisa Miller was Attilio Colonnello's most successful production here. His and Nathaniel Merrill's idea to play it within a proscenium of the period, stage boxes inhabited throughout the performance, was brilliant. The most startling thing about *Luisa Miller*, however, was Tucker, singing with a freshness as though his career had just begun. It recalled a letter Otto Kahn had written Caruso late in his career, when he was singing *L'Elisir d'Amore* and *Samson* in the same season. "To sing as you do," he wrote, "with the same artistic perfection heroic parts and lyric parts is a most outstanding artistic feat." Tucker later triumphed in *Luisa Miller* at La Scala.

Hansel and Gretel was given a long overdue revival in an enchanting new production by Merrill and O'Hearn, with Rosalind Elias and Teresa Stratas surely the most believable children ever to take on the title roles. This production out-Disneys the master. It has to be seen to be believed, and even then you can't quite believe it. The rocks and tree stumps and

Protagonist of Ponchielli's La Gioconda *in 1966–67 was the beloved Italian soprano Renata Tebaldi (above). The opulent décor for this new production (top right, Act I) was designed by Beni Montresor. The following season other Italians took the stage as the star-crossed lovers of Gounod's* Roméo et Juliette—*Franco Corelli, shown grieving over the dead Mercutio, John Reardon (bottom right), and Mirella Freni (below), at the moment Juliette contemplates taking the sleeping potion*

A quintet of Verdi productions at the new Metropolitan Opera House: Anna Moffo as Violetta in Act III of the 1966–67 Lunt/Beaton mounting of La Traviata *(left); Placido Domingo as Manrico in the 1968–69 Merrill/Colonnello production of* Il Trovatore *(below); the 1977–78 Dexter/Moiseiwitsch staging of* Rigoletto *(right), with Domingo as the carefree Duke of Mantua (top left), Ileana Cotrubas as Gilda and Sherrill Milnes as the Jester (top right), and the Act IV quartet (bottom), with these artists and Isola Jones as Maddalena; the Triumphal Scene of* Aida *(next two pages) in the Dexter/Reppa/Hall edition of 1975–76, with Cornell MacNeil as Amonasro, Leontyne Price as Aida, James Morris as the King of Egypt, Bonaldo Giaiotti as Ramfis and Marilyn Horne as Amneris; the celebrated Zeffirelli/Hall* Otello *from the 1971–72 season (subsequent two pages), with Milnes as Iago in Act II (top left), Teresa Zylis-Gara as Desdemona and Shirley Love as Emilia (top center), Milnes with James McCracken as the enraged Moor (bottom left), Zylis-Gara and McCracken during the dramatic ensemble of Act III, the arrival of the Venetian ambassadors (top right), and the final moment of Act IV, when Otello asks a final kiss of his dead wife*

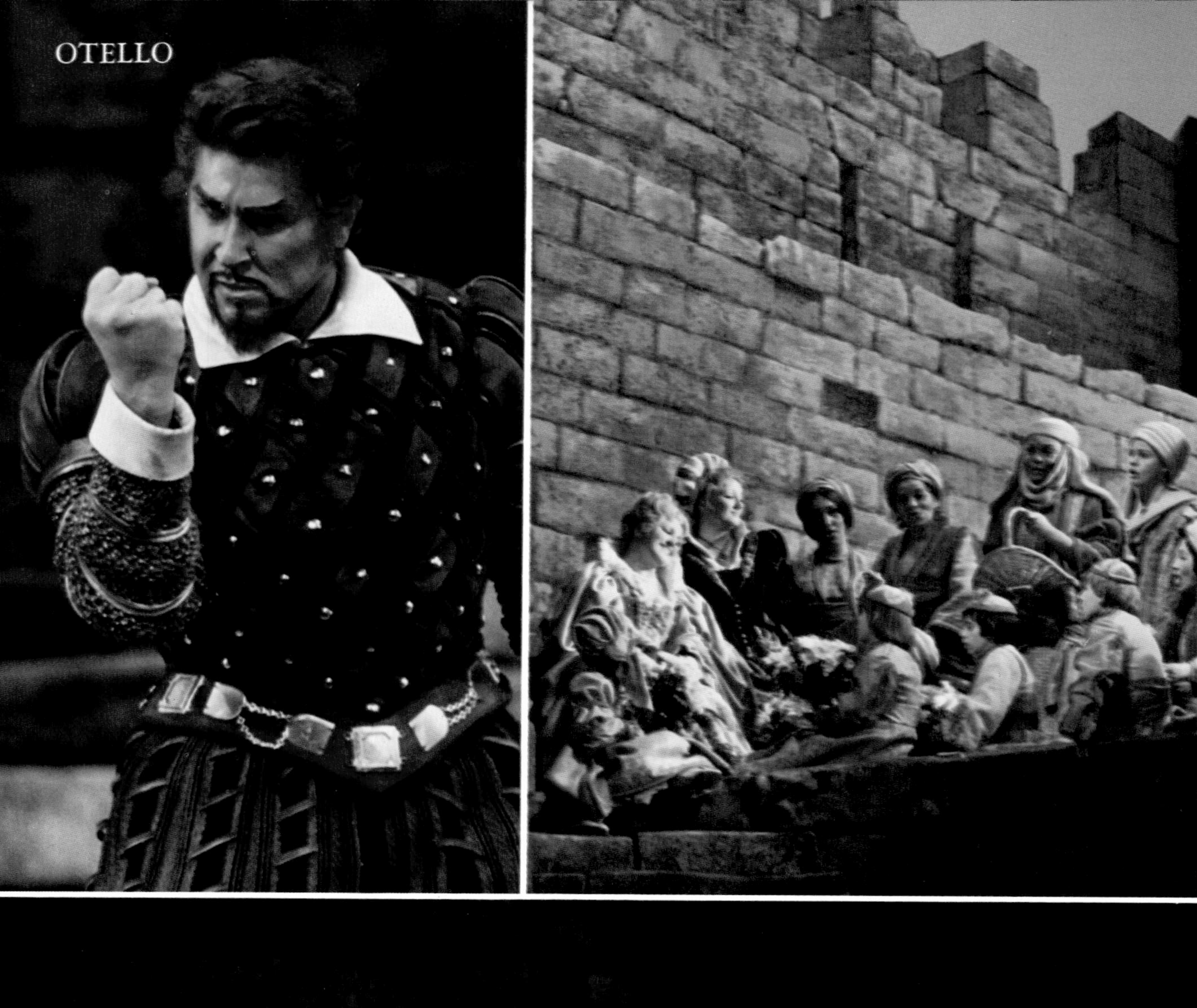

A triptych of new Puccini productions at the Metropolitan Opera: Il Tabarro *with Cornell MacNeil as Michele and Teresa Kubiak as Giorgetta (top left),* Suor Angelica *featuring Lili Chookasian as the Princess with Gilda Cruz-Romo as Angelica (top right), and* Gianni Schicchi *with Betsy Norden as Nella, Irene Dalis as Zita, Frank Guarrera as the title hero, Marcia Baldwin as Ciesca (bottom left), Raymond Gibbs as Rinuccio and Gene Boucher as Marco (below), a staging of* Il Trittico *unveiled between 1974 and 1975 by director Fabrizio Melano and designer David Reppa; Birgit Nilsson in the title role of* Tosca *with Gabriel Bacquier as Baron Scarpia (right), a Schenk/Heinrich collaboration of 1967–68; and the heralded 1976–77* La Bohème *televised coast to coast on PBS (previous two pages) in the Pier Luigi Pizzi décor and staged by Melano, with Renata Scotto and Luciano Pavarotti as Mimi and Rodolfo (far left and top right), Andrea Velis as Alcindoro and Maralin Niska as Musetta (top center), Paul Plishka as Colline during his touching coat song (bottom center), and Ingvar Wixell as Marcello (bottom right), comforting Rodolfo and the dying Mimi*

Wagner's epic Der Ring des Nibelungen *in the Karajan/Schneider-Siemssen/Wakhevitch production: Zoltán Kelemen as Alberich stealing the gold in* Das Rheingold *(top left), Thomas Stewart as Wotan confronting Birgit Nilsson as the errant warrior-maiden Brünnhilde in Act III of* Die Walküre *(bottom left), Jess Thomas in the title role of* Siegfried *(above) and Miss Nilsson as the* Götterdämmerung *Brünnhilde (below). At the premiere of* Götterdämmerung *Miss Nilsson gave new meaning to the term heroic soprano. A few days earlier she had dislocated her shoulder during rehearsal, and despite enormous pain, she sang the first performance with her arm in a sling, one of the more eloquent performances of her career*

toadstools are live little people, not to mention angels who really fly and witches who actually ride their brooms. Our president wanted to put it on the cover of our annual report that season, until we persuaded him to opt for something more serious.

The third season the new house saw the launching of the new *Ring* cycle, sponsored by Eastern Airlines. "Fly Eastern to Valhalla," one wag suggested as a sales pitch. Jonathan Rinehart, vice-president of Eastern, who was carrying the ball on the *Ring* sponsorship, said no.

The grandiose scheme was to bring in, one a season, Herbert von Karajan's production of the cycle for the Salzburg Easter Festival. When Rudolf Bing heard Karajan demanded—and got—eight full-length lighting rehearsals for one production, he said, "I could have got it that dark with one." Nevertheless, Karajan's conception of the *Ring* was as big as the work itself. It wasn't Shaw's allegory of Marxism but the corrupting power of power itself.

As chief designer for the Vienna State Opera, Günther Schneider-Siemssen had worked closely with Karajan, their first association being not on Wagner but on *Pelléas et Mélisande* in 1961. When he was starting out, Schneider-Siemssen could not decide whether to pursue a career as a designer or as a conductor. It was Clemens Krauss who advised him to "stick to the paintbrush instead of the baton." In Munich he studied with Emil Praetorius, the peerless designer of Bayreuth in the twenties and thirties.

A labor dispute, which cut nearly in half the season of 1969–70, delayed the sequence of the *Ring. Siegfried* did not get on until 1972–73, which time we had lost Karajan, but we did have Nilsson and Jess Thomas—and we had Erich Leinsdorf. *Götterdämmerung* came in the following season under Rafael Kubelik, and the entire cycle was completed the season of 1974–75, marking perhaps the last appearances in this country of Birgit Nilsson.

Someone once said of the late Tullio Serafin that when he came into the opera house even the cleaning women did their jobs better. This may or may not be true of Karajan, but he is emphatically more than an electrifying conductor. His ideas of stagecraft are amazing. The opening of *Das Rheingold* he and Schneider-Siemssen devised must be the most realistic water effect ever seen on a stage, and it was accomplished by the simplest of means. Wavy strips of shiny material about the length of a man's outstretched arms are attached to two drop scrims, one just back of the other. Slowly the scrims are raised and lowered in opposite directions. For the first time in history our dispensary had calls for seasick pills.

The new *Tosca* had effective, brooding scenery by Rudolf Heinrich and direction by Otto Schenk, the foremost actor of Middle Europe, though Sardou's and Puccini's melodrama gave him little rein for his greatest gift, which is comedy.

Der Rosenkavalier by the team of Merrill and O'Hearn was also a new production of 1968–69. One wild Saturday night there was a piece of stage business undreamed of by director, librettist, or composer. The spaniels of the Marschallin's levee mated right in front of the prompter's box. Even Dr. Böhm on the podium was convulsed, and the purveyors of our four-legged talent named one of the puppies Octavian. What else?

The bill for opening night that season was *Adriana Lecouvreur.* Maria Callas went backstage and laid to rest her ancient feud with Renata Tebaldi.

"A black orchid," the former soprano Margherita Sheridan used to call Callas, and the contrast of her dark beauty with the alabaster-skinned, blond-wigged Tebaldi created the "strange harmony of different beauties" that Tosca's lover sings about.

It was a vintage year for tenors, bringing about the Metropolitan debuts of both Placido Domingo and Luciano Pavarotti. Lauritz Melchior used to disappear into the wings for a beer during the long Grail Scene in the first act of *Parsifal.* Pavarotti's appetites lay in a different direction. During a June Festival matinee of *Rigoletto* he left the stage to bestow a bear hug and wet smack on a pretty blond girl he spied playing bassoon in the stage band.

Whatever went wrong in the overproduced *Antony and Cleopatra* Zeffirelli atoned for with *Cavalleria Rusticana* and *Pagliacci* on their delayed entry in 1969–70. We had been scheduled to open late September, but because of the labor dispute we did not get going until late December. The rehearsal of *Cavalleria* broke the silence. We reached an agreement at six o'clock on a Saturday evening. The company was summoned, and there was a rehearsal of *Cavalleria* onstage the next afternoon.

I wish there were a recording of Zeffirelli's pep talk to the company at that first rehearsal. He spoke of Duse, who had done the play, as though he had seen her. Grace Bumbry was Santuzza, Fiorenza Cossotto later assumed the role. When the first bars of Lola's whorey little ditty came from backstage Cossotto—without moving her head so much as a quarter of an inch—shot Corelli a look that could mean only one thing, castration.

Joan Sutherland as Norma in the only other new production of the season of 1969–70 was matched by Marilyn Horne, whose Metropolitan debut role was Adalgisa. The season made up in brilliance what it lacked in length. Horne's entrance in the first act was not a big voice cut down; it was a big voice far away, an eerie effect and a triumph of technique.

The new stage turntable, introduced in *Norma*, also was used with great effect as the Temple of the Grail swung into view while it moved forward in the new *Parsifal*. The turntable also allowed Merrill and O'Hearn, whose effect it was, to do *Die Frau ohne Schatten* as they had envisaged it four seasons before. Their round table in *Parsifal* is faced with carvings, exact copies of those that circle the great Chalice of Antioch.

The highlight of 1970–71 was the new *Fidelio*, which had its first performance on the 200th anniversary to the day of the composer's birth. Leonie Rysanek took the title role, Böhm conducted, Aronson was the designer, and Schenk the director.

One of the great scenes in all movies is the moment in *The Life of Émile Zola* when Joseph Schildkraut as Captain Dreyfus emerges from his prison on Devil's Island. We can feel the sting in his eyes, and we know he would run from the light had he not been denied it for so long. There is some of this in the last scene of *Fidelio* as brought to life by Aronson and Schenk. Admittedly, things had been churned up to quite a pitch in the pit by Dr. Böhm and the *Leonore* Overture No. 3 when the curtain rose on the final scene. The designer and director took it from there. Downstage on the raked platform stood the prisoners. Upstage, outside a giant, cruel gate, their families and friends waited, panting for it to rise. The light back of them was blinding. For a moment nothing moved. The suspense was almost unbearable. That picture said as much about justice and freedom, love and brotherhood as the music that inspired it.

Heroines for Verdi operas—Montserrat Caballé in Luisa Miller *(above), revived in a new Merrill/Colonnello production during the 1967–68 season, and Leontyne Price as Leonora in* Il Trovatore *(below), heard in the spring of 1969, still another Merrill/Colonnello effort. Franco Zeffirelli's spectacular productions of Mascagni's* Cavalleria Rusticana *with Grace Bumbry as Santuzza and Franco Corelli as Turiddu (top right) and Leoncavallo's* Pagliacci *with Sherrill Milnes as Tonio, Richard Tucker as Canio and Teresa Stratas as Nedda (bottom right) were first seen in 1969–70. That season balanced this verismo double bill with a bel canto masterpiece, Bellini's* Norma, *starring Marilyn Horne in her company debut as Adalgisa and Joan Sutherland as Norma (next two pages), in a production designed by Desmond Heeley and staged by Paul-Emile Deiber*

All of us at the Metropolitan have speakers in our offices connected to a microphone in the footlights. We can tune in on whatever goes on at rehearsals and performances. It is a major reward of the job. I can never forget Jon Vickers' sighs at the end of Florestan's great aria—sounds you would never hear in the auditorium, but there they were, not just finishing touches but part and parcel of an incomparable re-creation. It hangs in his gallery between Peter Grimes and Aeneas, not to mention Siegmund and Tristan.

At the first matinee of the June Festival of 1971 a young conductor made his Metropolitan Opera debut in *Tosca.* He was only twenty-eight. He was in pretty fast company—Bumbry, Corelli, Peter Glossop—but from the first crashing chords in the orchestra it was clear a master was at the helm and there was no limit to where he would go. Today he is the Metropolitan's music director, James Levine.

La Fille du Régiment, which had been a sensation at Covent Garden, was brought over, as the late S. Hurok used to say, "untact." Sir Rudolf, in his last season as general manager, deplored the production. It didn't matter. There was Sutherland shooting off sounds that were like showers of meteors in a winter sky. And there was Pavarotti, not only a vocal trapeze artist with his nine consecutive high C's but also displaying his rich comic gifts. Opera isn't often intentionally funny, but the spectacle of Pavarotti trying to hide behind Sutherland's skirts is something to be cherished forever.

The season also gave us *Tristan und Isolde* in a new production of surpassing imagination and almost unbearable impact. Wagner said the right kind of performance of *Tristan* would be more than the public could take. August Everding, the director, and Günther Schneider-Siemssen, the designer, came as near confirming the master's claim as has happened in our time.

They refused to be bound by anything save the immortal story they were retelling. In Act I the lights, scenery, everything, dissolved around the lovers, and imperceptibly they were lifted thirty feet in the air. You weren't in the slightest aware they were moving; you simply suddenly realized they were up there. The same thing happened in the love duet of Act II. Isolde's garden became a forest, a lake, the sky, anywhere to get lost.

Needless to say, Everding and Schneider-Siemssen were living up not only to Wagner but to Nilsson, Mignon Dunn, Jess Thomas (Vickers in a subsequent season joined Nilsson in a single, unforgettable performance), John Macurdy, Thomas Stewart, and Leinsdorf.

Another highlight of Bing's last season was the Zeffirelli *Otello* with costumes by Peter J. Hall—highly appropriate, since Verdi's penultimate masterpiece is one of Sir Rudolf's two favorite operas. Böhm conducted, while onstage, McCracken, Zylis-Gara, and Milnes outdid themselves. To point up the climax of Act III, Zeffirelli began the act in what appears to be an armory, gunmetal the prevailing color, with enormous swords and shields on the walls; when the brass announced the approach of the ambassadors, the stage blacked out. Without so much as a beat, on the first shout of the chorus, *"Evviva!,"* every light in the place came up again to reveal a scene of splendor rarely seen on a stage, all red and gold.

Sir Rudolf's last season had opened, as did his first, with a kingly Cesare Siepi in *Don Carlo.* Robert Merrill was again Rodrigo. The other principals were Martina Arroyo, who has had more opening nights at the Metropolitan

Cesare Siepi as Oroveso in Norma *(above), a role he sang at the Metropolitan opposite Zinka Milanov, Maria Callas and Joan Sutherland as the Druid priestess; Christa Ludwig with Franco Corelli in* Werther, *1970–71 (below); Miss Sutherland with Fernando Corena and Luciano Pavarotti in the Sequi/Anni/Escoffier production of* La Fille du Régiment, *1971–72 (top right); and, also from that season, Rudolf Bing's last as general manager, Judith Blegen as Mélisande and Thomas Stewart as Golaud in* Pelléas et Mélisande *(bottom right). Two years later came the Dexter/Svoboda/Skalicky staging of* I Vespri Siciliani *(next two pages), with Montserrat Caballé as Elena, Sherrill Milnes as Monforte and Nicolai Gedda as Arrigo*

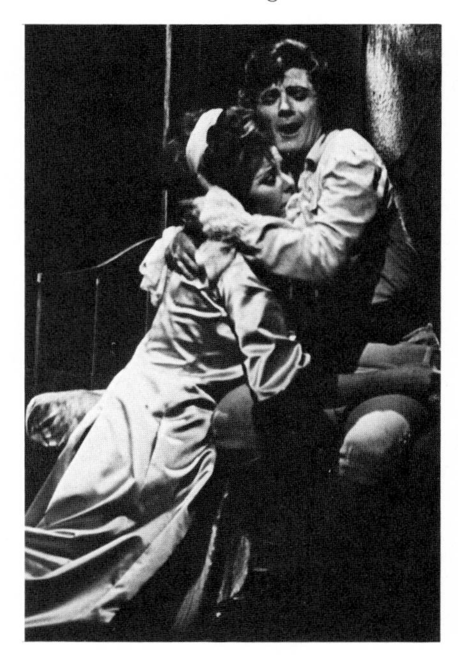

than any other prima donna in recent memory, plus Grace Bumbry and Domingo.

Goeran Gentele's production of *Carmen*, which was to have inaugurated the next season—his first as general manager—was carried out as nearly as possible according to his conception and kept its place in the calendar of 1972–73.

He and Leonard Bernstein had gone back to the original opéra-comique version, restoring the spoken dialogue instead of recitative. They went back even further to Mérimée's story, told in the first person by Don José in prison, awaiting execution for Carmen's murder. In Mérimée, José is not just a little mother's boy from the North. He is a loner, a loser, and he has killed a man, which may be one of the things that pulls Carmen to him. By restoring José to his important role in the story, Gentele raised this rough tale from the level of melodrama to tragedy. Marilyn Horne and James McCracken played it to the hilt.

There has never been as much light on a stage as in Josef Svoboda's first act of *Carmen*—128,000 watts. The curtain goes up on the "fate" motive in the prelude to reveal Don José in dim light, his back to the audience, standing guard at night. With that powerful unresolved chord on which the action begins, the switch is thrown, and immediately you are cooked by the heat of Seville at noon.

In spite of the little Christmas-tree lights on the bower above Lillas Pastia's inn, it is about as disreputable a dump as you would ever want not to enter. The mountain pass is as menacing as the "March of the Smugglers," but before we hear it a smuggler, center stage, his back to the public, waves a signal lamp. Way upstage, high up the canyon, a tiny light motions in reply. You know we are in for dark doings. Awful things are going to happen between those two lights. It's as though you had never seen *Carmen* before.

In the last act, the diagonal of the amphitheater—from the topmost corner of the proscenium stage left to the dull-red gates of the bullring just off center—is a masterstroke. From it the spectators rise into view from time to time during the bullfight, and at the end hats fly out of sight into the ring. In between a few notice another battle to the death going on below, between Carmen and Don José. Without a by-your-leave they turn right back to their national sport—a chilling piece of direction, quite beyond stagecraft.

An old hand at Berlioz, Rafael Kubelik gave the Metropolitan its first performance of *Les Troyens.* He had conducted it with great success at both La Scala and Covent Garden, where Jon Vickers had a personal triumph as Aeneas. New York had to wait 110 years for its first staged performance of *Les Troyens.* The production that Nathaniel Merrill and Peter Wexler created for it, not to mention the performances of Vickers, Shirley Verrett, Christa Ludwig, and the rest of a big and superb cast turned in, made it worth the wait. On the first night Miss Verrett accomplished the superhuman feat of singing on a few days' notice her own role of Cassandra plus Dido in place of Miss Ludwig, who was indisposed.

A brilliant *Contes d'Hoffmann* gave Richard Bonynge the opportunity to demonstrate why he is such a vitalizing force in the reemergence of French opera, at the same time providing Miss Sutherland with a four-wheeled vehicle and Domingo one of his best roles as the poet.

Astrid Varnay (above) portrayed the sexton's widow in Janáček's Jenufa *in 1974–75, with (top right) Teresa Kubiak as Jenufa, William Lewis as Steva and Jon Vickers as Laca. Another of the season's new productions follows (next two pages), Rossini's* L'Assedio di Corinto, *with Shirley Verrett as Neocle (top left), Harry Theyard as Cleomar, Beverly Sills as Pamira and Justino Díaz as Maometto (top center), Díaz alone (top right) and with Sills in Act II (bottom). The previous season, 1973–74, starred Placido Domingo as Hoffmann and Joan Sutherland as Antonia in Offenbach's* Les Contes d'Hoffmann *(below) and offered Rossini's* L'Italiana in Algeri *with Christine Weidinger as Elvira, Fernando Corena as Mustafà and Marilyn Horne as the Italian girl of the title, Isabella (bottom right)*

The theater is a strange place. When Katharine Cornell did *Romeo and Juliet*, Jo Mielziner designed a beautiful costume for her, filmy, virginal. You might have thought it just right if you hadn't seen what came later. A walk-on in the back row at the Capulets' ball was in a dress of gray flannel trimmed with orange and silver. The design had been stenciled on. Under the lights it was better than brocade. Her husband and director, Guthrie McClintic, decided that was the dress for Miss Cornell.

This story is told to illustrate how Ming Cho Lee's icons for *Boris Godunov* could be better—as indeed they were—than the priceless real ones the Bolshoi Opera brought during its visit in 1975. Ming had been delighting New York City Opera audiences for some time before he made his Metropolitan Opera debut with *Boris*. Everding was the director. Even the New York *Times* conceded that our *Boris* was better than the Russians'. It was a double first for the Metropolitan—the first time in Russian, and the first hearing of the Mussorgsky original score here.

Martti Talvela had made a big impression at his Metropolitan debut as the Grand Inquisitor in *Don Carlo* and later as Fasolt in *Rheingold*, but they weren't patches on the Finnish giant's overpowering Boris. Jerome Hines, who has passed his thirtieth milestone with the company, later reassumed the role of the guilt-crazed Czar.

At the opposite end of the scale was Benjamin Britten's *Death in Venice*, which came over from England in the original production and with the same direction and principals. There were those of us who wondered if Thomas Mann's painfully sensitive novella could travel to the opera house. It certainly didn't to the screen. The answer was a resounding yes, with highest marks to the composer. That hurdle out of the way, how would it fare in the vast spaces of the Metropolitan? Previously it had been heard only at Aldeburgh and in London. The answer again was yes, thanks to Peter Pears, John Shirley-Quirk, Steuart Bedford, Colin Graham, and John Piper.

The English invasion that came with *Death in Venice* looked in the announcements as though it might be some kind of British Mafia. Any possible apprehensions were unfounded. Never was there a more professional or pleasant team to work at the Metropolitan. New York had seen Piper's work in *The Rape of Lucretia* at the Ziegfeld Theatre some years back. Bedford and Graham, unknown quantities here, had performed their chores at the premiere and at Covent Garden, and they repeated their success here. Peter Pears as Mann's tortured author and John Shirley-Quirk in seven different roles were the last word.

The end of the 1974–75 season brought the long-awaited entry of Beverly Sills to the Metropolitan. *L'Assedio di Corinto* was the vehicle. It had also served to introduce Miss Sills to La Scala, but it was unknown here. She not only fulfilled every expectation but, hardy trouper that she is, took to the road with it and opened in every city that season with the unfamiliar Rossini work. Right up there with her was Shirley Verrett, who on tour the next season sang the first Normas of her career.

Aida passed the 600 mark during the 1975–76 season in a new production under Levine and Dexter, with scenery by David Reppa and costumes by Peter J. Hall. The unsurpassable lineup of principals included Leontyne Price, Marilyn Horne (later Mignon Dunn), James McCracken, Cornell MacNeil, and Bonaldo Giaiotti, adding up to the strongest musical performance of *Aida* in years.

Peter Pears as Aschenbach made his Metropolitan Opera debut during the 1974–75 season in the U.S. premiere of Britten's Death in Venice *(above). Bellini's final score,* I Puritani, *returned to the repertory during 1975–76, in a Sequi/Lee/Hall production that starred Joan Sutherland as Elvira and Luciano Pavarotti as Arturo (right). Also making a forceful impression in the important role of Sir Giorgio Walton was the young American bass James Morris (below), a protégé of no less a paragon of Bellini style than Rosa Ponselle. With Sherrill Milnes as Riccardo, the Metropolitan's quartet of stars rivaled Bellini's original cast—Grisi, Rubini, Tamburini and Lablache*

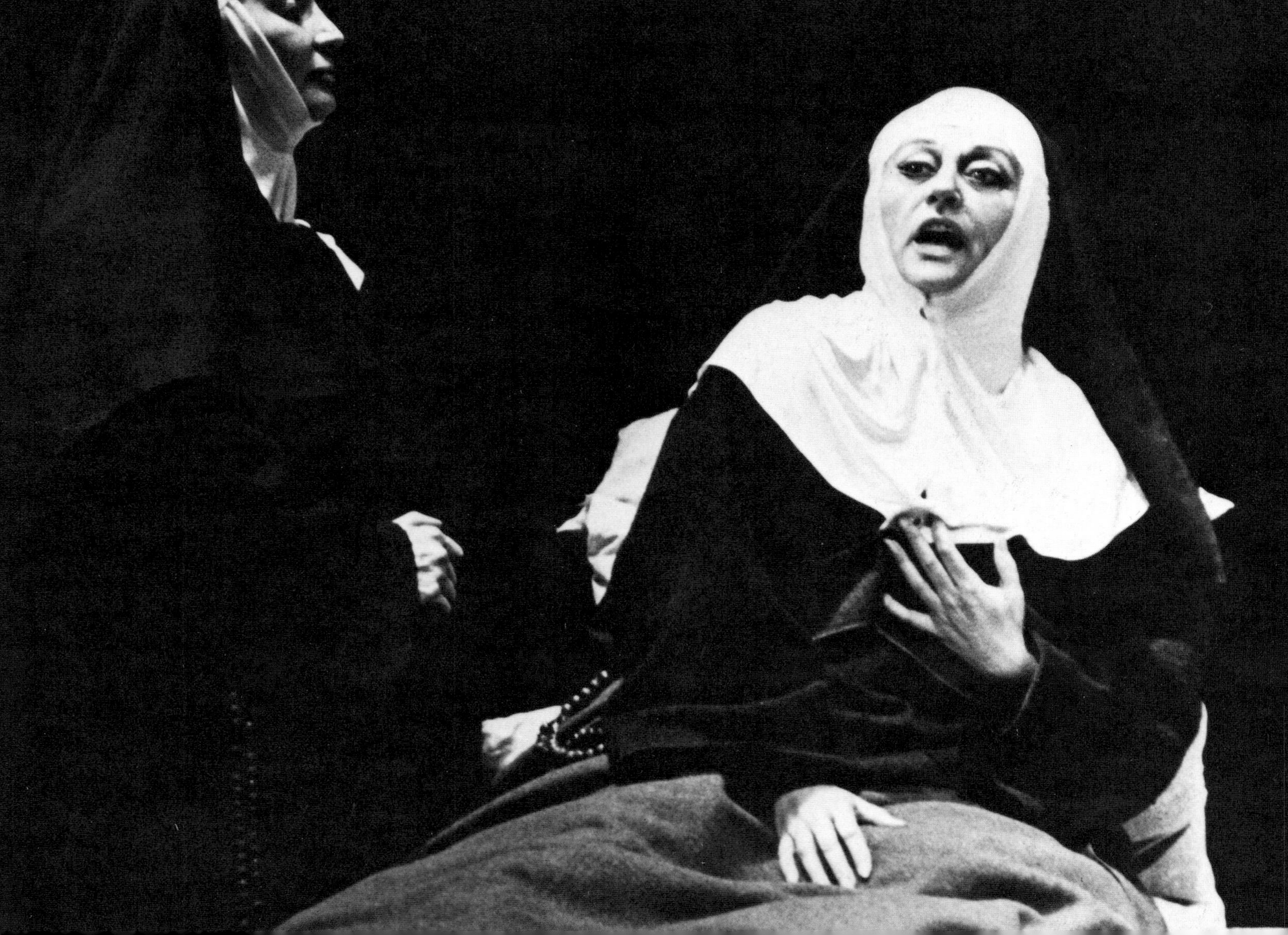

John Dexter's extraordinary stagings of two twentieth-century works never before heard at the Metropolitan shed true excitement on the season of 1976–77. Poulenc's Dialogues of the Carmelites *unfolded on a cross-shaped unit set (top left) and starred Mignon Dunn as Mother Marie and Régine Crespin as the Old Prioress (bottom left), shown here during her harrowing death scene. Alban Berg's* Lulu, *the third act of which had not yet been completed, featured Tatiana Troyanos as Countess Geschwitz (above), with Carole Farley as the amoral Lulu and Donald Gramm as Dr. Schön, her protector and victim (below). After Schön is fatally shot by Lulu, she is pursued by his son Alwa (next two pages), Miss Farley with William Lewis. When the Metropolitan gives* Lulu *again, it will be in the now-completed three-act version*

Dexter cut down on spectacle, though there was still plenty of that, and concentrated on the human side of the drama. He pointed out that most of *Aida* is one, two, or at most three people singing at a time. The ballet became a man-to-man gladiatorial encounter that was hair-raising.

From an earlier period came a more conventional production of Bellini's *Puritani*, absent from the boards of the Metropolitan for nearly half a century. Miss Sutherland, Pavarotti, Milnes, and James Morris turned in true bel canto performances. The duet of the baritone and bass will remain a peak in a lifetime of operagoing, and the delicately subdued stage pictures provided by Ming Cho Lee had the quality of tinted engravings right down to the frame, perfect for the period.

Miss Sills, who opened the season in a repeat of *L'Assedio di Corinto*, later melted us with a haunting *Traviata* under the baton of Sarah Caldwell, the first woman to conduct at the Metropolitan.

The *Trittico*, Puccini's trio of one-acters, was heard complete for the first time since the years of its world premiere at the Metropolitan. In two subsequent performances Renata Scotto's feat of singing the leading soprano roles in all three operas was an accomplishment without precedent in this theater.

How many opera houses can boast a resident designer of the versatility of David Reppa? The backdrop of *Il Tabarro* is a blow-up of photographs of rows of Paris houses. You smell the city immediately on the rise of the curtain.

Reppa and Fabrizio Melano made their joint debut with *Gianni Schicchi*, which the Metropolitan had produced before it undertook to restore the whole *Trittico.* Melano, the son of an Italian vice-consul in New York, attended the Sorbonne and Columbia University, has directed in Santa Fe, Dallas, Portland, and San Francisco, and for Miami he has staged *Les Pêcheurs de Perles.*

The fourth new production of 1975–76 was a handsome *Nozze di Figaro* with Evelyn Lear, Judith Blegen, and Frederica von Stade. Kiri Te Kanawa, the enchanting New Zealand soprano, who had made an unscheduled and highly acclaimed debut in *Otello* a few seasons before, took over as the Countess. Justino Díaz as Figaro fulfilled the promise of his beginnings.

Three of the six new productions brought out the season of 1976–77 were of works new to the Metropolitan. Two of these were masterpieces of the twentieth century, Alban Berg's *Lulu* and Francis Poulenc's *Dialogues of the Carmelites.* Both were sellouts and seem to have broken the curse on contemporary works at the Metropolitan. You couldn't juxtapose two works of wilder contrasts. During the overlapping rehearsal period of the two, John Dexter, who doesn't like interviews anyway, was heard to beg off a request for one on the grounds he was too busy "between my nuns and my whores."

Reeking with the decadence of Germany between two World Wars, *Lulu* is a shocker. Dexter's production was all the more effective for not going too far, and Jocelyn Herbert's compact settings and costumes brought back the time. James Levine got a virtuoso reading of the fiendish score from his orchestra and singers. The *Manchester Guardian* said *Lulu* "stirred not merely respect but genuine enthusiasm."

As the Countess Geschwitz, Tatiana Troyanos was curiously subdued, giving the character a strangely pitiful side, a dimension heretofore unsus-

pected. As Dr. Schön, Donald Gramm reconfirmed his right to a place in Polonius' company of "the best actors in the world, either for tragedy, comedy, history, pastoral," etc. The dual role of the Athlete and Ringmaster sent young Lenus Carlson two more rungs up the ladder.

Who will ever forget the picture of Dexter's nuns in *Dialogues of the Carmelites* prostrate on David Reppa's steeply raked cruciform stage? You were instantly prepared for the pity and terror and exultation to follow. After the experience of this piece, few can feel the same about life and death.

Régine Crespin's death scene at the end of Act I was spine-chilling. Alexander Woollcott once referred to Judith Anderson as a great tent pole holding up the billowing canvas of the play. That describes the performances of Mignon Dunn and Shirley Verrett as Mother Marie and Madame Lidoine. Betsy Norden made a charming Constance.

There are two schools of thought as to whether actors should cry real tears on the stage. Some big stars say no. It never seemed to hurt Ethel Barrymore, and Archbishop Sheen used to say, "If you would make me weep, you weep first." Maria Ewing as Blanche never came offstage that she wasn't dissolved in tears. Most of the audience was right with her. Michel Plasson, the young French conductor who had come here with the Paris Opera, in his Metropolitan Opera debut got as near perfection from his forces as can be imagined.

"A great event," Ruth Gordon called *Carmelites*, going on to write a friend, "When the nuns walked and the priest made the sign my heart stopped, or seemed to, not because they were going to their deaths, but because they believed. What a great experience. What a touching of the heights! And not in the theater, in an opera house. I would not believe such feeling could happen amidst crystal chandeliers up top and gold silk curtains waiting to come down, but no. Nothing came between us and faith." Poulenc would have liked that.

The third work new to the Metropolitan that season was *Esclarmonde*, which Mr. Bonynge had unearthed for Miss Sutherland. It explained to those of us who hadn't known the work why Massenet was called "Mademoiselle Wagner." Be sure to give Wagner here the French pronunciation. The production was borrowed from San Francisco. Beni Montresor, who had designed the scenery and costumes for *The Last Savage* and *La Gioconda* at the Metropolitan, hurled purples and reds in your face never dreamed of before, and Lotfi Mansouri, who directed, is now general manager of the Canadian Opera Company.

Miss Sutherland was Miss Sutherland. That doesn't mean we are taking her for granted. Far from it. You can't say more than that in the way of praise. Giacomo Aragall had been under the weather when he made his Metropolitan Opera debut a few seasons before. In *Esclarmonde* he came through as the sterling young tenor he is.

The absence of the swan in *Lohengrin* set off some lively arguments. There were even those who swore they had seen it, proving how much better than any molting Thanksgiving turkey was the shaft of light among Ming Cho Lee's downstage rushes to signal the coming of the Swan Knight. Peter J. Hall designed the costumes. René Kollo, making his Metropolitan Opera debut, and Pilar Lorengar in radiant white were a dream pair. Ming's foreshortening of the minster was awesome, and Max Reinhardt in his best

French rarities: Joan Sutherland as heroine of the Metropolitan premiere of Massenet's Esclarmonde *(above), staged during 1976–77, with Spanish tenor Giacomo Aragall as the knight Roland (below); the same season's Dexter/Wexler production of Meyerbeer's* Le Prophète *(top right), a work absent from the company's repertory for half a century, starring James McCracken as Jean of Leyden (bottom right), shown at the banquet preceding the fiery denouement; and, from the 1977–78 season, Massenet's* Thaïs *(next two pages), with Beverly Sills as the Alexandrian courtesan and Sherrill Milnes as the fanatical Cenobite priest Athanaël, who, tempted by her charms, forgets his holy vows*

The emergence in recent years of bel canto specialists, among them Shirley Verrett, Luciano Pavarotti and Sherrill Milnes, made possible a new production of La Favorita *during the season of 1977–78, the Metropolitan Opera's first staging of this Donizetti tragedy in more than threescore years and ten. Miss Verrett assumed the pivotal role of Leonora, the king's favorite (above)*

Milnes was cast as her consort, Alfonso (below). Also shown is the final scene (left), one of Donizetti's finest, when the penitent Leonora dies in a monastery while searching for the holy man she loves, Fernando, sung by Pavarotti

days couldn't have maneuvered crowds with more power than Everding handled his—the slow, massive advance of the knights to the banks of the Scheldt at the beginning and the end of the opera, the suspense of the bridal procession at the end of Act II. James Levine brought out unplumbed beauties in the score. The work of the chorus was spectacular.

"The meaning of *Lohengrin* today," Everding said of his production of 1976–77, "is that our world is so dark, so full of woe, full of envy and quarreling, and in an instant a kind of heaven opens up." All this was clear in his direction.

Mignon Dunn made Ortrud, though evil, a figure of towering tragedy. Donald McIntyre was hard to hate as Telramund, and Bonaldo Giaiotti was a sonorous King Henry.

Le Prophète had not been heard at the Metropolitan since 1928. Marilyn Horne's performance as Fidès did not suffer by comparison with Schumann-Heink and Matzenauer. When has there been a voice of such color and range, flexibility and power? James McCracken's John of Leyden was in the great line, and Renata Scotto's brilliant aria was a show stopper right at the rise of the curtain. Peter Wexler's stage pictures were Brueghels come to life. For *Le Prophète* he and John Dexter devised a unit set that resembled the skeleton of a cathedral. Nine wagons were modified to suggest various locales. The stagehands were costumed, and the action recalled what must have gone on when the morality plays set up shop in the town square. To start the snowfall you saw a little man climb a ladder and shake confetti from a bag; then flakes began to fall from the flies, and illusion took over.

The skaters' ballet, with choreography by Stuart Sebastian, was an utter delight. The couple teaching their youngster to skate was a wonderful touch, and Anthony Santiago in red, the only dot of bright color in the wintry scene, was as good as Brian Shaw in green had been in Sadler's Wells' *Patineurs*.

It was more than an eye on the exchequer that prompted Dexter to hold his productions down on *Le Prophète* and *Carmelites*. "All this technical equipment is fine," he said, "but if it stunts the audience's imagination it is no good. The audience should be looking for faces, not windmills."

Pier Luigi Pizzi's scenery and costumes for *La Bohème* were borrowed from the Lyric Opera of Chicago. When Thomas Schippers became ill, shortly before rehearsals began, Maestro Levine took over. Fabrizio Melano directed with some highly original and effective strokes. The production, which moves the period from the 1830s of Murger's novel to the 1880s of Puccini, is realistic but also highly romantic.

Renata Scotto and Maralin Niska were Mimi and Musetta. Pavarotti, Ingvar Wixell, Allan Monk, and Paul Plishka were the quartet of bohemians. This was the cast of the first complete opera to be telecast from the new house on March 15, 1977.

Four new productions were unveiled during 1977–78, *Rigoletto*, *Tannhäuser*, *Thaïs*, and *La Favorita*. Maestro Levine and Dexter gave new life to *Rigoletto* by sweeping away many of the encrustations of a century and a quarter—the held notes, the interpolated high notes, etc. We now knew what Verdi meant when he replied to an admirer's praise of *Otello*, "I could write another *Otello*. I could never write another *Rigoletto*."

Forsaking the North Sea of *Peter Grimes*, Tanya Moiseiwitsch came up with a revolving unit set which, according to the *Times*, "might represent

The Tower of Babel, or one of Sodom's more interesting structures, or the court of Mantua." It is unmistakably infested with Rigoletto "clambering up and down it," in the words of Peter G. Davis of the *Times*, "like some kind of scurrying, repulsive spider." It also becomes the creepy house of Rigoletto and the unsavory inn of the killer. On tour, whenever we want to describe a suspicious hostelry, we call it "a Sparafucile joint."

The arrangement of the acts was as Verdi intended, three instead of four, with the first two scenes joined. Rigoletto collapses in a heap on the floor under Monterone's curse, isolated by a spotlight which *Newsweek* said was "like the finger of God." He lies there, and the spotlight stays on him during the scene change. He is lying in the street in front of his house when the lights go up on Act II.

One age-old problem with *Rigoletto* has been how to get from the Duke's palace to the jester's house without a twenty-minute scene change. In the old Metropolitan production, the first intermission was longer than the first act! "We can't stop the momentum here," Dexter says. "This great, decaying Renaissance tower turns slowly, a giant silhouette in the darkness. Suddenly we are in front of Rigoletto's house. As he gets up, with the curse still ringing in his ears, he bitterly wipes off his court jester's makeup, and the stage is set for his sinister meeting with the assassin Sparafucile."

A farewell and a debut were made during 1978–79 with the John Dexter/Desmond Heeley production of Don Pasquale: *Beverly Sills bade adieu to the company as Norina while Haken Hagegard made his bow as Malatesta (right). Gabriel Bacquier sang Pasquale (above with Hagegard's Malatesta), and Nicolai Gedda was Ernesto, Pasquale's nephew (below). Among three other new stagings that season by Dexter was* Don Carlo, *with sets by David Reppa and costumes by Ray Diffen (next two pages). The cast included Renata Scotto as Elisabetta (top left), Sherrill Milnes as Rodrigo (bottom left), Nicolai Ghiaurov as Philip II (top right) and Marilyn Horne as Eboli (bottom right). Also shown are the sets for the monastery of St. Just (top center) and the cathedral square (bottom center), with Scotto, Milnes, Ghiaurov and Giuseppe Giacomini as Don Carlo*

Sherrill Milnes sang the first performance in place of Cornell MacNeil, who was ill. MacNeil later took over the role of his Metropolitan Opera debut. Ileana Cotrubas was all youth and innocence as Gilda; Placido Domingo as the gay and unprincipled Duke was later replaced by Neil Shicoff, who made good the promise of his debut the season before in *Gianni Schicchi;* and Justino Díaz was a stellar Sparafucile, as Pinza had been thirty years before him.

When the new production of *Tannhäuser* was unveiled in 1977–78, the last time a Metropolitan audience had heard the Festival March was closing night in the old house. Günther Schneider-Siemssen's scenery looked as though the New Bayreuth had never existed. The valley of the Wartburg was right out of the Thuringian landscape. The sturdy arches of the Hall of Song were the best German Romanesque this side of Worms, and the grotto of Venus might have been one of those that Mad King Ludwig dreamed up for his fairy-tale castles.

Patricia Zipprodt was already established as a quadruple success on Broadway, in movies, television, opera, and ballet before her Metropolitan Opera debut. Her costumes for *Fiddler on the Roof* and *Cabaret* had won Tony awards. In films she dressed Katharine Hepburn in *The Glass Menagerie* and Anne Bancroft in *The Graduate.* She also designed costumes for Miss Bancroft's television special *Annie, the Women in the Life of a Man.* For the New York City Opera she was responsible for costumes for *Katerina Ismailova*, and for the New York City Ballet *Watermill* and *Les Noces.*

Even this impressive record was insufficient preparation for the marvelous costumes she provided *Tannhäuser.* Her subdued but glowing colors were like tapestries and seemed to blend right into Schneider-Siemssen's frescoes. You could hardly tell the sitters in the choir-stall-like ring around the wall from the paintings above.

It was Levine's first *Tannhäuser*, but nowhere did this show. From his forces he got a reading that was authoritative and utterly convincing, no mean feat, considering how views of sex and religion have changed since 1845. Schenk's direction was in the same vein.

A folio of three new Wagner productions at the Metropolitan Opera: the 1976–77 Everding/Lee/Hall Lohengrin *with Pilar Lorengar as Elsa (left), René Kollo as the Swan Knight in prayer (top left) and after his arrival in Act I with Lorengar and Bonaldo Giaiotti as King Henry (top right), the confrontation during the bridal procession of Act II (bottom right), with Donald McIntyre as Telramund, Giaiotti and Lorengar, and Mignon Dunn as Ortrud with McIntyre (below); the acclaimed 1971–72 Everding/Schneider-Siemssen evocation of* Tristan und Isolde *(next two pages) with Birgit Nilsson (top left) and Jess Thomas (bottom right) as the tragic lovers and the sets for the Act I ship (top right) and the second-act love duet (bottom left); and the no-less-lauded Schenk/Schneider-Siemssen/Zipprodt* Tannhäuser *of 1977–78 (subsequent two pages) showing nymphs and satyrs in the Venusburg grotto (top left), James McCracken as Tannhäuser serenading Grace Bumbry as the Goddess of Love (bottom left), the Act II Hall of Song, with Leonie Rysanek as Elisabeth and John Macurdy as Landgraf Hermann (top center), and Misha Raitzin as Walther and Bernd Weikl as Wolfram (top right) and the Valley of the Wartburg, with Rysanek as Elisabeth in prayer while Weikl as Wolfram faithfully watches (bottom right)*

A trio of new Strauss productions at the Metropolitan Opera: the heralded company premiere of Die Frau ohne Schatten *in 1966–67, a Merrill/O'Hearn collaboration with James King and Leonie Rysanek as the Emperor and Empress (top left), Walter Berry and Christa Ludwig as the dyer Barak and his Wife (bottom left); the same season's Graf/Heinrich edition of* Elektra *with Regina Resnik as the guilt-torn Klytämnestra (right) and Birgit Nilsson with William Dooley as Elektra and Orest (below); and the Merrill/O'Hearn* Der Rosenkavalier *(previous two pages), introduced during the 1968–69 season with Rysanek as the Marschallin in the Act I finale (top left), Reri Grist as Sophie and Ludwig as Octavian during the presentation of the silver rose (top center) and Berry as the wounded Baron Ochs with Rosalind Elias as the letter-bearing Annina (top right). Also shown is Faninal's overblown reception hall of Act II (bottom), at the moment Octavian, Count Rofrano, takes up the sword to protect Sophie from her boorish suitor, Baron Ochs, with Rudolf Knoll as Faninal, Elias, Berry, Andrea Velis as Valzacchi, Judith De Paul as Marianne, Ludwig and Grist*

A storm of controversy arose in the spring of 1979 with the first staging in New York of Jean-Pierre Ponnelle's unconventional production of Wagner's Der Fliegende Holländer, *which the French designer-director presented in a single act—actually the composer's original intention—but with the story unfolding as the nightmare of a young Steersman on Daland's ship. For three of the principal roles, conductor James Levine chose Carol Neblett, in her Metropolitan Opera debut, as the haunted Senta (left), Jose Van Dam as the man in her visions, the accursed Dutchman (above), with William Lewis as the Steersman (below), who during the course of his dreams assumes the character of the huntsman Erik. When the curtain finally fell on the two-and-a-half-hour premiere, the entire audience rose to its collective feet, some cheering, some jeering. The reaction to this fresh view of an old favorite was decidedly mixed, but no one was bored*

McCracken not only sang the errant knight but acted him. Leonie Rysanek, the most touching Elisabeth in memory, scored another triumph. Who can forget her in her blue gown and veil, prostrate at the wayside shrine, then going among the pilgrims to search in vain for the returning Tannhäuser? Her reckless fall on both knees for the prayer was literally an act of self-sacrifice.

Making his debut as Wolfram, Bernd Weikl was handsome as a Greek god and sang and acted with dignity and complete understanding. John Macurdy was a majestic and resonant Landgrave. Norbert Vesak's ballet was appropriate to the music of the Bacchanale.

In the words of the New York *Times*, Grace Bumbry, who stood Bayreuth on its ear as Venus, all black and gold, "contrives to be a symbol without losing credibility as a woman."

The late Lawrence Gilman wrote there would always be revivals of *Thaïs* as long as beautiful babies were born who grew up to be beautiful opera singers. That being the case, it was inevitable Beverly Sills would take on *Thaïs.* Gilman wrote that in 1939, when Helen Jepson sang the courtesan of Alexandria. There hadn't been a Thaïs at the Metropolitan since.

Opposite Miss Sills was Sherrill Milnes as Athanaël, the cenobite monk, who tries to save the soul of Thaïs and loses his own, a kind of earlier-day Rev. Henry Davidson in *Rain.*

The production was appropriately lavish and decadent, with a great swinging bed in Thaïs' mirrored boudoir. The scenery and costumes by Carl Toms were borrowed from the San Francisco Opera, and Tito Capobianco directed. Capobianco, for years a guiding light at the New York City Opera, is now putting San Diego on the opera map as artistic director of the company there. Dennis Seetoo, also making his Metropolitan debut, was responsible for the orgiastic choreography. The violin solo of the famous Meditation, telling of the conversion of Thaïs, was another memorable contribution by our concertmaster, Raymond Gniewek.

Raymond Gibbs and Jean van Ree alternated in the role of Nicias. That same season Gibbs was Pelléas in the loveliest recreation of Debussy's masterpiece in memory. So carefully was this moonstruck work served up that the conductor, James Levine, avoided applause at the beginning by entering the pit in the pitch dark.

La Favorita had not been heard at the Metropolitan since Caruso, and early Caruso at that, 1905. This time it had Pavarotti at the top of his form, singing "*Spirto gentil.*" Shirley Verrett sang "*O mio Fernando*" and the duet with Sherrill Milnes and the rest of Leonora's music sumptuously. Bonaldo Giaiotti was a high-powered Baldassare. Jesús López-Cobos, who had made his Metropolitan Opera debut with *Adriana Lecouvreur,* was the conductor, and Patrick Tavernia brought more than a score of years' experience on our stage to the direction. The scenery by Ming Cho Lee and costumes by Jane Greenwood were borrowed from San Francisco.

Billy Budd, in 1978–79, was another smash hit for John Dexter, with Peter Pears returning as Captain Vere and Richard Stilwell a touching Billy.

Forthcoming seasons will see the Metropolitan orbit farther into the twentieth century. Schoenberg's *Moses and Aaron* and Weill's *Rise and Fall of the City of Mahagonny,* are on the agenda. With *Carmelites*, *Billy Budd*, and *Lulu* it was demonstrated there need not be collisions with the older and more familiar works. Undoubtedly there will be commissioned works.

CONDUCTORS

In one of his excursions from the story line of *War and Peace*, Tolstoy says that 300 sheep led by a sheep will fight like sheep but 300 sheep led by a lion will fight like lions. The same is true of an orchestra, but God help you if you have, as in the case of the Metropolitan Opera Orchestra, a hundred lions through some inexplicable miscalculation led by a sheep.

The emergence of the conductor as a stellar quantity is a comparatively recent development in the 400-year history of opera. Nevertheless, the Metropolitan had its share of lions on the podium from the very beginning.

Two conductors were listed on the roster that first season. If you ask even an opera expert who Auguste Vianesi was, he wouldn't know. Put the question another way, and ask who conducted the first performance of the Metropolitan Opera: the answer would be the same.

Cleofonte Campanini, the other conductor of the Metropolitan's first season, is another story. After the disaster of that inaugural semester, Campanini returned to Europe and conducted at La Scala and Covent Garden, among other things the disastrous world premiere of *Madama Butterfly* in 1906. He then came back to America as music director and chief conductor for Oscar Hammerstein, who gave the Metropolitan such a run for its money they had to pay him to leave town. Campanini's next move was to Chicago as general manager. He engaged Galli-Curci after the Metropolitan had given her the cold shoulder. Three years after her debut there, that dear lady sang at his funeral on the stage of Chicago's old Auditorium.

The Metropolitan Opera's first conductor, Auguste Vianesi (above), and its second, Cleofonte Campanini (right). In 1907, at Oscar Hammerstein's Manhattan Opera, Campanini was on the podium for Mary Garden's U.S. debut in Massenet's Thaïs. *He also presided over the U.S. premiere of Debussy's* Pelléas et Mélisande *there, with the incomparable Garden, who had created the role in Paris, as heroine (below)*

The younger brother of Italo Campanini, who sang the title role of *Faust* when the Metropolitan threw open its doors for the first time, Cleofonte was born in Parma, which has the most savage opera audience in the world. He survived a debut there conducting *Carmen* the same year he came to the Metropolitan. He was only twenty-three.

In moments of stress the hair dye would mingle with the perspiration and come trickling down, and Campanini was the most superstitious of men in a world where superstition is both religion and law. He could not resist a bent nail. The old Auditorium in Chicago was connected to the Congress Hotel by tunnel. Some members of the opera company never breathed fresh air or saw daylight from one season's end to the next. A wretch among them strewed the tunnel with bent nails. Campanini arrived at rehearsal barely able to walk under the weight in his pockets.

If he saw a hat on a bed, he would hurl it into the street below. He would gallantly replace it with a new one, but at about half the price you had paid.

"What is your fee?" he asked a luckless tenor after an audition. "Two thousand dollars a performance," the tenor replied. "I'll give you two hundred," Campanini shot back without changing tone. "I'll take it." This is a true story.

After its first season, the Metropolitan became to all intents and purposes a German house. Leopold Damrosch had founded the Oratorio Society and the New York Symphony, and he conducted the Philharmonic as well as at the Metropolitan. His older son, Frank, became chorus master at the Metropolitan and later director of the Institute of Musical Art, now the Juilliard School. Walter Damrosch succeeded his father as conductor of

Metropolitan Opera House,

SEASON 1884-5.

The opera season will extend over thirteen weeks, which will include thirty-eight subscription nights and twelve matinees. For these performances arrangements have been made with the distinguished European artists whose names are appended.

Sopranos.

Frau MATERNA,
Imperial Theatre, Vienna.
Frau SCHROEDER-HANFSTAENGL,
Grand Opera, Frankfort.
Frau ROBINSON,
Grand Opera, Hamburg.
Frau A. KRAUS,
Grand Opera, Bremen.
Frl. H. BELY,
Grand Opera, Hamburg.
Frl. A. SLACH,
Grand Opera, Prague.
Frl. STERN,
Hamburg.

Mezzo-Sopranos and Contraltos.

Frl. MARIANNE BRANDT,
Imperial Theatre, Berlin.
Frl. GUTJAR,
Berlin.
Miss CARRIE MORSE,
New York.

Tenors.

Herr ANTON SCHOTT,
Royal Opera House, Hanover.
Herr ANTON UDVARDY,
Royal Opera House, Pesth.
Herr TIFERRO,
Royal Opera House, Graz.
Herr KEMLITZ,
Royal Opera House, Hanover.

Baritones and Basses.

Herr ADOLF ROBINSON,
Grand Opera, Hamburg.
Herr A. BLUM,
Royal Opera, Wiesbaden.
Herr JOSEPH STAUDIGL,
Grand Ducal Opera, Karlsruhe.
Herr JOSEPH KOEGEL,
Grand Opera, Hamburg.
Herr JOSEPH MILLER,
Kroll's Opera, Berlin.
Herr L. WOLFF,
City Theatre, Zurich.

Musical Director and Conductor,

Dr. LEOPOLD DAMROSCH.

Stage Manager,

Herr WILHELM HOCK,
Grand Opera, Hamburg.

Chorus Masters,

Herr LUND, Herr REICHELT.

Leader of Orchestra,

Herr REINHARD RICHTER.

Ballet Master,

Monsieur BAPTISTIN.

Prime Ballerine,

Mlle. ZOLLIA, Mlle. CORMANI, Mlle. TORRI, } From La Scala, Milan.

The Metropolitan Opera's 1884–85 prospectus (above) did not announce Walter Damrosch as a conductor, but when his father, Leopold, died, the young man (below left) assumed command with assurance. Born in Breslau in 1862, he formed his own opera troupe during the nineties, touring Wagner's works widely. His first opera as composer to reach the stage was The Scarlet Letter, *in 1886, the Metropolitan mounting his* Cyrano De Bergerac *in 1913. He achieved distinction as a symphonic conductor and in his late years (below), he won new laurels as one who purveyed classical music to young people via radio*

METROPOLITAN OPERA HOUSE,

Thursday, March 31, 1898.

MEMORIAL SERVICES,

ANTON SEIDL,

Born May 7, 1850. Died March 28, 1898.

ORDER OF EXERCISES:

1. DIRGE, - Musical Mutual Protective Union. Conductor: Nahan Franko.
2. MALE CHORUS, "Wenn Zwei Freunde Scheiden." Arion Society. Conductor: Julius Lorenz.
3. "ADAGIO LAMENTOSO" from Symphonie Pathetique, - Tschaikowsky. Philharmonic Orchestra. Conductor: Richard Arnold.
4. "HELDEN REQUIEM," - - H. Zoellner. Deutscher Liederkranz. Conductor: H. Zoellner.
5. ADDRESS by the Rev. Merle St. Croix Wright.
6. "SIEGFRIED'S FUNERAL MARCH," Wagner. Philharmonic Orchestra. Conductor: Henry Schmitt.

Anton Seidl (below), a native of Pest, was principal conductor at the Metropolitan during its German years, the 1880s. He led the first U.S. performances of many Wagner scores at the Opera House, including Die Meistersinger. *His wife, the Viennese soprano Auguste Seidl-Kraus, sang Aïda (below right) and numerous other roles under his baton. Seidl was highly respected by the public and when he died, in 1898, he was accorded a unique honor: his funeral services were conducted on the stage of the Metropolitan (above)*

the Oratorio and New York Symphony Societies and was later conductor of the Philharmonic. It was he who persuaded Andrew Carnegie to build Music Hall, which was later given the philanthropist's name.

Three operas by Walter Damrosch were produced by the Metropolitan. None of them held a place in the repertory. The last was *The Man Without a Country* in 1937. When Edward Ziegler saw the grand old man coming in for the first night, resplendent in white tie and tails, he said, "There goes the man without an opera." But that night he did have a real soprano, making her debut at the Metropolitan. "I brought Gadski to this country," Dr. Damrosch said to Helen Traubel, "and I had to come to St. Louis to find you!"

Fifty years ago, Dr. Damrosch was the Lenny Bernstein of his day, with his "Music Appreciation Hour" on NBC. His "Good afternoon, my young friends," in a faintly German-flavored accent, brought joy to hundreds of thousands. The outdoor bandshell at Lincoln Center is named Damrosch Park for this family, whose influence on the musical life of this country is inestimable.

Leopold Damrosch died during that first German season. Walter and the manager, Edmond C. Stanton, were sent to Europe to seek talent and came back with commitments from Lilli Lehmann, Max Alvary, and Emil Fischer, who was to introduce Hans Sachs to America. They also signed Anton Seidl, who was a friend of Wagner, had lived six years in his house, and had assisted the Master at the first complete production of the *Ring*. Seidl remained the peerless champion of Wagner's music dramas and gave the United States its first performances of the *Ring* and *Tristan und Isolde*. His wife, Auguste Seidl-Kraus, was the first Eva in this country.

"Although 'Hojotoho'-ing' Brünnhildes were enthusiastically acclaimed by New York's German-American population," Edward R. Lerner records in an article for *Columbia Library Columns*, "the boxholders eventually tired of helmets and spears. Even during the early years of Seidl's rule, they induced the director to internationalize the repertory by curtailing the presentations of Wagner's works. Finally a new management, favoring Italian singers, was installed for the 1891–92 season. Three new conductors were employed for operatic performances, while Seidl, shunted to the background, was assigned only Sunday evening concerts." He was out a season, but the public and Jean de Reszke, the only tenor Caruso was ever jealous of, clamored for the return of Wagner—and Seidl—and he resumed his place.

One heir to the conducting mantle of Anton Seidl was Frankfurt-born Alfred Hertz (bottom left), who arrived in 1902. His service to the Metropolitan was long and diligent, thirteen seasons. During his tenure he supervised several U.S. premieres, including Parsifal *with Milka Ternina as Kundry (above),* Königskinder *with Geraldine Farrar (top right) and* Der Rosenkavalier *with Margarete Ober as Octavian and Frieda Hempel the Marschallin (below)*

Seidl distinguished himself in New York outside the opera house as well as at the Metropolitan. He succeeded Theodore Thomas as conductor of the Philharmonic Society and conducted the first performance anywhere of Dvorak's symphony *From the New World.*

His standards were the highest, and there was apprehension that he might forsake America. To forestall this, a group of his friends were forming a permanent orchestra for him when he suddenly died. There was a memorial service to him on the stage of the Metropolitan. He was the first to have such an honor.

Alfred Hertz conducted the pirated Metropolitan production of *Parsifal*, the first staged production outside Bayreuth, in 1903, and the American premiere of *Der Rosenkavalier*, which took place at the Metropolitan. He also conducted the world premiere of *Königskinder* at the Metropolitan, for which Engelbert Humperdinck, the composer, came to New York, and which provided Geraldine Farrar as the Goose Girl with what she called "this sweetest of roles." On her retirement Henry E. Krehbiel wrote in the *Tribune*:

> With what exquisite charm Miss Farrar was likely to invest so romantic a heroine the artist's admirers might easily have guessed; but it is doubtless if any imagination ever reached the figure she bodied forth. She was a vision of tender loveliness, as perfect in poetical conception as in execution. Memories of the picture she presented walking through the massive town-gates, followed and surrounded by her white flock, will die only with the generation that witnessed it.

Hertz went on to conduct the San Francisco Symphony.

When Gustav Mahler made his Metropolitan Opera debut, the same Henry E. Krehbiel reported, "Mr. Mahler did honor to himself, Wagner's music, and the New York public." It was a livelier *Tristan* than they were accustomed to at the time, but, Mr. Krehbiel went on, "inasmuch as the acceleration of tempo in nearly every instance inured to the benefit of the dramatic effect, to that extent admirable—eloquent in phrasing, rich in color, elastic in movement, and always sympathetic with the singers.

Such diverse works as *The Bartered Bride* and *Pique Dame*, both having their first American performances, benefited from Mahler's leadership. The latter had "remarkable finish, delicacy and finesse and a strong vitality," according to the *Times.*

The path of Gustav Mahler (bottom right) at the Opera House proved less smooth than that of Hertz, but it was of the highest artistic standard. He made his debut in 1907 following a brilliant reign at the Vienna State Opera and he conducted eight works during three seasons on the roster, including Don Giovanni, Fidelio *and* Die Walküre

White

TOSCANINI CONDUCTING A REHEARSAL

Arturo Toscanini (left) spent seven seasons, 1908–15, on the podium of the Metropolitan Opera, leading 373 performances there. Coming to New York with the company's new general manager, Giulio Gatti-Casazza, the conductor from Parma, who had already served as the musical czar of La Scala, soon proved his powers in a stunning variety of works, thirty in number, including the U.S. premieres of Mussorgsky's Boris Godunov, *Puccini's* Le Villi, *Catalani's* La Wally. *Dukas's* Ariane et Barbe-Bleue, *Wolf-Ferrari's* Le Donne Curiose *and Montemezzi's* L'Amore dei Tre Re. *Toscanini's interpretive intensity blazed even during rehearsal, and at one for* Tristan und Isolde, *Olive Fremstad (below) had to excuse herself because of the artistic pressure whipped up by the Maestro*

Arturo Toscanini made his Metropolitan bow the opening night of Mahler's second season and immediately helped himself to the Wagner goodies. *Aida* was his debut, but *Götterdämmerung* was his first rehearsal. After Toscanini's second season, Mahler was out in the cold. Toscanini's repertory included French as well as German and Italian works. His *Carmen* and *Manon* with Caruso and Farrar made history.

From the beginning, Toscanini was a fire-eater. In his first weeks, years before there was any such thing as a grievance committee, a delegation of the men sought an audience with the general manager. What, Mr. Gatti asked, were the foul names the new conductor hurled at them? Blushingly, the men repeated the malodorous epithets. "You think that is bad," Mr. Gatti said. "You should hear what he calls *me.*"

But what music! What wouldn't you give to have been hidden somewhere in the auditorium the day the Maestro whipped things up to such a heat the rehearsal couldn't go on? Fremstad was the Isolde, and Mary Watkins Cushing, who was the soprano's secretary, describes it in her book, *The Rainbow Bridge*:

> The music began, announcing an unusual excitement at the first note. It quieted, only to rise again with electrifying sweep and power, catching up the soprano and carrying her to emotional heights even beyond herself. A strange and magical antiphony now developed without apparent cause. Enkindled by Isolde's growing exaltation, the Maestro in his turn sent the flames of his own inspiration crackling higher and higher. Tossing the torch back and forth to each other, always with an upward lift, the two artists were soon standing alone together in a high, fire-girt world quite beyond the vision of ordinary mortals. The tension continued to mount, became painful, then suddenly was no longer to be borne. Beads of perspiration broke out on the Maestro's brow, and he groaned and moaned in a hoarse, unmusical voice, the baton quivering in his hand. The men in the orchestra began to mutter, and on the stage there was sudden silence. Fremstad left her place and walked uncertainly toward the footlights, her face wet with tears and her arms flung out in protest.
>
> "*Maestro, non posso più!* I beg you, let us go no further!" The Maestro shook his head sadly, shrugged his shoulders, and gave the signal for dismissal.

They said Toscanini took everything fast, faster as the years went on to avoid any notion that he might be getting old. There isn't that much difference in the timings on the scores at the Metropolitan between his and other conductors' tempos. It was pacing, emphasis, involvement. He simply had no equal.

"*Canta, canta,*" he would beg, cajole, command his musicians—"Sing, sing," and he would sing himself in a sound never heard on land or sea, more like a croak. You can hear it on the recording of *La Bohème* on the fiftieth anniversary of the world premiere, which he had conducted. He joins Peerce and Albanese and turns the love duet which concludes Act I into a trio. Rosa Raisa, the first Turandot, wired Toscanini after that historic broadcast, "Dear Maestro, It was so good to hear you sing again."

There is a famous Toscanini story that tells only half of what happened. Perhaps it's time to set the record straight. There was some disagreement at rehearsal between the Maestro and Miss Farrar. Coming down to the footlights, the soprano said, "May I remind you I am the star here."

"Madame," Toscanini replied, "the only stars are in heaven." And there the story has stopped all these years. The Toscanini camp has suppressed what followed. Miss Farrar fired right back—and survived. "But the public pays to see my face, not your back." Some face; some back.

After Toscanini's defection, in 1915, Giorgio Polacco became the leading Italian conductor at the Metropolitan. He and Bori made their debuts the same night with *Manon Lescaut.* He later went to Chicago as chief conductor and eventually general manager, taking with him his lovely wife, Edith Mason. Puccini wrote Liù for Mason, but when *Turandot* had its world premiere she was having a baby and could not deliver in two areas at the same time.

Although the title had not been introduced at the Metropolitan, Artur Bodanzky was virtually Gatti's music director after Toscanini left. The departures of Toscanini and Hertz had sent the general manager searching for a new conductor for his German wing. He found Bodanzky, who had just conducted the first performance in Britain of *Parsifal.*

A native of Vienna, Bodanzky was born in 1877 on Beethoven's birthday, December 16. He studied at the Vienna Conservatory and at twenty was a violinist at the Court Opera and with the Gesellschaft der Musikfreunde, where he played under Brahms. Later he was assistant to Mahler, who was then general manager of the Vienna Opera.

Bodanzky's record at the Metropolitan is astounding, 795 performances of forty-five works. The variety of his repertory is equally impressive, and you have to swoop down to the present, when James Levine will take on two performances of *Pelléas et Mélisande* and two of *Eugene Onegin* in a single week, to meet its match.

Bodanzky conducted Caruso's last performance, was present at Flagstad's audition for the Metropolitan in Switzerland, and presided at her debut and that of virtually every other important Wagner singer of the period—Melchior, Schorr, Leider, Lehmann, Thorborg. The white heat of his performances made the orchestra men cry out in all seriousness, "Thank God, Wagner didn't write four-act operas!" Like Strauss, he was a card shark and gave big parties in his house.

*Artur Bodanzky (above) followed Toscanini as the Metropolitan Opera's major Wagner conductor and he maintained his eminence in this repertoire for twenty-four seasons, 1915–39. During the late 1930s, when the company's roster brought a new Golden Age to Wagnerian singing—*Tristan und Isolde, *for example, with Kirsten Flagstad and Lauritz Melchior in the title roles (right) and Karin Branzell as Brangäne (below)—Bodanzky was inspired to surpass himself, leading performances of incandescent splendor. Wagner became the company's greatest drawing card, with Standing Room Only signs the rule. After his death, Mozart's Masonic Funeral Music was played between the second and third acts of an* Orfeo *he would have conducted*

MORTON

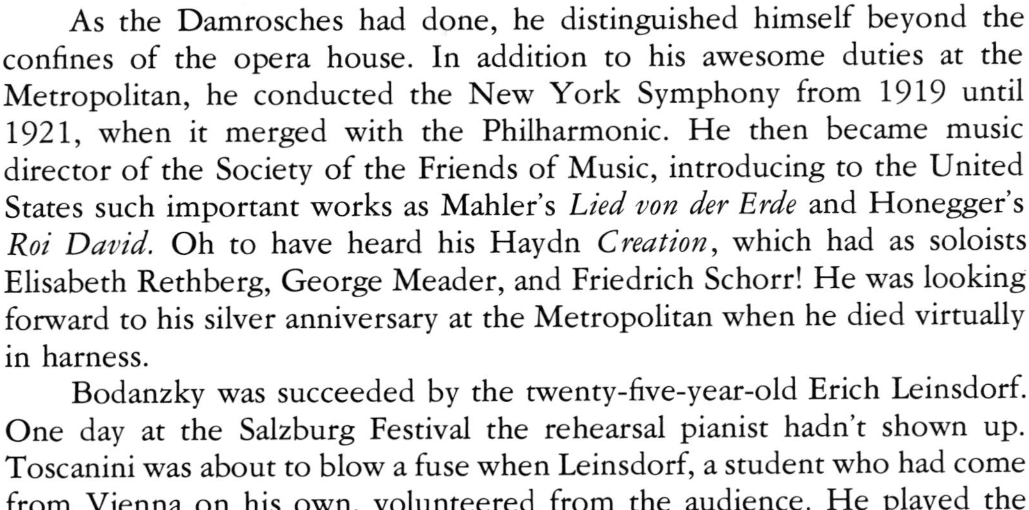

Tullio Serafin and Ottorino Respighi, conductor and composer, posed by the podium of the Metropolitan in 1928 at a rehearsal for the American premiere of La Campana Sommersa *(left). Other novelties of Serafin's decade, 1924–34, included the first U.S. performances of Giordano's* La Cena delle Beffe *and Puccini's* Turandot *as well as the world premieres of two scores by an American composer, Deems Taylor,* The King's Henchman *and* Peter Ibbetson. *Like Toscanini before him, Serafin also conducted Wagner at the Opera House,* Siegfried *and* Parsifal. *Pierre Monteux (below) had two periods with the company, 1917–19 and 1953–56, both outstanding. During his first tour of duty he took charge of the Metropolitan premieres of Rimsky-Korsakov's* Le Coq d'Or, *Rabaud's* Marouf *and Leroux's* La Reine Fiammette, *all introduced to help fill the void left in the repertory by a World War I ban on German works. Monteux returned at seventy-eight to lead* Faust, Carmen, Manon, Les Contes d'Hoffmann, Samson et Dalila *and* Orfeo *as only he could*

As the Damrosches had done, he distinguished himself beyond the confines of the opera house. In addition to his awesome duties at the Metropolitan, he conducted the New York Symphony from 1919 until 1921, when it merged with the Philharmonic. He then became music director of the Society of the Friends of Music, introducing to the United States such important works as Mahler's *Lied von der Erde* and Honegger's *Roi David.* Oh to have heard his Haydn *Creation*, which had as soloists Elisabeth Rethberg, George Meader, and Friedrich Schorr! He was looking forward to his silver anniversary at the Metropolitan when he died virtually in harness.

Bodanzky was succeeded by the twenty-five-year-old Erich Leinsdorf. One day at the Salzburg Festival the rehearsal pianist hadn't shown up. Toscanini was about to blow a fuse when Leinsdorf, a student who had come from Vienna on his own, volunteered from the audience. He played the rehearsal and from then on was in. From the Metropolitan he went to the orchestras of Cleveland, Rochester, and Boston, returning to us from time to time for memorable performances.

Stravinsky, who was hard on conductors, said of Pierre Monteux, "Of all the conductors his beat seems to be more for the orchestra and less for the public." Monteux had conducted the world premieres of *Petrouchka* and *Le Sacre du Printemps* when he came to the house with the Diaghilev Ballet. He was subsequently engaged by the Metropolitan, and Rudolf Bing brought him back to open the season of 1953–54 with *Faust*, the work with which he had made his debut in 1917.

It was the seventieth anniversary of the house in 1953–54, and a new production of *Faust*, the work which had opened it, was chosen to celebrate the occasion. Peter Brook, the director, and Rolf Gérard, the designer, decided to advance it to the nineteenth century, the period of Gounod. They were not the first to do this. The Theatre Guild had moved up to the time of Goethe when they produced the play.

Actually it was a very effective production, but Monteux had nothing but scorn for it and didn't hesitate to say so in a Sunday interview the day before the opening. He particularly disliked the Louisiana plantation Gérard had designed for the garden scene. When he saw it the first time, he observed, "*Marguerite est donc millionaire.*"

In the garden scene Martha asks Méphistophélès, "*Ainsi, vous voyagez toujours?*" And so, you are always traveling? "*Dure nécessité, madame,*" he replies, "*dure nécessité,*" Hard necessity, madame. Until 1961 the Metropolitan used to journey to Philadelphia every Tuesday evening—over in the afternoon, back that night. It was backbreaking. We had just returned from Philadelphia after the 1953 *Faust*, trudging through Pennsylvania Station at 2:30 in the morning. John Gutman in flawless French asked Monteux, then seventy-eight and very well off, "Maître, why do you do it?" Under the famous walrus mustache the old boy whistled the music of "*Dure nécessité.*"

After his first stint with the Metropolitan, Monteux went on to the Boston and San Francisco symphonies, and Wilfrid Pelletier inherited the French repertory from Monteux but was by no means confined to it. It was Pelletier who brooded over the "Auditions of the Air" and had a great deal to do with starting the careers of Leonard Warren, Eleanor Steber, and Robert Merrill. His wife is the beautiful Rose Bampton, who sang both mezzo and soprano roles at the Metropolitan. The Salle Wilfrid Pelletier in the Place des Arts in his native Montreal perpetuates the conductor's name.

When Tullio Serafin made his debut with the opening night *Aida* the season of 1924–25, the old *Literary Digest* headed its review, "The Opera's New Star." The American singer never had a better friend, and it was he who guided the careers of Rosa Ponselle and Lawrence Tibbett, pointing them respectively to *Norma* and *Simon Boccanegra.* Later he proved to be the great artistic force in the early career of Maria Callas. When Serafin returned to Italy he was succeeded as the leading Italian conductor at the Metropolitan by Ettore Panizza. Right hand of Toscanini at the Scala, Panizza supervised the long overdue revivals at the Metropolitan of *Otello, Le Nozze di Figaro,* and *Un. Ballo in Maschera.*

One of the better by-products of World War II was to make available to Edward Johnson the services of Bruno Walter, George Szell, and Sir Thomas Beecham. Walter gave us a *Don Giovanni* which Claudia Cassidy said confirmed our right as "keeper of the operatic keys" in this country, plus a matchless *Fidelio* and an English *Bartered Bride* in which he insisted Pinza had no accent; but it was in Verdi that he perhaps reached his greatest heights. There was a *Forza del Destino* with Milanov, Petina, Baum, Tibbett, Pinza, and Baccaloni, and a *Ballo in Maschera* with Milanov, Thorborg, Peerce, and Warren, finally the Requiem.

One of Bing's first moves was to abolish the traditional Good Friday *Parsifal*, probably the only religious observance ever undertaken by some of our subscribers. He substituted the Verdi Requiem with Milanov, Nikolaidi, Peerce, Siepi, Bruno Walter, and our chorus and orchestra. Old Maestro Polacco said it for us all afterward: "I want to go and find some dark place to cry."

Bing, who had reunited Bruno Walter and the Vienna Philharmonic at the Edinburgh Festival after the war, persuaded him to come back to the Metropolitan. When he outlined the splendors of the *Fidelio* cast—Flagstad, etc.—Dr. Walter quietly asked, "Who is the First Prisoner?"

"*Lasst uns musizieren,*" he used to say to his singers and musicians—"Let's make music," and they did.

Sir Thomas shook the dust out of the dovecotes by giving the French repertory—*Faust*, *Carmen*, *Manon*, *Mignon*, *Louise* (Grace Moore)—a pretty thorough workout, not to mention taking on *Tristan und Isolde* with Marjorie Lawrence. His debut was a double bill which only Sir Thomas would have dreamed up, Bach's *Phoebus and Pan* and *Le Coq d'Or.* "Sir Thomas Beecham and Johann Sebastian Bach entered the Metropolitan cheek by jowl last night," Robert Bagar reported in the *World-Telegram.*

Often late (the Philadelphia Orchestra once began a concert where he was guest conductor without him), Sir Thomas raced to the podium to give the downbeat at the first rehearsal of the double bill. There was some confusion. Half the orchestra had the music of *Le Coq d'Or* and the other half had *Phoebus and Pan.*

After a *Faust* in Public Auditorium, Cleveland, capacity 8,573, Sir Thomas was asked how the performance had gone. "From the conductor's point of view, *mahr-ve-lous*," he snorted. "Not once did I hear the singers."

In 1943 New York finally got around to some attempt at enforcing gas rationing. If your license plate was sighted at the track, maybe your A-card would be taken away. Sir Thomas came out of his apartment up on Park Avenue one evening and hailed a cab. "The Metropolitan Opera House," he directed loftily. The driver didn't move. "I can't take you there, mac," he snapped. "Why not, may I ask?" "I can't take you to a place of amusement."

Ettore Panizza (above), the Argentine maestro of Italian heritage who from 1934 to 1942 ranked among the Metropolitan Opera's most accomplished conductors. Bruno Walter (below), whose eloquent debut in 1941 leading Beethoven's Fidelio *seemed one German emigre's noble response to Hitler's tyranny. The goateed Sir Thomas Beecham (top right), a three-season wartime windfall, 1941–44, seated with stage director Désiré Defrère to rehearse Charpentier's* Louise *with the Mother and Julien of the production, Doris Doe and René Maison. Fritz Stiedry (bottom right), with the company a dozen seasons, 1946–58, works to prepare Verdi's* Don Carlo*—with Delia Rigal, Robert Merrill, Jussi Bjoerling and Fedora Barbieri, the Elisabetta, Rodrigo, Carlo and Eboli of the first night of the Bing era, 1950–51*

George Szell (above with Désiré Defrère), a taskmaster from Budapest, gave the Opera House five seasons, starting with Salome *in 1942 and ending with an unannounced departure after a 1954* Tannhäuser. *In addition to the music of Strauss and Wagner, which he read with intense feeling, he brought forth the heroic dimensions of Mussorgsky's* Boris Godunov, *which launched the 1943–44 season. Fritz Reiner, another Hungarian, also made his debut with* Salome, *but he was blessed with the new Bulgarian soprano Ljuba Welitsch as his Princess of Judaea (left). Reiner tallied five seasons with the company, 1949–54. Fritz Busch, another peerless musician (below), had preceded Reiner on the roster and was introduced with* Lohengrin, *the 1945–46 opener. He stayed four terms, with Mozart and Verdi performances milestones for him and for the Metropolitan. Those who heard him also still speak of his lyrical reading of* Tristan und Isolde

It was the opening Sir Thomas had been waiting for for years. "My good man," he replied patronizingly, "be under *no* misapprehension. The Metropolitan Opera House is not a place of amusement."

Another giant of the Johnson era who came over into Bing's, but not for long, was George Szell. He had his greatest glory with the Cleveland Orchestra, and there is a story that seems to sum him up; in fact *Time* magazine concluded its cover story on him with it. He was conducting the Berlin Philharmonic and making life hell for Westermann, the manager, the son of the statesman.

"Come, come, Szell," Westermann protested mildly, "you are going at this as if it were a matter of life and death."

"Don't you see?" Szell said, very near apoplexy, "It is! It is!"

The three Fritzes—Busch, Stiedry, and Reiner—were also jewels in the Johnson crown. Busch came in the opening night of 1945–46 with *Lohengrin* and conducted the first telecast of the Metropolitan Opera opening night of 1948, his masterful *Otello* with Vinay, Albanese, and Warren. *Otello* with that cast went on tour everywhere that season, and we little realized that in Minneapolis we were saying good-bye to Dr. Busch for the last time.

There hadn't been a new mounting of the *Ring* at the house for thirty-five years when the Metropolitan Opera Guild gave us the Lee Simonson production in 1948. Stiedry conducted, and we had a new, youthfully believable Siegfried in Set Svanholm. Stiedry, who had known Rudolf Bing in Vienna, conducted the splendid *Don Carlo* the first opening night of the Bing regime. He had figured in the Verdi revival of the late twenties and early thirties, which began in Germany. His *Parsifal* was deeply moving, and he proved equally adept at Mozart in the sparkling new *Così Fan Tutte* directed by Alfred Lunt, a plum of Bing's second season.

The roar that went up a February night in 1949 after the joint debuts in *Salome* of Ljuba Welitch and Fritz Reiner is still in the ears of those who heard it. Reiner had come from the Pittsburgh Symphony. He left us for the Chicago Symphony, but he was first—as were most European conductors—an opera man. The government of Hungary had sent him to Bayreuth when he was still a teen-ager, and he was running the Dresden Opera at twenty-six. He engaged Elisabeth Rethberg before she was old enough to sign a contract. Her father had to come up to Dresden from the Black Forest to do it for her.

One evening after a performance, as Dr. Reiner was having supper at Reuben's, Regina Resnik came in from another performance. "What did you do tonight?" the soprano asked. "I don't know what *they* did," Reiner said, not missing a spoonful of his soup. "*I* conducted *Meistersinger.*" And what a *Meistersinger* it was. He did it all over on the tour of 1950. The climaxes were overwhelming, and you discovered things in the orchestra in the quieter moments, such as on Walther's entrance in the last scene, you had never heard before.

It was Reiner who conducted Flagstad's postwar return to the Metropolitan. They had first done *Tristan* at Covent Garden, and a decade later they again worked perfectly together. Bing brought him back in 1963 to conduct *Götterdämmerung*, but he got only through the dress rehearsal of one act. We were doing them a day at a time. He died exactly a week before Kennedy was assassinated.

Fausto Cleva (above)—proudly wearing the ribboned cross of a Grand Ufficiale al Merito of the Italian government, an honor bestowed on him by consul general Vieri Traxler—addresses family and friends at a party in the Opera House in 1971 marking his fiftieth anniversary with the Metropolitan. Among those gathered near the Trieste-born conductor, who was to die three months later during an Orfeo ed Euridice *at the Athens Festival, are Mrs. William Francis Gibbs of the Metropolitan's Board of Directors, Mrs. Cleva, the sopranos Zinka Milanov and, all but hidden by her hat, Maria Jeritza, William Hadley, the Richard Tuckers, Francis Robinson, Maestro Cleva's daughter, Wally (Mrs. Charles Riecker), and, behind the figure of Mr. Traxler, Bruno Zirato, who once served Caruso as his secretary*

Reiner always wanted to conduct *La Bohème* at the Metropolitan. His *Carmen* was definitive, and he wrought miracles with a beat that had to be measured in quarter inches. Frank St. Leger used to give an imitation of his cue for the Armageddon that ends *Der Fliegende Holländer.* Senta jumps off the cliff, and the haunted ship splits and sinks, to the loudest noise ever heard indoors. Reiner's signal for this cataclysm was a look over his glasses and the slightest nod in the direction of the timpani, to his right. "It's my business to make the audience sweat," he used to paraphrase his friend, Richard Strauss, without bestowing those little quotation marks—"not sweat myself."

Fausto Cleva had a half-century association with the Metropolitan. He was almost a beardless youth when he was appointed assistant chorus master to Giulio Setti, who had come with Gatti and Toscanini. The season of 1938–39 he was engaged as conductor. After the collapse of Samuel Insull's empire he went to Chicago for several seasons to try to resurrect the opera there. Cesare Sodero, a pioneer in radio and recording, took over the

During his long tenure with the Metropolitan Opera, Cleva was on the podium for eight opening nights: Aida *(1951), a televised Gala Performance (1954),* Norma *(1956),* Il Trovatore *(1959),* La Fanciulla del West *(1961),* Andrea Chénier *(1962),* La Traviata *(1967) and* Adriana Lecouvreur *(1968). These titles give an indication of the repertoire that was his, excluding French works, for which he demonstrated real affinity. As Bing's most trusted general in the Italian wing, Cleva presided at new productions of* La Gioconda *and* Pagliacci *at the new Opera House, and with this last walked off with new critical raves. He was a true master of his art, one who served the Metropolitan with uncommon excellence and devotion. His son-in-law, Charles Riecker, now serves the company's artistic administration*

Italian repertory at the Metropolitan. Both were flawless musicians, and in his first season Bing brought Cleva back to what amounted to a new career.

There was never a more informed tribute paid a conductor than a remark our contrabassoon, Hugo Burghauser, former president of the Vienna Philharmonic, made about Cleva. The Vienna Philharmonic is autonomous. It was organized by the orchestra of the Vienna Opera to give themselves the opportunity to get away from oom-pah-pah. They choose their own conductor and select their own soloists. It was Burghauser who brought Toscanini to Vienna for the first time. When he spoke, all Vienna trembled. About conductors, Professor Burghauser had few illusions. Of Cleva he said, "When we make a mistake, it's our fault, not his."

The first important conductor not to be inherited by Bing from Johnson was Dimitri Mitropoulos, who came to us from the Philharmonic. Mitropoulos was a beloved man. When commended—and thanked—for having saved a green young tenor from catastrophe in his unscheduled debut, he shrugged. "I like to improvise." He collapsed during a rehearsal of the Mahler Third at La Scala and died on the way to the hospital.

Illness had prevented Mitropoulos from conducting the new production of *Turandot.* In spite of a broken hip only a few weeks before at the age of nearly eighty, Leopold Stokowski can be said to have leaped into the breach. He entered on crutches, attended by a nurse, but led a performance the critics called "powerful, magical." Before each act and at the end the audience rose to greet him. Four standing ovations in one evening must be some kind of record.

Stokowski had conducted his Philadelphians in the Metropolitan Opera House before, a *Sacre du Printemps* with Martha Graham, no less, as the Chosen One, and the New York premiere of *Wozzeck* with Nelson Eddy as the Drum Major, but *Turandot* was his debut with the company. Nilsson used to say, "Wagner made me famous, but Puccini made me rich." She and Corelli were at their very peak, and the rest of the cast was likewise gilt-edged—Moffo as Liù, De Paolis as the old Emperor, Guarrera, Nagy, and Anthony as Ping, Pang, and Pong.

Eugene Ormandy, Stokowski's successor in Philadelphia, had come in Bing's first season to conduct *Fledermaus*, which broke all records before or since—nineteen performances in one season and never an unsold seat.

To our regret and subsequent loss, Rudolf Kempe didn't seem to like it here. He made his debut with a superb *Tannhäuser* and conducted the first Metropolitan Opera production of *Arabella.* Arthur Judson, the all-powerful manager, at one time of both the Philadelphia Orchestra and the New York Philharmonic, who jockeyed conductors around the country as though they were chessmen, came to a matinee, had Kempe to tea afterward, and offered him the world. Kempe was unimpressed. He stayed only two seasons.

Thomas Schippers was only twenty-five when he made his Metropolitan Opera debut. There had been only two native Americans before him. Schippers had conducted the Philadelphia Orchestra before he came to the Metropolitan, and he became conductor of the Cincinnati Symphony while continuing his opera engagements here and elsewhere. He led the world premiere of Samuel Barber's *Antony and Cleopatra*, which Bing commissioned to inaugurate the opera house at Lincoln Center, and his conducting of the new *Boris Godunov*, going back to Mussorgsky's original, did full justice to that great work.

On Broadway, Schippers had conducted Menotti's *Consul*, and on television his *Amahl and the Night Visitors.* As artistic director of the Spoleto Festival he gave opportunity to countless other young Americans. His huge repertory embraced all schools. He died pathetically young.

Another link between our present music director and the great recent past was Jean Morel. James Levine was a pupil of Maestro Morel at Juilliard. Morel was also the teacher of another splendid young conductor now at the Metropolitan, James Conlon. When Morel died, Conlon led the Juilliard Orchestra in a performance of Mahler's Sixth Symphony in his memory. Conlon's *Zauberflöte* in New York and on tour was a highlight of 1976–77. He took over the new *Bohème* in 1977, with *Tosca* following in 1978.

It is impossible to think of a finer musician than Morel. His ear was uncanny, his personality and wit everything you think of as Gallic, and of course in French music he was supreme.

His debut was the Metropolitan premiere of *La Perichole*, and he served up Offenbach with as much care as he would have Mozart. "Is my music

Eugene Ormandy (above), the Hungarian music director of the Philadelphia Orchestra, made appearances with the Metropolitan Opera for two seasons, 1950–52, sparking its hit production of Johann Strauss' Fledermaus. *Dimitri Mitropoulos (top right, rehearsing with Giorgio Tozzi) was another musician first known in the concert hall; the Greek conductor gave the Opera House six seasons starting in 1954, with* Salome, Eugene Onegin, Tosca, Simon Boccanegra *and the world premiere of Barber's* Vanessa *among his finest hours. In 1961 the legendary Leopold Stokowski (bottom right, with stage director Nathaniel Merrill) made an indelible impression with a single work,* Turandot. *Jean Morel (below) began a nine-season stint in 1956, sticking to the French repertory—his debut was Offenbach's frothy* La Perichole—*except for an exceptionally moving account of* Madama Butterfly

light?" he liked to quote Offenbach. "Then it has less chance to fall down." On his own he said of Offenbach's music, "It is lucid, limpid, and never hollow." To watch him contemplate a wine list, cigarette dangling to the point where one more centimeter would have found the ashes on the lapel of his gray sharkskin, was one of the pleasures of a lifetime. He would order some heavenly label, then return to an exposition of Bizet.

Recently the torch of French opera has been carried by Georges Prêtre, who conducted *Faust* the last opening night in the old house. He is equally strong in the Italian and German schools, having conducted *Il Trovatore*, and *La Traviata*, as well as *Tristan, Parsifal,* and *Arabella.* A graduate of the Paris Conservatory with first prize, he also studied with the late André Cluytens. Prêtre is possibly the only conductor in the world to have won his black belt in karate.

Karl Böhm entered the Metropolitan in high and has remained there. His introduction was a new *Don Giovanni* designed by Eugene Berman and directed by Herbert Graf, with a perfect cast—Siepi, Steber, Della Casa, Peters, Valletti, Tozzi, Corena, Uppman. It was at the time *My Fair Lady* was packing them in on Broadway, and we called that glorious Mozart revival *Our Fair Lady.* It never played to an unsold seat.

The postwar era produced a new generation of conductors and many of the most gifted appeared at the Metropolitan. American-born Thomas Schippers (top left) was a key figure on the roster for over two decades, from his debut Don Pasquale *in 1955 to a final* L'Assedio di Corinto *in 1975. Georges Prêtre of Paris (above) made his bow with* Samson et Dalila *in 1964 but he soon proved to have a catholic musical gift. Georg Solti (bottom left)—Hungarian like Szell and Reiner before him—arrived in 1960 with* Tannhäuser, *putting in three seasons. In 1962–63 Lorin Maazel, an American (below), showed great potential with* Der Rosenkavalier, *staged by Lotte Lehmann, and* Don Giovanni. *Grand old man at the Opera House, old in years not spirit, is octogenarian Karl Böhm of Austria (next two pages), who has made the music of Mozart, Beethoven, Wagner and his friend Richard Strauss glow with new life*

As great in its way was *Die Frau ohne Schatten,* which had its first performance at the Metropolitan the third week in the new house. Dr. Böhm has a direct line to Richard Strauss. The score of *Daphne* is dedicated to him, and in Vienna he conducted *Ariadne auf Naxos* in honor of the composer's eightieth birthday. It is hard to believe it was any finer than the *Ariadne* he gave us when he conducted the first performance of that work at the Metropolitan with Rysanek, Kerstin Meyer, and Jess Thomas, with scenery and costumes by Oliver Messel and thirty-eight virtuosos from the Metropolitan Opera Orchestra.

Böhm began his career in his hometown of Graz. He thought the forces of the theater inadequate to do justice to a masterpiece like *Lohengrin*, so he marshaled the local church choirs, the Mäennerchor, a high school chorus—in all about 200 voices—and they sang as only amateurs can when inspired.

It just happened that a great conductor from Berlin was on holiday in Graz, and having nothing else to do that evening, he went to *Lohengrin.* He came backstage and introduced himself. It was another Karl—Karl Muck. "Everything was very good, even though you conducted the Bridal Chorus as if it were a polka," Dr. Muck said. "Come and visit me sometime, and I will study all the Wagner scores with you." Böhm was on his way. "You never know who is out front," Katharine Cornell used to say.

"One mounts the podium," Böhm quotes yet another Karl, Karl Richter, "and either one knows how to conduct or one will never learn it!"

We had Solti before he became Sir Georg and a cult figure, here as well as in Chicago, but not before he had reached the plane of his unsurpassable recording of the *Ring*, the first complete *Ring* on records and the best to date. Solti's *Rheingold* is one of the two finest complete opera recordings ever made. His *Otello* at the Metropolitan brought James McCracken's return as a star. Then he had a new production of *Aida* on opening night of 1963–64, *Die Walküre* and *Tristan*, all with Nilsson, and we look to his return.

Despite his relative youth, Lorin Maazel had appeared in Bayreuth before he came to the Metropolitan, where he conducted Crespin's debut in *Der Rosenkavalier* under the stage direction of Lotte Lehmann. He later was

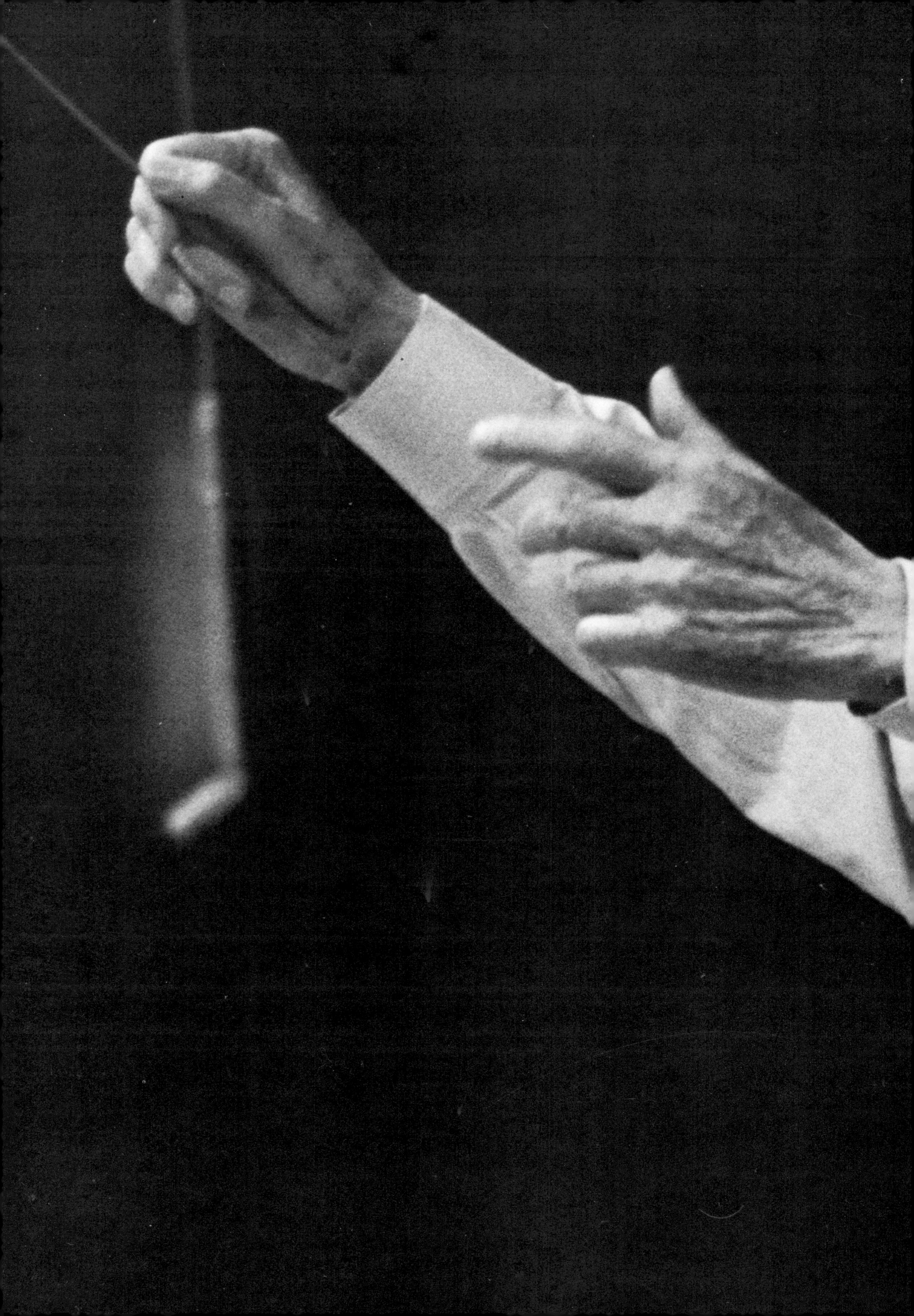

boss of the opera in West Berlin. His commitment to Cleveland, where he is the worthy inheritor of George Szell's mantle, has somewhat limited his appearances in opera, which is opera's loss.

Ernest Ansermet had conducted at the Metropolitan with the Diaghilev Ballet during its visit in 1917, sharing the podium with Monteux. He joined the company over half a century later to conduct a performance of Falla's *Atlantida* at Philharmonic (now Avery Fisher) Hall as the Metropolitan's participation in the opening festivities of Lincoln Center. A long-time friend of Debussy as well as of Falla, he went on that year to conduct a beautiful *Pelléas et Mélisande* in the old house.

To some observers *Falstaff* didn't seem like Leonard Bernstein's kind of music when he was announced to conduct a new production of Verdi's last work in connection with the 400th anniversary of the birth of Shakespeare. From the first day of rehearsal he swept away every reservation and bowled everybody over. He had mastered every bar, every note, and the result was as near perfection as you are likely to find in the opera house. Equally inspired, the décors and direction were by Franco Zeffirelli, also making his Metropolitan Opera debut.

The final season in the old house saw the advent of another glamour boy who could also conduct and is now Bernstein's successor at the Philharmonic, Zubin Mehta. In his first season Bing had tried to get William Steinberg. He was then conductor in Buffalo, and his Metropolitan debut did not take place until well into his Pittsburgh and Boston careers. There have been few of the top conductors the Metropolitan hasn't gone after and in most cases succeeded in getting.

Josef Krips conducted the happiest *Zauberflöte* at the Met up to his time. Was ever a house blessed with three such Papagenos as Ted Uppman, Hermann Prey, and now Donald Gramm? Krips' first was Prey, of whom a fan said, "I want him for Christmas."

The Metropolitan public gave its seal of approval to Richard Bonynge before Queen Elizabeth put him on her Silver Jubilee honors list for Order of the British Empire. If for nothing else we would be forever in his debt for having guided his wife, Joan Sutherland, to bel canto.

Three superstars who have given of their best to the Metropolitan Opera: Leonard Bernstein (above, in a chorus rehearsal with David Stivender at the piano), Zubin Mehta (right) and Herbert von Karajan (below). Bernstein has conducted new productions of Falstaff, Cavalleria Rusticana *and* Carmen, *always proving himself the true man of the theater, equally attuned to stage and pit. Mehta, a native of Bombay, made his debut in 1965 with* Aida *and has done* Turandot, *the world premiere of* Mourning Becomes Electra *and* Il Trovatore *in subsequent years. In the late 1960s, Karajan led the first two installments of his own production of the* Ring *Cycle,* Das Rheingold *and* Die Walküre, *which originated at his Salzburg Easter Festival*

Richard Bonynge and his wife, Joan Sutherland (top left), have specialized in the bel canto repertoire, though on occasion at the Metropolitan the conductor has branched out to lead Gluck's Orfeo ed Euridice *and French fare—Massenet's* Werther *and* Esclarmonde, *Offenbach's* Les Contes d'Hoffmann*—which have revealed new facets of his gifts. Bonynge's debut took place at the new Opera House in 1966, a* Lucia di Lammermoor *starring Miss Sutherland. Despite responsibilities as music director of the Australian Opera, he remains a Metropolitan regular. Henry Lewis (bottom left) made front-page news at his debut in 1972 as the first black to conduct at the Metropolitan, but the real news was published on the music page—that a musician of real talent had arrived on the podium. Lewis' assignments have included* La Bohème, Carmen, Roméo et Juliette *and the new production of* Le Prophète. *More headlines were made in 1976 by Sarah Caldwell (below), the first woman conductor in Metropolitan history. La Maestra followed up her highly successful debut with* La Traviata *by a heartfelt reading of* L'Elisir d'Amore. *Most of Miss Caldwell's energies, however, are absorbed by her own Opera Company of Boston, where she doubles as conductor and stage director, overseeing every detail of production*

Herbert von Karajan is an absolute. When you see him come slowly from the pit after a performance, sit between his curtain calls, then, coat around his shoulders, go straight to his waiting car, you know it is no act. He is spent. He has given everything, and that cannot be measured or described. His first season he had us all worried. He did not bring his orchestra up from the rehearsal room into the auditorium until the dress rehearsal of *Die Walküre*, but when it finally happened, he knew exactly what he had—balance, volume, everything. He is also one of the few conductors not to make a stop within the first ten bars at rehearsal. He goes right through and then comes back and cleans up with unbelievable precision. Nothing has escaped him. A true master.

Henry Lewis began as a double-bass player in the Los Angeles Philharmonic. He was drafted into the Army and on duty in Germany organized the Seventh Army Orchestra, which attracted world-wide attention. Back in Los Angeles, he resumed his place on his stool in the double-bass section, but when Igor Markevitch fell ill and was unable to fill a guest engagement, Lewis stepped in and was on his way. Fritz Reiner always said, "Prepare for the emergency." One of Reiner's pupils, Leonard Bernstein (he was Reiner's before he was Koussevitzky's), made it that way; so did Toscanini. The list is long. Hamlet said it: "The readiness is all."

Kazimierz Kord, the young Pole who prepared in Russia, had already established himself at the Metropolitan and with *Boris* when he was chosen to open the season of 1977–78.

Richard Woitach is one of our own. He began with us as an assistant conductor, then went to San Francisco, where he was a major force in the organization of Western Opera Theatre. He is back as a conductor of the first rank. Sarah Caldwell, Giuseppe Patané, John Pritchard, Jesús López-Cobos all come from widely different backgrounds, bringing their special and peculiar gifts to their tasks. The clarity of Miss Caldwell's *Traviata*, the meaningful pauses, restored to the beloved old work some of the life squeezed out of it by routine performances.

When he made his debut at the Metropolitan in 1971, James Levine said he had fifty-five operas "almost at my fingertips." He now knows twice that number. As a boy he had haunted the Cincinnati Opera, which used to perform summer seasons at the city zoo. In San Francisco he showed Dorothy Kirsten the score she had signed for him when he was a boy in Cincinnati, and he had told her he would be conducting for her one day. "I didn't know a twenty-seven-year-old could tell me anything about *Tosca*," Dorothy said in amazement, "but he did!"

Three young men who conducted in the first dozen years of the new Metropolitan Opera House now guide the musical destinies of three of the world's foremost opera houses. Colin Davis, who gave us unforgettable performances of *Wozzeck, Pelléas,* and *Peter Grimes*, is music director of the Royal Opera House, Covent Garden. Claudio Abbado, who conducted *Don Carlo*, is artistic director at La Scala, that shrine of Italian opera, which as this is being written is entering its third century. And then, of course, there is our own James Levine.

Nor does it end here. Christopher Keene is head of the Festival of Two Worlds in Spoleto. John Nelson acquitted himself with *Jenufa* and *Les Troyens*, John Mauceri with *Fidelio*, Conlon and Woitach with numerous works. If there were no other signs than these young men with baton, there would be hope for the future of opera.

SINGERS

To Leontyne Price went the honor of creating the role of Cleopatra in Samuel Barber's *Antony and Cleopatra*, which opened the new Metropolitan Opera House. In a way, Miss Price was speaking for all of us when she said, "The ghosts from the old house—Caruso, Flagstad, all of them—moved uptown, too. When I'd look up at that gold ceiling, there they'd be, saying to me, 'Lee, you mess it up and we'll take care of you!'"

Needless to say, Miss Price did not mess it up, but the spirits of the great who forged the Metropolitan still keep watch, and many of them peer right at you from their portraits in the concourse of the opera house. A few singers and conductors who did not appear at the Metropolitan are represented, but they are not out of place, and four of the sixty-four subjects have more than one likeness in this unique gallery.

There are some gaps, notably Rosa Ponselle, but they will be taken care of in time. The Chinese say, "A good house is never finished," and the Metropolitan is a good house. A life-size, near-full-length oil portrait of Miss Ponselle, hanging over the fireplace of the drawing room of Villa Pace, her home outside Baltimore, will one day come to us.

The principal ringer is Jenny Lind, who died in 1887, four years after the Metropolitan raised its first curtain, but Jenny was the first big international star to come to these shores. Her presence in our pantheon is also a tribute to her native Sweden which for its size and population has sent us more great voices than any other country.

Although our podium was never honored by Richard Strauss, he is shown both in a bronze head and in an oil portrait. In the painting he is conducting at the Vienna Opera, and the score on the stand is *Così Fan Tutte.* He was a better conductor than most composers, and they say he took everything at quite a clip in order to get back to his cronies and the nightly game of skat.

Richard Strauss (above), whose operas are among the most frequently performed at the Metropolitan Opera, in an oil painting in Founders Hall, a gallery of great artists located on the concourse level of the new Opera House. The central area (below), at the foot of the grand staircase, contains an honor roll of contributors to the building of the theater, a Caesar-like bronze bust of Enrico Caruso—a name still synonymous with the Metropolitan—and display cases holding memorabilia. Among singers' portraits is Lotte Lehmann as the Marschallin in Der Rosenkavalier *(right). The great German soprano sang Strauss, Wagner and Puccini with the company for twelve seasons, 1934–46*

Giuseppe De Luca is remembered in Founders Hall with a portrait as Verdi's Rigoletto (top left). A Roman by birth, the baritone made his Metropolitan debut in 1915 as Figaro in Il Barbiere di Siviglia *and had his name on the roster for twenty-two seasons, until 1946. Among world premieres, De Luca created the title role in Puccini's* Gianni Schicchi. *Another Italian, though from Milan, was Amelita Galli-Curci (top right), shown as Rosina in* Il Barbiere di Siviglia. *Her roles at the Opera House between 1921 and 1930 included Violetta, Gilda and the mad heroine of* Lucia di Lammermoor. *Elisabeth Rethberg's Aida (bottom left) set a standard at the Metropolitan for two decades, 1922–42. This German soprano excelled in Verdi, Puccini, Mozart and Wagner, with Elisabeth in* Tannhäuser *a role she endowed with heavenly radiance. The dashing Ezio Pinza is displayed as Don Giovanni (bottom right). Like De Luca, this bass was a native of Rome and remained with the company for twenty-two seasons, 1926–48. Outstanding among his fifty-one roles were Mozart's Figaro, Méphistophélès in* Faust, *Fiesco in* Simon Boccanegra *and Boris Godunov. Louise Homer, the Pittsburgh-born contralto whose portrait as Orfeo in Gluck's* Orfeo ed Euridice *(below) could be mistaken for the Muse of Music, was the aunt of Samuel Barber, composer of* Vanessa *and* Antony and Cleopatra, *both produced at the Metropolitan. Homer managed to combine a busy home life—six children—with twenty-one seasons on the roster, between the years 1900 and 1930. Her debut was as Amneris in* Aïda *and among other major roles she sang Fidès in* Le Prophète, *Dalila, Azucena, Fricka and Brangäne*

There are two portraits of Lucrezia Bori, so different as to be almost unrecognizable as the same person. One must be from the very beginning of her career, smiling and eager. It almost jumps out of the frame at you. The other is more sophisticated, cool, reserved, a little withdrawn, which Bori rarely was. It hung over the fireplace of her apartment in East Sixty-sixth Street. Martinelli rates both a bronze head and an oil portrait.

By all odds the one with the most representations is Caruso, and that is as it should be. He sang his last in 1920 and died the following year. The mail on him to the opera house is more than on all the other singers, living and dead combined. Four times he appears in the gallery, and there are a couple of oil portraits of him elsewhere in the house. The heroic bronze head in Founders Hall, center area of the concourse, was placed in the Broadway lobby of the old house the year after his death. Looking more like a Caesar than the most beloved singer in history, it was as famous a meeting place as Scott Fitzgerald's Biltmore clock. "Meet me at the Caruso statue," you would say to your date if there wasn't time to foregather earlier.

Balancing him is a larger-than-life marble bust of Gatti-Casazza in full evening attire, which used to dominate the Thirty-ninth Street lobby of the old house. That was the carriage trade entrance, and not even Mr. Gatti's glowering visage could discourage some of the antics certain first-nighters during the forties seemed to delight in.

Stroll to the left from Founders Hall. The first portrait is of Louise Homer as Orpheus in Toscanini's re-creation of Gluck's masterpiece, which was also illuminated by Johanna Gadski and the beloved Alma Gluck as the Happy Shade. Alma Gluck was the first Victor Red Seal artist to sell a million records. A portrait of her in the Metropolitan Opera House would be in order.

In his autobiography, *Memories of Opera*, Mr. Gatti writes, "It is said the art of bel canto is finished. But this is not true. Artists like De Luca and Rosa Ponselle, Elisabeth Rethberg and Lily Pons demonstrate the truth of what I assert." The first named is shown as Rigoletto. He came to us in 1915 and returned after World War II at the age of seventy, still a master of bel canto.

Ezio Pinza brought back *Don Giovanni* and Mozart generally to the Metropolitan. There had been no Don since Scotti, no Figaro since De Luca—absences of more than twenty years each—until Pinza came along, and here he is, looking as though he were about ready to go into "Là ci darem la mano."

Il Barbiere di Siviglia was the work in which Amelita Galli-Curci sang her farewell to the Metropolitan, but there is no sadness in the portrait of her as Rosina, which had a prominent place in all three of her homes in California.

Lauritz Melchior is seen as Tristan, but Kirsten Flagstad, who shared curtain calls with him in so many legendary performances at the Metropolitan, is in a concert gown. Her lovely portrait is the gift of her grandson, Sigurd Dusenberry. Lawrence Tibbett's portrait is the thing you remember best about his apartment in the Savoy-Plaza Hotel, alas no longer standing. Grace Moore also lived at the Savoy-Plaza and, rather than make the journey twenty blocks south and two blocks west, would sometimes summon her colleagues to rehearse there.

A cast of Gemito's great bronze head of Verdi is one of our authentic treasures. The old man is deep in thought, the head bowed so low you cannot tell whether the eyes are open or not—a great work of art and the sovereign likeness of a giant.

Sargent would have been proud to sign the full-length portrait of Emma Eames by her first husband, Julian Story. Madame Eames divorced Story to marry Emilio de Gogorza, the baritone. She later divorced him. Although she was born in Shanghai and presided over the most select salon of Paris, Madame Eames was a Yankee and had a devastating wit. She dealt Don Emilio the most withering epitaph a man ever had. When notified of his death there was a moment's pause and then the blockbuster fell. "He was a fine artist—but not much of a husband."

To the right of Madame Eames are man and wife, two of the most beloved artists in the history of the Metropolitan, Elisabeth Rethberg and George Cehanovsky, she as Aida (Grove's Dictionary just comes out and says it: "There was no finer Aida in her generation"), he as Brétigny in *Manon.* After forty years as a singer, George remains invaluable to the Metropolitan as the official language coach, now that we are doing *Boris* and *Onegin* in their original language.

Emanuel List is shown as Baron Ochs in *Der Rosenkavalier*, a role he made his own as surely as Lotte Lehmann laid unchallenged claim to the Marschallin. His comic gifts were as outsized as his frame, but he excelled in serious roles as well. He was Hunding in the historic recording of the first act of *Die Walküre* with Madame Lehmann, Lauritz Melchior, and the Vienna Philharmonic under Bruno Walter.

An elfin pastel of Emma Calvé leaves you wondering how she could have been the reigning Carmen of her day. The first opening night of the Bing regime is remembered by the portrait of Delia Rigal as Elisabetta in *Don Carlo*, a beautiful and queenly lady with a beautiful voice. Another pastel shows Nina Morgana—wife of Bruno Zirato, who was Caruso's secretary and later manager of the New York Philharmonic. This darling girl from Buffalo shared honors with Caruso on the concert stage as well as in the opera house.

What Van Dyck was to the Stuart kings, Artur Halmi was to the sopranos of the first third of this century. He was the prima donna's best friend, and his signature crops up four times on a walk through the Metropolitan's gallery. Calvé and Frances Alda are lovely, full of atmosphere, and evocative of their subjects. Farrar and Garden are less successful. There was a ravishing Halmi pastel of Jeritza that we never had the pleasure of displaying and never will. Madame Jeritza insists on having live candles on her Christmas tree, and one Yuletide this beautiful work of art went up in smoke.

Beside the latter Bori portrait is an oil of Caruso during one of his mustache periods. These came and went. After his first season at the Metropolitan, Chaliapin left, vowing never to return. Although the public recognized a genius, his Mefistofele and Don Basilio were too strong for some of the powerful but finicky press. He did return, however, and sang *Boris Godunov.* Appropriately, it is in this greatest role of his that he is pictured at the Metropolitan.

John Brownlee was a mainstay at Glyndebourne before he came to this country, and we see him here as the Count in *Le Nozze di Figaro*, which he sang in the great 1940 revival with Pinza, Rethberg, Stevens, and Sayão. Marion Telva was Adalgisa to Ponselle's Norma, but it is a straight portrait we have of the St. Louis mezzo-soprano, who was a friend and neighbor of

Emma Eames (right, full length), one of the Metropolitan Opera's earliest American divas, appeared as Juliette, the Countess, Elsa, Desdemona and other heroines between 1891 and 1909. Her style was so cool that after an Aïda in Boston, a critic quipped the Nile was still frozen over. Warmth was an outstanding quality of Tennessee-born Grace Moore (top right), and she exuded it throughout fifteen seasons, from a 1928 debut as Mimi in La Bohème *through a final Tosca in 1946. The soprano developed into an outstanding actress, acclaimed for Charpentier's* Louise *and Montemezzi's* L'Amore dei Tre Re. *The renowned Swedish soprano Jenny Lind (bottom right) was sixty-three when the Metropolitan opened in 1883, so her career predated the theater. Her portrait recalls her pioneering tours of the United States under P. T. Barnum's banner. Olive Fremstad is seen as Carmen (next page far left, full length) doing the Gypsy Song. Swedish-Norwegian and a protégée of Lilli Lehmann, she made her debut in 1903 as Sieglinde in* Die Walküre. *During eleven seasons she was hailed as a consummate artist in all she undertook. Nineteen solo curtain calls greeted the soprano's farewell in 1914. Lawrence Tibbett, who arrived in 1923 (top center left), was the son of a California sheriff. His name conjures up twenty-seven seasons when he did the major baritone leads—Amonasro, Wolfram, Iago, Boccanegra, Scarpia—and such novelties as* The Emperor Jones *and* Jonny Spielt Auf. *Emanuel List as Baron Ochs (bottom center left) summons memories of his seventy-five performances of* Der Rosenkavalier *between 1935 and 1950. Lily Pons (top center right) adorned the roster twenty-eight seasons, her debut in* Lucia di Lammermoor *creating a sensation in 1931. She made quite a sensation when she bared her navel as Lakmé, another speciality of the tiny coloratura from Cannes. Giovanni Martinelli's Otello (bottom center right) was the crowning achievement of his thirty-two seasons at the Opera House. The tenor made his debut in 1913 as Rodolfo in* La Bohème *and he had a voice bright and penetrating as a platinum trumpet. Maria Jeritza is costumed as Octavian in* Der Rosenkavalier *(far right, full length). The darling of Strauss, the Czech soprano was no less admired by Puccini, whose Tosca, Minnie and Turandot were cheered during her decade on stage, 1921–31. In 1951 she returned for one night as Rosalinda in a gala* Fledermaus *at the special invitation of Rudolf Bing. Mme. Jeritza, who is still blond and glamorous, for many years has been a regular subscriber to the Metropolitan Opera, always preferring to sit in row A of the Orchestra section—as close to the stage as is possible*

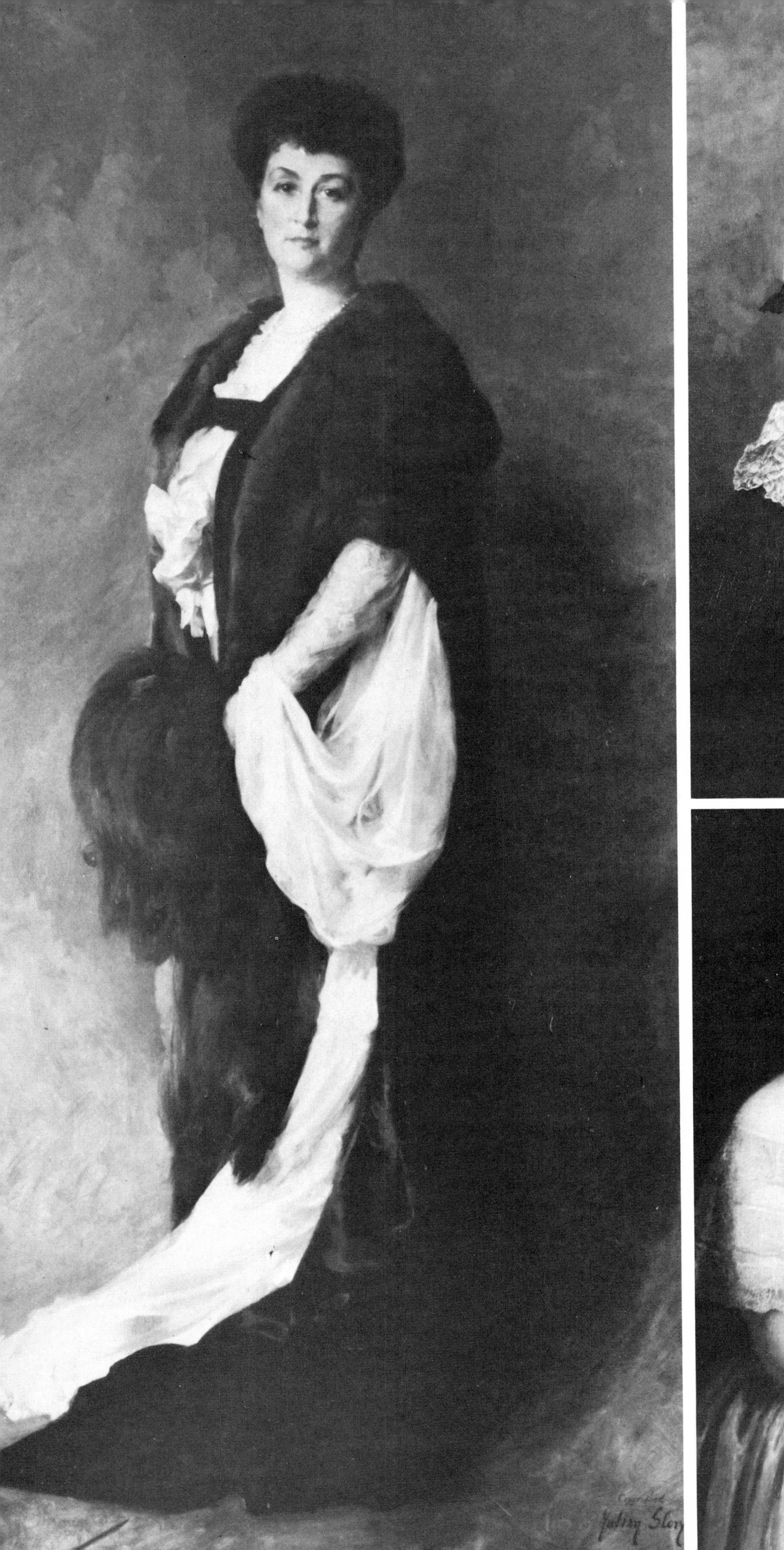

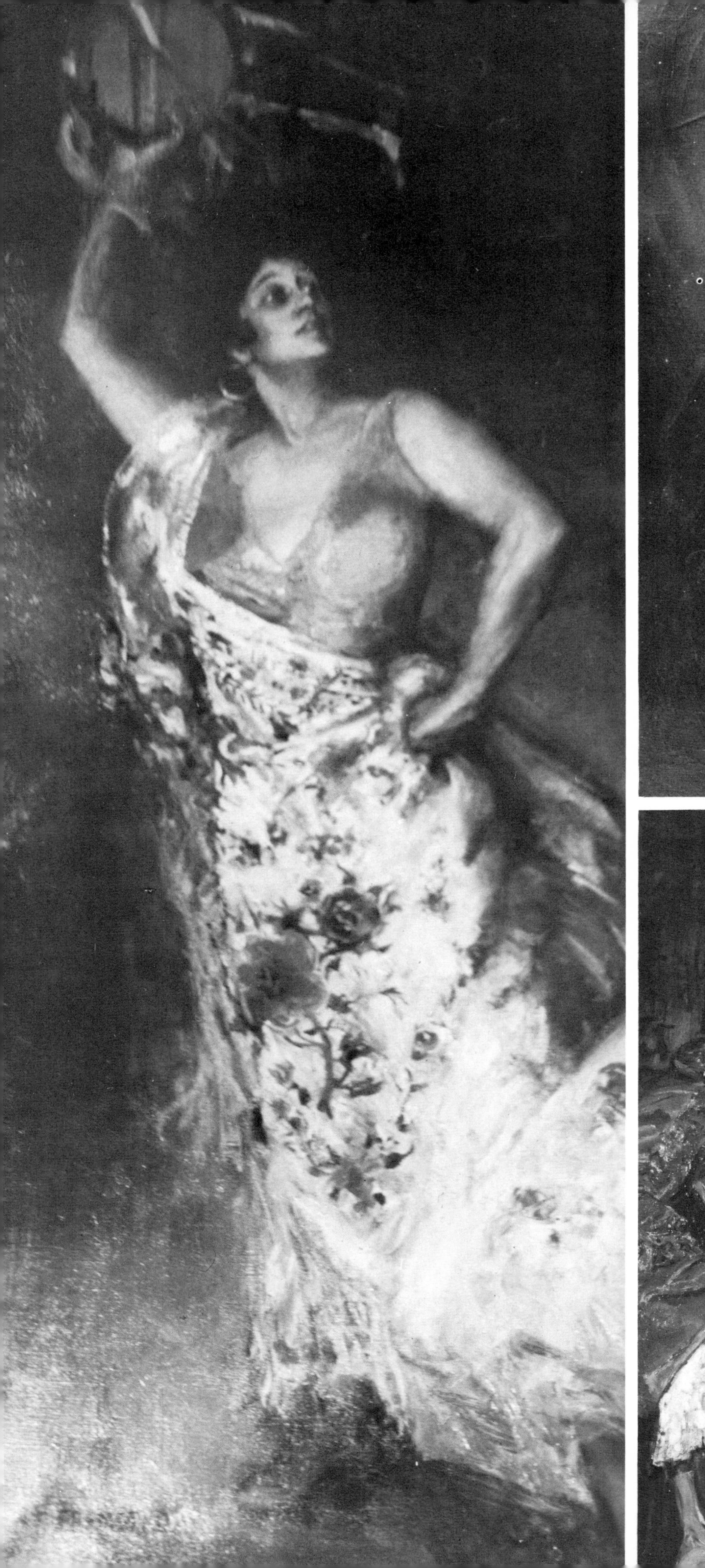

Kirsten Flagstad (above) appeared as if from the blue when the Metropolitan needed her most, in the depths of the great depression. The Norwegian soprano's debut as Sieglinde in Die Walküre *was totally unheralded. Her portrayals of all the major Wagnerian heroines, Beethoven's Fidelio and, in 1952, Gluck's Alcestis, were a guarantee of extraordinary artistry and a sold-out theater. Nellie Melba (left) made child's play of the most difficult coloratura feats during her period at the Opera House, 1893–1911. The soprano's performances in* Lucia di Lammermoor *and as the Queen in* Les Huguenots, *to name but two of her many roles, were invitations to brilliance, the kind served up today by another Australian, Joan Sutherland. Edward Johnson (below), Metropolitan general manager 1935–50, previously earned fame in tenor leads, 1922–35*

Miss Farrar. At one time the famous Farrar ankle-length chinchilla was one of only three in the world. When Miss Farrar retired, it was divided into three shoulder wraps, and Telva was one of the lucky girls.

Anton Seidl glares through his pince-nez as though somebody had not given a dotted eighth its just due. Jenny Lind is between him and Giuseppe Danise, the Metropolitan's first Gérard in *Andrea Chénier.* We haven't had a William Tell since Danise, and the fact that he persuaded Bidù Sayão to marry him is another of his claims to fame.

When asked what Madame Schumann-Heink was like, Frank La Forge, her accompanist, replied, "She was a great natural phenomenon. She was like Niagara Falls." The legendary contralto is pictured as Azucena in uncharacteristic repose. She made a recording of "Ai nostri monti" with Caruso, whose pet name for her was *"Nonna,"* Grandma. That is how she signed her cablegram of sympathy to Mrs. Caruso when the great man died.

The portrait of the delicious Sayão as Violetta is reproduced on the jacket of her record of Villa-Lobos' *Bachianas Brasileiras* No. 5, coupled with arias from *La Traviata*, *Manon*, *Le Nozze di Figaro*, and *Don Giovanni.* Next comes Nellie Melba, the Metropolitan's first Mimi and the prima donna assoluta of her day. The toast that is supposed to make you thinner, the peach-and-ice-cream dessert that is sure to make you fat or a little fatter, a cigar, a lipstick, a theater in Dallas, and any number of little girls born around a certain time, all were named Melba.

Before she became the first black artist to join the company, Marian Anderson gave an annual Easter Sunday afternoon concert at the Metropolitan. When she reported for the first rehearsal for her debut as Ulrica in *Un Ballo in Maschera*, a member of the staff said, "Welcome home." She is here forever in a splendid bronze head. Bruno Walter is also in bronze, head lifted, a little beatific. Arturo Toscanini, another bronze, seems to be singing along while conducting, as was his wont.

Giovanni Martinelli, more of whom later, has another bronze in the Opera Club where he was, as everywhere, a great favorite. Leo Slezak as Otello is the gift of his son, Walter, and beside him is Olive Fremstad in *Carmen*, which she sang in San Francisco with Caruso the night before the earthquake and fire. She makes a rather Nordic and heroic gypsy, and Richard Strauss in bronze looks rather dour. If there is a smiling likeness of Strauss, it has never come to light.

The portrait of Grace Moore by Rosko is the gift of the late soprano's brother, Richard L. Moore. Originally Mr. Moore thought of commissioning a painting of his sister, who was killed in a plane crash on a concert tour of Scandinavia in 1947, from photographs. Rarely are these efforts successful, and he was persuaded to part with this period portrait, probably done about the time she was in Irving Berlin's *Music Box Revues.* She was the first to sing "Always" and "All Alone" in those delightful musicals.

The head of the incomparable Jussi Björling was unveiled at the new opera house by Princess Christina of Sweden in the presence of the tenor's widow and one of his sons. Between Björling and Giacomo Lauri-Volpi is a captivating model of the proscenium of the old opera house—the gold curtain up, the stage set as for the first act of *La Bohème* circa 1903. This genuine relic was given in memory of Cornelius N. Bliss. Lauri-Volpi, he of the heroic high notes, Pollione to Ponselle's *Norma* and Radames on the great recording of the Nile Scene from *Aida* with Rethberg and De Luca, now lives in Valencia, where he teaches and has a street named after him. Among the luminaries who have studied with him is Franco Corelli. His bronze head is the result of efforts of fans in Milwaukee!

A full-length, life-size Jeritza, creator of the leads in *Ariadne auf Naxos* and *Die Frau ohne Schatten*, is just about to present the silver rose as the Rosenkavalier, head on. Posing with a live bird on a finger would, for any other coloratura, be carrying things too far, but on Lily Pons it looks good. It's naive as a fox, and Lily wears an elaborate concert outfit of blue velvet, complete with fur cuffs and tiny matching fur hat—very chic and very different from Lotte Lehmann, who comes next.

Madame Lehmann is seen in the last-act costume of her most famous role, the Marschallin. In one of his autobiographies, Vincent Sheehan wrote of her, "The peculiar melancholy expressiveness of her voice, the beauty of her style in the theater, the general sense that her every performance was a work of art, lovingly elaborated in the secret places and brought forth with matchless authority before our eyes, made her a delight that never staled. She was like that Chinese empress of the ancient days who commanded the flowers to bloom, except for Lotte they did." Harold C. Schonberg summed it up when he wrote, "She generated love." Can more be said of any artist?

Edward Johnson deserves better than the portrait contrived at the time of his retirement as general manager. He is sitting onstage in a business suit, the Canio hat and Lohengrin helmet of his singing days lying self-consciously about.

Marcella Sembrich was the prima donna of the Metropolitan Opera's second performance, *Lucia di Lammermoor* on October 24, 1883. When she retired, in 1909, Mahler took part in the ceremonies. She taught at Juilliard and Curtis Institute in Philadelphia and remained a beloved figure on the musical scene until her death in 1935. Her portrait in a gold evening dress and a cape trimmed with ermine tails was a fixture on the east wall of Sherry's in the old house.

It is hard to believe there was no *Otello* at the Metropolitan for twenty-four years, from Slezak in 1913 to Martinelli in 1937. The Divo, as his circle of admirers called Martinelli, is shown as the Moor. He used to get more applause than some of the people onstage when he strode, white mane rampant, to his place in the fifth row of the orchestra on a Monday night.

Of more recent history is the bronze bust of Sir Rudolf Bing by Betti Richard, an American sculptor, who is also responsible for the busts of Mozart and Wagner at the end in the north room of the concourse. They flank the portrait of Gluck by Joseph Sifrede Duplessis (1725–1802), which we are told is the original—the one in Vienna being a copy.

The left passage to the north might be called baritones' row. Three are grouped near Sir Rudolf, a superb bronze of Antonio Scotti as Scarpia, a small painting of Pasquale Amato as a haughty Count di Luna, and a giant one of Leonard Warren as Simon Boccanegra. Like their colleague and friend Caruso, Scotti and Amato were Neapolitans. Scarpia was Scotti's most famous role. Seventeen Toscas over a period of thirty-four years he pursued around the sinister baron's apartment in the Farnese Palace.

The opera department Huey Long established at Louisiana State University was the first opera school attached to a state university in this country, and Amato was brought to Baton Rouge to be the first head of it. He loved the place so much that he is buried there. Warren died in the

The bust of Marian Anderson (above) commemorates her historic debut at the Opera House in 1955, as Ulrica in Un Ballo in Maschera. *She was the first black to be engaged to sing a solo role with the Metropolitan. Before this, the distinguished contralto from Philadelphia had appeared at the theater only in recital. In the north corridor of Founders Hall (top right) are the portraits of Jeritza, Pons, Lotte Lehmann, Strauss, Johnson, Sembrich and Martinelli. Leonard Warren's likeness as Simon Boccanegra (bottom right) dominates another wall of that corridor. The New York baritone was an indispensable to the roster for twenty-two years, starting in 1939 with his debut as Paolo in* Simon Boccanegra. *A sculpture of Antonio Scotti as Baron Scarpia in* Tosca *(below) pays tribute to this baritone's thirty-four-year record. Born in Naples, Scotti first took center stage at the Opera House in 1899 as Don Giovanni. He said goodbye in 1933 with his* cavallo di battaglia, *as Chim-Fen in Franco Leoni's* L'Oracolo

Feodor Chaliapin as Boris Godunov (above) captures the giant Russian bass in his most celebrated role, one he did often during nine seasons at the Metropolitan, 1907–29. Leo Slezak's Otello (top left) served for the Czech tenor's debut in 1909–10, first of his four New York seasons. Margarete Matzenauer (top right) is costumed in an unidentified role. This Hungarian contralto made her bow in 1911 as Amneris in Aida *and remained nineteen seasons, sometimes taking on soprano roles. Marcella Sembrich (bottom left) was a much loved artist from the company's second night, a* Lucia di Lammermoor *in 1883, and she did not retire until 1909. Lilli Lehmann (bottom right), a master musician and vocalist from Germany, was undaunted by Donna Anna, Carmen, Isolde, Norma or anything else during seven seasons of the 1880s and '90s. The contralto Ernestine Schumann-Heink, as Azucena (below), began in 1899 with Ortrud in* Lohengrin *and ended in 1932, at age seventy-one, as Erda in* Siegfried, *even at this advanced age a peerless Wagnerian*

middle of a performance of *La Forza del Destino* on March 4, 1960. Three nights before, he had sung the title role in a new production of *Boccanegra.*

An unrecognizably slender Matzenauer comes as an unidentified character with dagger. Azucena? This noble mezzo could also take on the soprano repertory. She was, moreover, a great musician. George E. Judd, late manager of the Boston Symphony, said no matter how new or difficult the work—Stravinsky's *Oedipus* or whatever—Matzenauer would arrive at the first rehearsal without the book, letter-perfect. Never did she require so much as a glance at the score.

Mrs. Caruso gave the silver bust of her husband to the Metropolitan in 1946, and it stood in the Family Circle of the old house. It bears a Latin inscription, *"Per artem ad astra,"* Through art to the stars.

Gladys Swarthout wears a formal, long-sleeved Valentina gown of red with a fetching skullcap to match, smart to this day. She regularly made the ten-best-dressed-women list and had a haunting wood-wind mezzo to the bargain. The bronze head of Dimitri Mitropoulos is as unadorned as he was in life, the hair that was left shaved, almost primitive, a contradiction in so cultivated a man and conductor.

Karin Branzell, who came back to sing Erda in the Bing regime, is shown as Brangäne, the role she so often performed with Flagstad. When the Norwegian soprano died, Branzell's tribute was one of the most eloquent. "She was a rock," she said, "we all clung to." Geraldine Farrar is done less than justice by the small Halmi head. A colleague—it was Emilio de Gogorza—said of her, "Her voice was like herself, beautiful as a ray of sunshine."

Martha was Victoria de los Angeles' last new role at the Metropolitan. Frank St. Leger said of the lovely Spanish soprano, "For a vocalism like that you have to go back to Melba." He knew. He had been Melba's accompanist.

Risë Stevens sang the role of Carmen more often than any of her predecessors, including Calvé and Farrar. Her leave-taking of the Metropolitan as a singer is the classiest of any artist I know about. On each dressing-room door is a little frame into which the name of the artist who occupies that room is inserted before each performance. On the evening of April 12, 1961, Walter Surovy, Miss Stevens' husband, noticed her name was not in the frame. "Is this it?" he asked. "Yes," she said quietly. She had slipped the card out as she came in.

Fortunately for us, Miss Stevens by no means left the Metropolitan. She is a member of the Association and was chairman of our annual bazaar. For several years she did a splendid job as president of the Mannes College of Music.

Miss Stevens is shown as Orfeo, and this is apostolic succession. The role was written for a male alto. Gluck's noble work had virtually gone into oblivion when Berlioz made a version of it for the female voice, which he persuaded Pauline Viardot to do. Viardot had a pupil named Anna Eugenie Schoen-René, who came to the Juilliard School, where she had a pupil named Risë Stevens.

After a *Meistersinger* in the thirties Lawrence Gilman wrote, "This utterance of a rich and tranquil spirit, so warm and humorous and so deeply wise, must remain among those things which live for the unfailing reassurance of the minds of men." Gilman was of course writing about Richard

Wagner, but it would be just as true of Friedrich Schorr as Hans Sachs, and that's how we have him, reading his Bible at the beginning of the third act of what Gilman called "this most endearing of all scores." The portrait is by the baritone's brother, Dr. Eugene Schorr.

The bronze head of Fausto Cleva has a good deal of the power with which he infused his performances. By him is a portrait of Heinrich Conried, who brought Caruso to this country. It is the gift of his son, Richard G. Conried, who should have been in the theater. He would have made a splendid actor, but his father would have none of it, so he settled for a seat on the New York Stock Exchange.

The portrait of Marjorie Lawrence is the gift of Dr. John M. Yarborough, Jr., of New Orleans. There is no more heroic story in the history of opera than the Australian soprano's. Stricken with polio just as her career was going gloriously, she came back to the Metropolitan to sing Isolde and Venus in *Tannhäuser* from a couch. She was a distinguished teacher and an example of shining and indestructible courage. In 1943 President Roosevelt closed a letter to her, "Mirrored in your great victory for many years to come, those beset with burdens and harassed with handicaps will see the glory and the satisfaction of the good fight—well won. From an old veteran to a young recruit, my message to you is 'Carry on.'"

If Zinka Milanov had been around in Mr. Gatti's time, she would have been included in his list of exponents of bel canto. A great deal of nonsense has been written about bel canto. Irving Kolodin, the dean of music critics, calls it simply "a beautiful way of saying *beautiful singing*" and went on to say, "the great tradition of bel canto . . . can be heard at its best in the singing of Zinka Milanov." She is shown as Leonora in *La Forza del Destino*, which she sang under Bruno Walter and with which she opened the season of 1952–53 in a new production with Tucker, Warren, and Siepi.

The Metropolitan's first Isolde and first Norma were one and the same, Lilli Lehmann. She was also the teacher of Geraldine Farrar, and the portrait we have of the great lady hung in Miss Farrar's living room in Ridgefield, Connecticut. After Miss Farrar's death it was given us by her faithful Sylvia Blein.

Historic counterparts Richard Tucker in the title role of Giordano's Andrea Chénier *(above left) and Enrico Caruso as Eléazar in Halévy's* La Juive *(above). Through the years legions of young tenors have been inspired by the voice of Caruso. A case in point was Brooklyn-born Tucker, though he was only a child when the great Italian singer died. As a young man, he listened to the hundreds of records issued from the time of Caruso's Metropolitan Opera debut, in 1903, until his final performance, as Eléazar in 1920. Tucker's career at the Opera House began a quarter century after Caruso's death, in 1945, and lasted until his own death in 1975. Many Caruso roles became Tucker roles. In the end, Tucker, like Caruso, died at the peak of his powers, virtually in harness. It is fitting that portraits of the two men are placed side by side in Founders Hall. But there is a double irony in the arrangement. In 1920 Caruso had looked forward to singing in* Andrea Chénier *at the Metropolitan. Fatal illness kept him from fulfilling this hope. (The opera went instead to a young tenor from Italy, Beniamino Gigli, who then shared the Caruso roles with Giovanni Martinelli and Giacomo Lauri-Volpi.) Giordano's early verismo work was one day to provide Tucker with one of his finest vehicles, so much so that it was selected for his official portrait. Now for the other side of the irony. Tucker, as a fervently religious man and one who revered the achievements of Caruso, held onto a lifelong ambition to one day sing in* La Juive *at the Metropolitan. Though he got to do Eléazar elsewhere, he did not live to perform the role in New York. All things, alas, come to no man. Not a Tucker. Not a Caruso*

Lucrezia Bori (above), an exquisite soprano from Valencia, made her Metropolitan debut at the 1912–13 opening opposite Caruso in Manon Lescaut, *which she had earlier done with the company during a tour to Paris. At once a favorite with the public, she soon added other roles, which through the years came to number twenty-nine, with Iris, Violetta, Fiora, Mélisande, Manon and Louise among them. In 1915 a throat ailment necessitated Bori take a prolonged absence from the stage, but when she returned, in 1921 as Mimi in* La Bohème, *her popularity was undiminished. This second career lasted through the 1935–36 season, which concluded with a gala farewell. She had already joined the Board of Directors and helped found the Metropolitan Opera Guild. Not far from Bori's portrait in Founders Hall stands a bust of Gioacchino Rossini (below)*

Lillian Nordica, born Lillian Norton in Farmington, Maine, was already a big international star before there was a Metropolitan. She was here only eleven seasons, but she sang twenty-one roles, nearly two hundred performances in the house, and almost as many on tour—everything from the high coloratura of Philine in *Mignon* to Isolde. Can you think of any other soprano who sang both Susanna in *Figaro* and Donna Anna? Elsa, the role she performed here most often, she was invited to sing at Bayreuth. She took all three Brünnhildes in stride, and it is as Wotan's favorite daughter that she is shown, full-length and life-size. Her portrait is the gift of Norman Kelley, the tenor, another singer from Maine.

Mary Garden sang a number of times in the old house but never as a member of the company. She came as a visitor with the Hammerstein forces, which had moved to Philadelphia, notably in Victor Herbert's *Natoma.* Halmi, usually the last word on prima donnas, simply doesn't catch her magnetism and glamour.

Jarmila Novotná, a radiant member of the company for sixteen seasons, is pictured as Manon. Her St. Sulpice scene added up to one of the more elegant and important seductions in all opera. She was an enchanting Bartered Bride, which had an added poignancy since it was during World War II when the powers of evil had done everything they could to wipe out her homeland.

The bronze head of John McCormack is by Mario Korbel, who did the statue of St. Theresa in the chapel dedicated to her in St. Patrick's Cathedral. When McCormack acquired Moore Abbey in Ireland as his home, he commissioned Korbel to do a statue of the recently canonized St. Theresa in silver for the chapel. The sculptor asked Bori—who, McCormack always said, was his favorite of his eighteen Mimis—to let him use her hands as his model. They might well have belonged to the Little Flower of Lisieux, who said, "After my death I shall let fall a shower of roses." A bronze of Bori's hands by another sculptor is in the Belmont Room.

The bronze head of Bodanzky is by Malvina Hoffman, who comes honestly by her feeling for musicians. Her father was pianist and an assisting artist when Jenny Lind made her American debut at Castle Garden. There is a fine head of Beethoven, then the young Bori.

The most recent entry in the Metropolitan's Hall of Fame is Richard Tucker. In twenty-one seasons with the company he sang 499 performances of thirty roles. Before his untimely death in 1975 he was already an immortal. Kenneth van Rensselaer shows him as Andrea Chénier. The last painting is Caruso in the last role he ever studied and the last role he ever sang, Eléazar in *La Juive.* No one could have guessed that Christmas Eve in 1920 was his farewell.

But there is one remaining head, a classic marble of Rossini who gave us his recipe for opera "Voice, voice and more voice," not an inappropriate thought in this very special gallery. Edward Johnson said, "Every age has its Golden Age singers," and he was right.

His predecessor, Mr. Gatti, said, "Don't make *comparisions,*" a better word than the original—it rhymes with derisions, which is what comparisons usually are.

The Bible tells us, "There is one glory of the sun, and another glory of the moon, and another glory of the stars: for one star differeth from another star in glory." If the Corinthians had had an opera house, the Apostle may well have been thinking of its roster when he wrote that last.

DIRECTORS AND DESIGNERS

If the conductor as star is a relatively late phenomenon in opera, the rise of the stage director (in England and on the Continent they call him producer) is still more recent. For the first time the Metropolitan has a director of production.

When *Madama Butterfly* was introduced to the Metropolitan, in 1907, the composer was brought over to "supervise" the production, but neither the director nor the designer was mentioned in the program or the reviews.

It was different three years later, when *La Fanciulla del West* was given its world premiere by the Metropolitan. Puccini was here again, but David Belasco, on whose plays both *Madama Butterfly* and *La Fanciulla del West* are based, was the director. You may be sure he received full screen credit. "The Wizard," as Belasco was known on Broadway—theater owner, playwright, producer, director, and a one-time actor too—would have seen to that, even if the Metropolitan hadn't known it had something to crow about and acted accordingly.

David Belasco, Arturo Toscanini and Giacomo Puccini (right), the stage director, conductor and composer of La Fanciulla del West, *at the Metropolitan before the opera's world premiere, December 10, 1910. Belasco's activities in the legitimate theater included the authorship of a Wild West drama,* The Girl of the Golden West, *which Puccini set to music with extraordinary fidelity. The plot culminates with the attempted hanging of a handsome bandit, Ramerrez, alias Dick Johnson, who was created by no less than Enrico Caruso (below). His savior, the pure-hearted barmaid Minnie, was played by Emmy Destinn, with Pasquale Amato cast as their adversary, Sheriff Jack Rance. The opening night proved a triumph for all concerned*

EB

During the 1920s and '30s the stage director Wilhelm von Wymetal and the designer Joseph Urban (top left) were collaborators on many productions at the Metropolitan Opera. Among Urban's countless designs was a poetically atmospheric Parsifal *(top right, Act I, Scene 1), which exerted its magic from 1919 into the mid-1950s*

Max Reinhardt directed the first performance on any stage of *Ariadne auf Naxos* in Stuttgart, but these were isolated cases, and at that premiere *Le Bourgeois Gentilhomme* was involved in *Ariadne.* The complete Molière play was incorporated in the original version. Jeritza, who created the title role, always said Reinhardt molded her into the actress she became.

In her second season at the Metropolitan, Wilhelm von Wymetal followed Jeritza from Vienna, probably at her behest. He made his debut here directing Jeritza in *Der Rosenkavalier* and was in charge of stage matters when she sang the title role in the first American production of *Turandot.*

The first really important designer at the Metropolitan was Joseph Urban, who was responsible for the scenery and costumes of that *Turandot.* Born in Vienna, he couldn't have been better named. He was summoned to Egypt by no less than the khedive to build a palace. In his home city he remodeled a castle for one of the Esterházys, and in St. Petersburg he built the Czar's bridge over the Neva. Just the kind to attract Florenz Ziegfeld, he collaborated with the great man on glorifying the American girl and was responsible for the scenery and costumes for twelve editions of the *Follies.* His finest monument was the Ziegfeld Theatre, alas no longer standing, on Sixth Avenue at Fifty-fourth Street, and he was the architect of the new Metropolitan Opera House that Otto Kahn planned for West Fifty-seventh Street.

When Urban designed scenery, a tree was a tree and a leaf was a leaf, but he created some of the most evocative settings ever seen at the Metropolitan. *Parsifal* will never be forgotten by those of us who experienced it. The dim religious light in the vast Temple of the Grail and the tender young spring of the Good Friday Spell were a study in contrasts. He designed the Metropolitan's first *Pelléas et Mélisande* and succeeded totally in capturing the poetry of that elusive work. His *Faust* lasted until 1951 and his *Tristan* until 1959, and what wouldn't we give to see his lights of Paris come on again in the last act of *Louise?*

*Comparable to Wymetal and Urban during the 1950s and '60s were the director Herbert Graf and the designer Eugene Berman (bottom right), who did four productions as a team—*Rigoletto *(1951),* La Forza del Destino *(1952),* Don Giovanni *(1957) and* Otello *(1963). The settings for* Forza *(bottom left, Act II) are still in service, with a new staging devised by John Dexter. The Berman-Graf* Otello *(below, costume sketch for the Moor) is retired, having given way to a newer mounting by designer/director Franco Zeffirelli*

Another Viennese import, by way of Salzburg and Philadelphia, was Herbert Graf, son of Max Graf, the critic. After twenty years his superb *Don Giovanni* is still in the repertory, the longest run of any production current. He had staged *Die Meistersinger* when Toscanini conducted it at Salzburg, and Fritz Reiner brought him to this country for the short-lived but brilliant Philadelphia Opera. Admittedly a traditionalist, he was weighted down with *Samson et Dalila* for his Metropolitan debut, but he survived to do among other works two new *Otellos*, the historic *Figaro* under Johnson, and thirteen productions under Bing, including the Berman *Rigoletto*, *La Forza del Destino*, and *Don Giovanni.*

There was movement in the direction of beautiful stage pictures and action, but as recently as the late forties old Désiré Defrère, who had begun life as a baritone, got up to leads, and then become a régisseur, would brag he could put on *Aida* with one three-hour rehearsal. Remember, the playing time of *Aida* is minimum three hours and a half.

From his first opening night Rudolf Bing demanded a change in all this. He brought in Margaret Webster, the daughter of Dame May Whitty and Ben Webster, herself an actress and director of Maurice Evans' Shakespeare productions, including his full-length *Hamlet.* When Leonard Warren wasn't available for rehearsal, Bing yanked him out of *Don Carlo* and put in Robert Merrill. Miss Webster staged two other Verdi works at the Metropolitan, *Aida* and *Simon Boccanegra.*

Bing's first designer was Rolf Gérard. He became virtually the court painter, with scenery and costumes for no less than eighteen productions and costumes for another to his credit plus the ballet *Les Sylphides.* The son of Mafalda Salvatini, the noted soprano, and a famous physicist, Gérard also took a degree in medicine, but the lure of the theater was too strong. On Broadway he designed *That Lady* for Katharine Cornell, Shaw's *Caesar and Cleopatra* for Lilli Palmer and Cedric Hardwicke, and the one-woman revue of his friend Beatrice Lillie.

Gérard could get some stunning effects with almost nothing. The chandeliers in *Così Fan Tutte* were two-dimensional, little more than coat-hangers with candles stuck in them. They were clever, stylish, and attractive as could be. When Christian Bérard's scenery for Louis Jouvet's company was unveiled here, lo and behold, there were the same chandeliers. A friend called Rolf on this. "I did it first," he insisted—and he had, in *Così* at Glyndebourne.

Bing's first real Broadway-Hollywood type was Garson Kanin. He wrote the book and directed the sensationally successful *Fledermaus.* Ljuba Welitsch, then the hottest name on the roster, he called "Red" and lived to tell the tale. He hung numbers around the necks of the chorus and ordered them around like field hands. They didn't like it at first, but we got no protest from AGMA. Everything worked in that production. Howard Dietz wrote the lyrics, and Gérard supplied the charming décors.

Bing had offered Rosalinda to Dorothy Kirsten. She turned it down, and Welitsch was a riot. What Welitsch unwittingly did to some of Kanin's text is unprintable. Bing's first choice for Adele was Lily Pons. After Patrice Munsel stood the town on its ear as the coloratura minx, Lily recovered quickly. "That's what I've always said—this girl is for Broadway." Risë Stevens really didn't want to do Orlofsky. "The best Orlofsky in the business is Irra Petina," she told Bing. Irra used to wear her father's czarist colonel's uniform, and her accent was authentic, but Risë let herself be talked into it, and Orlofsky turned out to be one of the biggest successes of her career. *Fledermaus* was Bing's and Kanin's Christmas present to and from New York that first Bing season. For some visiting Scandinavian royalty the president of our board of directors had to go to a scalper for tickets.

Alfred Lunt had always been in love with opera. As a boy in Milwaukee he had a miniature stage and made his own production of *Parsifal*, which was big news at the time by virtue of its pirated performance at the Metropolitan. Alfred claimed his was really the first on this continent. When Bing invited him to stage *Così Fan Tutte*, Lunt was ecstatic. He seized the chance of a lifetime and burst onstage just before the overture, resplendent in black satin and jet. John Gutman in the right stage box had a carefully staged fit of coughing. Lunt shot him a searing stare and slowly shook a reproving finger. He bowed to a stray latecomer—in *The Taming of the Shrew* he used to tell them the plot up to where they came in!—and then set about the chore at hand. With a taper as long as a coachman's whip he ceremoniously went through the business of "lighting" the candles behind their old-time big shades. They obliged, one at a time. Back to center stage, he gave the downbeat to Fritz Stiedry, who relayed it to the orchestra as Lunt disappeared in the part of the curtain. It was sheer heaven and set the mood perfectly. What went on after was on the same level.

The designer Rolf Gérard and the Metropolitan Opera's director of ballet Alicia Markova (top right), working on the set model for their 1964 production of Les Sylphides, *which shared a double bill with* Don Pasquale. *Gérard was the designer most frequently engaged by Rudolf Bing, turning out nineteen productions over two decades, 1950–70. These ranged from the universally admired* Don Carlo *that launched the Bing regime (next two pages, Act I, Scene 2) to the hotly controversial 1953–54* Faust, *in which the libretto's period was updated to Gounod's time and Méphistophélès wore a top hat (above)—all in the cause of revivifying an old masterpiece*

Margaret Webster, seen rehearsing with Ezio Flagello and Nicola Moscona (bottom right), first worked at the Metropolitan in 1950, staging Don Carlo. *Her distinguished record in the legitimate theater, especially the Shakespearean repertory, served her well and she made* Don Carlo *a landmark production. Miss Webster returned for two other Verdi projects:* Aïda *in 1951 and* Simon Boccanegra *in 1960*

Eleanor Steber in peach satin and Blanche Thebom in changeable blue-green looked like Dresden figures. At one point he had them sit on the floor practically on the footlights, backs to the audience and their parasols open, while their lovers went through their paces upstage. Munsel must have been the Despina of Mozart's dreams. Tucker and Guarrera and Brownlee went just far enough and no further.

"Matched pearls on a string," Lunt used to say of Mozart's music. And again, "He brings you to the brink of slapstick, and then there is something about him so childlike that he pulls you back."

"Now is the time to make the scene," Stiedry whispered to Lunt one day at rehearsal when opening night was getting nearer and results weren't. "You all," Alfred roared, feigning a tantrum, "look like bowls of rancid oatmeal." Things improved perceptibly from that moment.

Stylish, sophisticated comedy came to the Opera House in 1951 with a Gérard-designed production of Mozart's Così Fan Tutte *staged by the eminent American actor Alfred Lunt (right) and featuring Eleanor Steber as Fiordiligi (above), a role of grueling vocal demands*

Think of a season that could boast both Lunt and Tyrone Guthrie. That was 1951–52, before Stratford, Ontario, or Minneapolis were even gleams in Guthrie's eye. He and Gérard again made a virtue of necessity. We ran out of money and couldn't afford an outdoor set for the last act of *Carmen.* Instead of being played in front of the bullring, the final act was moved to the toreador's dressing room, and it worked beautifully. There is a full-length mirror and the madonna, as authentic as Hemingway.

The chorus, the ladies all in red of one kind or another, come down to the footlights and appear to be watching the parade of the bullfighters from a balcony. The railing and arches of the balcony fly. Escamillo takes his leave of Carmen. She quenches the lights in the candelabra with her fingers and turns to be confronted by Don José, who has entered rear center and plunged his switchblade into Escamillo's trunk. Perhaps symbolic, but he is ready for action, and by this gesture he announces it.

They tear into each other like savage beasts, and when the moment of truth arrives, José has Carmen backed against the rear wall. With his left hand around her throat he plunges his knife into her groin and the first night an incredible thing happened. There was the *sound* of a stabbing. In the old days of radio we used to do it with a butcher knife into a ripe melon. Whether it was mass hypnosis we will never know, but a gasp went through the entire house.

The elegant Lunt, costumed as a servant (below), acted out an amusing little pantomime just before the curtain rose. The production's first cast, shown here in the ebullient finale of Act II (bottom right), was Frank Guarrera as Guglielmo, Miss Steber as Fiordiligi, Patrice Munsel as Despina, John Brownlee as Alfonso, Blanche Thebom as Dorabella and Richard Tucker as Ferrando

Carmen staggers to a great high window as though for air or to call Escamillo. She makes not a sound. She clasps the tattered red curtain at the window, which falls slowly ring by ring. Risë Stevens played this for all it was worth, and Frank Guarrera made the most of his big break as Escamillo. Robert Merrill was to have done it, but Bing had exiled him for most of the season when he went to Hollywood without leave.

"As an actor Richard Tucker is all right," Guthrie said, "if you give him something to clutch." Guthrie followed his own rule, and before his untimely death Richard was regularly clutching all our hearts.

Guthrie was not so successful with *La Traviata.* Leonard Warren bitterly resented the notion that the elder Germont might also be a candidate for Violetta's favors, and at one point in the scene at Flora's Guthrie wanted Miss Tebaldi to jump playfully up on the gaming table. A crisis was precipitated at rehearsal, and the leap did not go into the show.

There was no such nonsense about *Peter Grimes* in the new house. This was Guthrie's meat, and he had the ideal partner in Tanya Moiseiwitsch as designer. Daughter of the celebrated pianist Benno Moiseiwitsch, she had

come from the Abbey and the Old Vic and had done *Peter Grimes* with Guthrie at Covent Garden. Never was gloom more deep, doom more real.

The opera-in-English people have strong arguments on their side, and Bing yielded to the extent of offering a new production of *La Bohème* alternately in English and Italian. The Italian outdrew the English every time. Howard Dietz was as wrong for *La Bohème* as he had been right for *Fledermaus.* The real villain, however, was the director, Joseph Mankiewiecz. He was a big man in Hollywood (*All About Eve*, Elizabeth Taylor in *Cleopatra* to come, etc.), but he was anti the spirit of *La Bohème.* At the end of the first act he had Rodolfo close the door with one hand as he embraces Mimi with the other, still inside, mind you, the implication being they are not going right away to join the other bohemians at the Café Momus. Now Rodolfo may not have been the first young man in Mimi's life, but we can't be led to believe she is a pushover, not to that music. This deplorable bit of business didn't stay in very long.

The Rake's Progress by Stravinsky had its champions and its detractors, but there was nothing wrong with George Balanchine's direction or Fritz Reiner's conducting, and it was something to have those three geniuses under the roof at the same time, let alone working on the same production.

The Brook-Gérard-Monteux *Faust* had a marvelous cast. Victoria de los Angeles, who had made her debut in the same role three seasons before, was Marguerite, Jussi Bjoerling was Faust, Robert Merrill was Valentin and Nicola Rossi-Lemeni was Méphistophélès in top hat, white tie and tails, with a red-lined cape. The final scene has never been brought off better. The low roof of the prison rose to allow the bars to become the gates of a sanctuary. The backdrop was like a great monstrance of white and gold with a dove in the center, rays streaming out from it against a background of pale blue. The gates opened by themselves, allowing Marguerite to walk slowly through, so different from that Sunday School pageant of ballet girls as angels with molting wings to which we had for eons been subjected.

Peter Brook was anathema to Ljuba Welitsch after the weird Salvador

Tyrone Guthrie (right) created three new productions for the Metropolitan Opera: Carmen *in 1952 with Richard Tucker as Don José and Risë Stevens as Carmen (above, in Act I),* La Traviata *in 1957 and, at the new theater,* Peter Grimes *in 1967, this last becoming a fixture in regular repertory*

George Balanchine and Horace Armistead (below), director and designer for the U.S. premiere of Stravinsky's The Rake's Progress, *1953*

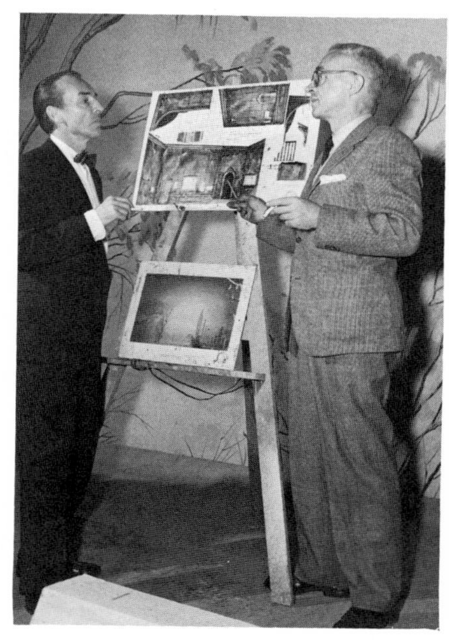

·PULL·
·PULL·

Cyril Ritchard, seen with Rudolf Bing during a rehearsal for La Perichole *(top left), brought laughter to the Opera House many times. On twenty-six occasions the merriment was induced by his own portrayal of Don Andres, the delightfully naughty Viceroy of Peru in Offenbach's comedy, which he staged in 1956. A highpoint of the first act was Patrice Munsel as the title heroine reeling through a drunken wedding song (bottom left), with Ritchard in full regalia looking on in self-satisfied rapture. Another credit for the production was a charming performance of the street-singer Paquillo by Theodor Uppman, who was dressed in blue satin when presented at the Viceroy's court (below). Including* La Perichole, *Ritchard directed five operas during the Bing era:* Il Barbiere di Siviglia *in 1954,* Les Contes d'Hoffmann *in 1955,* Le Nozze di Figaro *and* The Gypsy Baron *in 1959*

Dali *Salome* they did together in London. David Webster invited her to lunch at Claridge's one day and giving her the address said, "It's in Brook Street." She let out a howl, threw a minor tantrum, and almost had to be coaxed to enter a thoroughfare so named. Brook didn't have this effect on us and was invited to return to direct *Eugene Onegin.* It was the same season he was doing *The Visit* for the Lunts and *The Little Hut.* Miss Fontanne was upset by the thought that he was getting three round-trip fares from England, one for each assignment.

Taking a cue from Lunt, Cyril Ritchard appeared as a non-singing, non-speaking servant in his *Barbiere di Siviglia*, and Eugene Berman's portrait of Dr. Bartolo in the second and third acts is really a self-likeness. Well, Michelangelo and El Greco painted themselves in.

Cyril Ritchard's second production was *Les Contes d'Hoffmann* under Pierre Monteux. It opened the season of 1955–56 and was atmospheric, particularly the Venetian scene, with Santa Maria della Salute right out there. It was *La Perichole*, however, before Ritchard hit his stride, and it was his peak. He loved to crack, "I am the only artist ever engaged by the Metropolitan in spite of an audition." *Le Nozze di Figaro* had incredibly beautiful scenery and costumes by Oliver Messel, and you would have thought it would be Cyril's dish, but it wasn't. There was a clothesline in Act I with some of Susanna's (or the Countess'?) unmentionables dangling from it, not out of place really, but it brought some of our friends to the brink of apoplexy.

His *Gypsy Baron* not only didn't stay in the repertory, it faded almost before the season was out; but *Perichole* was champagne. Patrice Munsel and Theodor Uppman as the barefoot balladeers were adorable. As Adele, Despina, and Perichole, everything Pat did was right. She can feign the most titillating naughtiness, and you somehow know she is still that nice girl from Spokane, fresh as a May morning. When she sang the letter song from *Perichole*, in the translation of Maurice Valency, who gave us the English version of *The Madwoman of Chaillot*, she tugged your heart.

An example of his deft rendering are these verses from the letter song, the music of which was made famous in this country by the waltz from *Gaîté Parisienne*:

Can I always be true and faithful
  While my body is starved for bread?
Oh how hard it is not to surrender
  When love itself cries to be fed!

It is hard for me to write this,
  But I write it from my soul,
And I sign myself despite this,
  Ever yours your Perichole.

I shall laugh with other laughter,
  I shall weep with other pain,
But despite what comes hereafter,
  I shall never love again!

Ted rivaled *The Blue Boy* in his Act II azure satin costume, and all over the lot was Cyril, outrageous as the Viceroy, one of the great clowns. His masquerade as the jailer was wild. Once introducing an artist at a Guild luncheon he confided, "And he sings in five languages," with such a leer you thought it was something to be X-rated.

Aided and abetted by Cecil Beaton's atmospheric décors, Gian Carlo Menotti worked wonders with Samuel Barber's *Vanessa.* He had a cast to work them with—Steber in the title role, Rosalind Elias as the younger sister, Regina Resnik in the almost mute role of the old Baroness. Miss Resnik topped even this characterization with her portrait of the old Countess in *Pique-Dame.* Nicolai Gedda was the young Anatol, George Cehanovsky the perfect butler, and Giorgio Tozzi the doctor right out of Chekhov. There were recollections of Isak Dinesen and anticipations of Ingmar Bergman, and not once was the strange mood broken. You felt the cold, the isolation of the whole unhealthy scene.

As might be expected, Menotti gave a lively account of his own *Last Savage*, which introduced Beni Montresor to the Metropolitan with some truly lovely sets. They would do for *Lakmé* today if we still did *Lakmé.*

Cornelius V. Starr donated a stunning new production of *Madama Butterfly* in 1957–58. Having made a fortune in the East, he was an avid orientalist. Not even in opera, he maintained, should chrysanthemums and cherry blossoms be blooming onstage at the same time, as they had in the Metropolitan's old production. We went straight to headquarters and got a Japanese director and a Japanese designer, Yoshio Aoyama and Motohiro Nagasaka.

Aoyama took some liberties with Puccini's stage directions. Butterfly does not make little holes in the shoji, the sliding paper panel, for herself and Suzuki and Trouble to watch for Pinkerton. "No Japanese would punch holes in the wall," Mr. Aoyama said. And Butterfly does not blindfold Trouble before she kills herself. She sends him into the garden, which conforms with Butterfly's last words, "*Va, gioca,*" (Go, play). She binds her legs in the kneeling position so there will be no struggle. Pinkerton and Sharpless do not reenter. Pinkerton's cry comes from offstage, and Butterfly dying alone amid the falling cherry blossom petals makes a more heart-rending finish than we had before. The tiny screen falls forward under her, and the petals are puffed upward, as though Butterfly's troubled spirit is at last released.

Verdi's *Macbeth* was an auspicious Metropolitan first. It marked Carl Ebert's debut at the house, with Leonard Warren in the title role and Leonie Rysanek stepping in for the recently ejected Maria Callas. One of Germany's most distinguished actors (he looked like Goethe), Ebert actually was responsible for Bing's entry into opera. He had turned from acting to management and one day appeared at the agency where Bing was working to give a job description of the assistant he wanted for Darmstadt. "Do you know someone?" he asked. "Yes," Bing answered. "Me."

He and Bing were colleagues in Berlin as well as Darmstadt, and later at Glyndebourne. His Berlin production of *Macbeth*, designed by Caspar Neher, was tied up with the Verdi renaissance, and they repeated their success at Glyndebourne. It was less successful at the Metropolitan, partly because Neher's heavy sets and costumes were a little old hat, somewhat reminiscent of Germany of the early thirties. Neher's *Wozzeck*, however, directed by Graf, was marvelous. The production reflected perfectly the nightmare quality of the work. Our stage crew performed miracles with the fifteen scenes that have to shift to Berg's music, sometimes in segments of only twenty seconds. The next-to-last scene, with the pond lit by a blood-drenched moon, was terrifying.

Günther Rennert (top left) was the director for seven major new productions for the Metropolitan Opera: Nabucco, *1960;* Un Ballo in Maschera, *1962;* Manon, *1963;* Salome, *1965;* Die Zauberflöte, *1967;* Jenufa, *1974; and* Le Nozze di Figaro, *1975. Designer Beni Montresor, who in 1965 collaborated with Rennert on a production of* La Cenerentola *for the Metropolitan Opera National Company, was aligned with the composer-director Gian Carlo Menotti (top right) for the U.S. premiere of* The Last Savage *in 1964. Montresor went on to display other works at the new Opera House—*La Gioconda *in 1966,* Esclarmonde *in 1976. Menotti had already been associated with the theater, for the premieres of two of his early operas,* Amelia al Ballo *and* The Island God, *and, in 1958, as stage director for the world premiere of Barber's* Vanessa, *for which Menotti wrote the libretto. Other European guests of the period included the noted German designer Caspar Neher and the director Carl Ebert, who posed on a set for their 1959 production of* Macbeth *with the conductor, Erich Leinsdorf (bottom right). Neher also did the decor that season for the Metropolitan Opera premiere of Alban Berg's* Wozzeck *(next two pages), a milestone for the company, proving that twentieth-century works can succeed at the box office. Ebert's other credits as director included* Martha *in 1961 and* Ariadne auf Naxos *in 1962. A guest from the Far East, Yoshio Aoyama, taught Antonietta Stella (below) authentic geisha gestures for her portrayal of Cio-Cio-San in his 1958 staging of* Madama Butterfly, *designed by another Japanese, Motohiro Nagasaka. The production remains one of the staples of the Opera House*

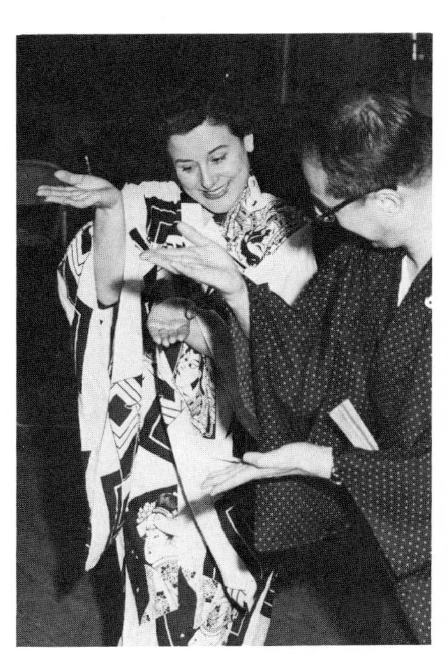

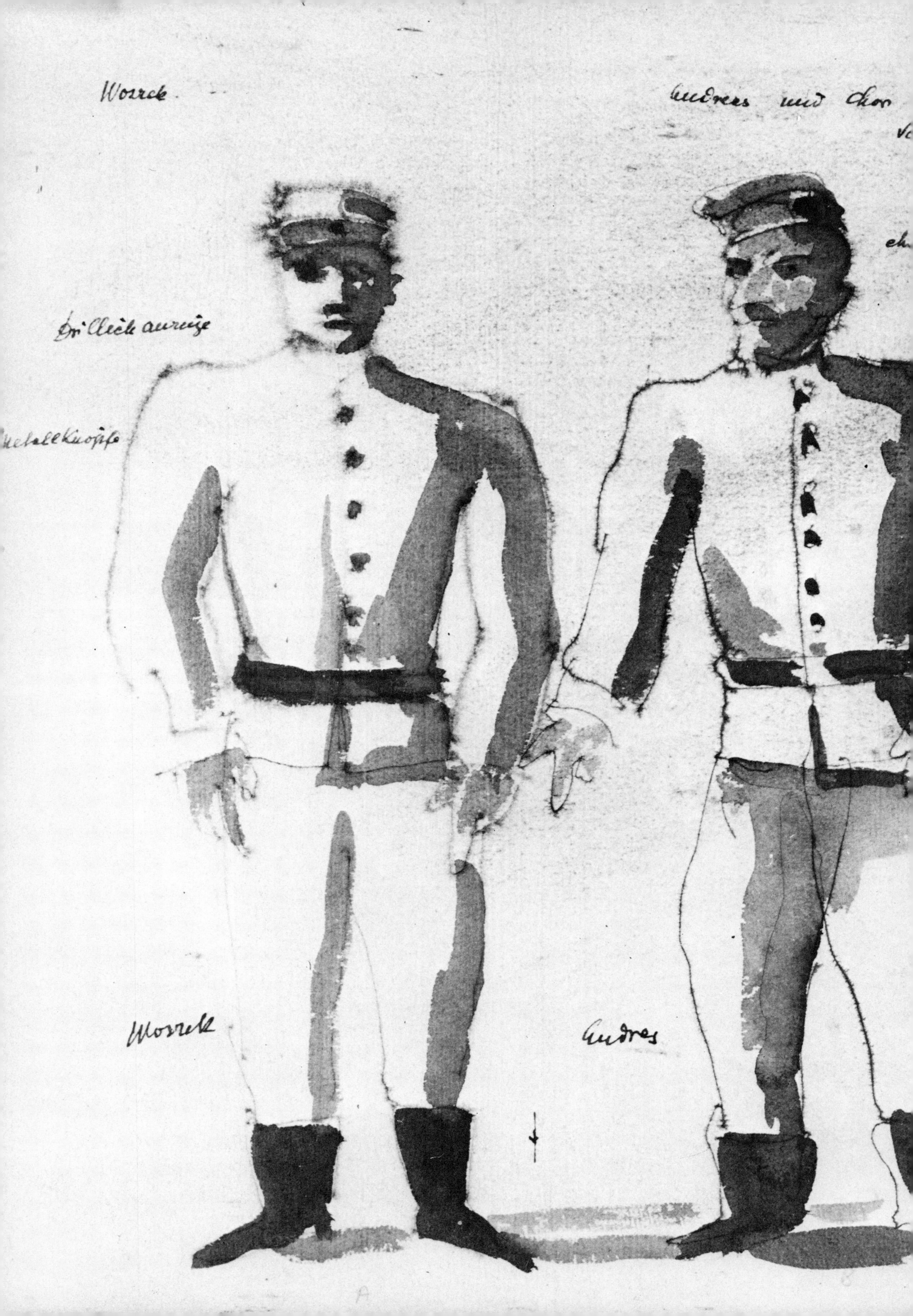

Wozzeck

Andres und Chor

Drilleich anzüge

Metallknöpfe

Wozzeck

Andres

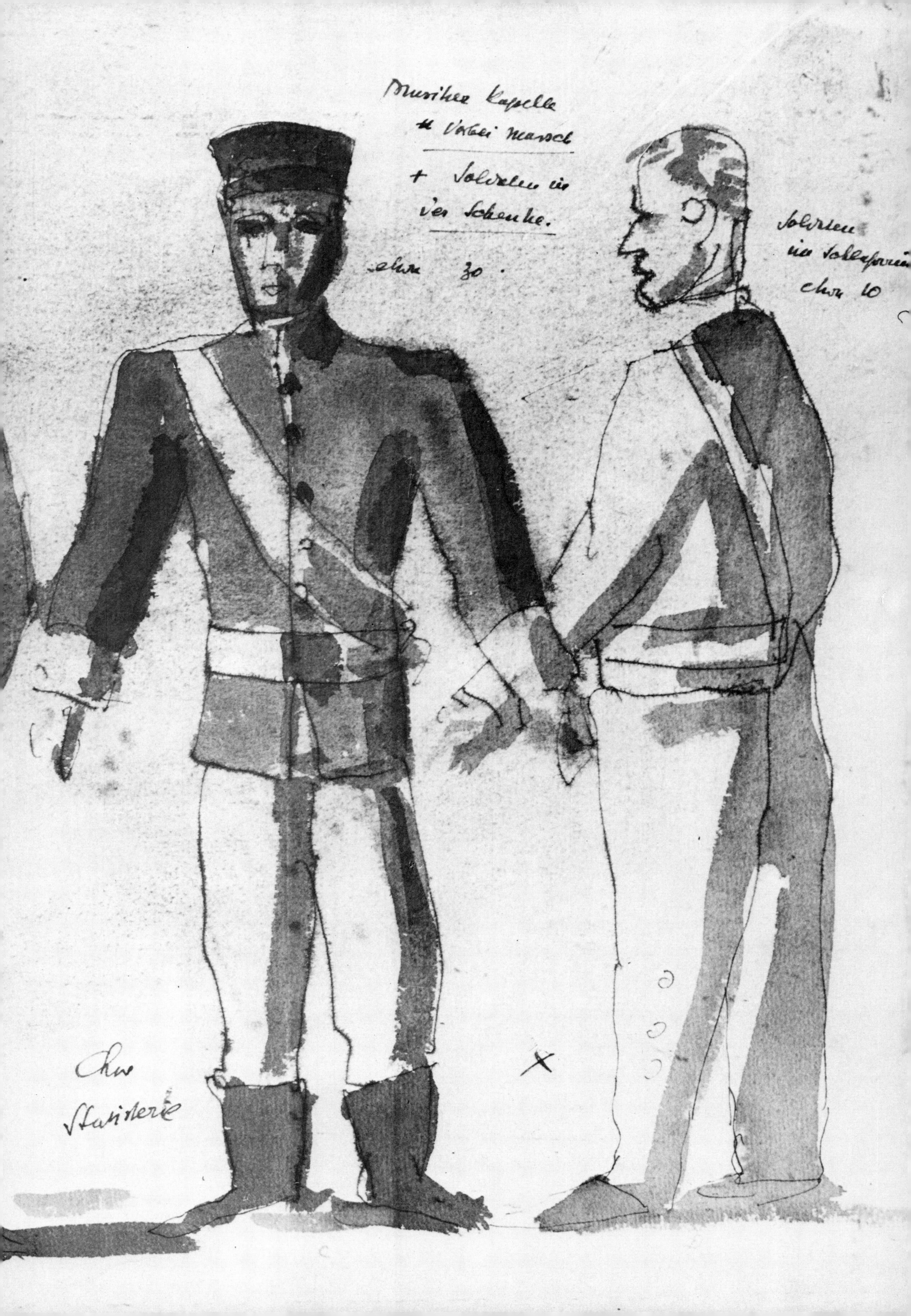
+ Soldaten in der Schenke.
Chor 30.
Soldaten
Chor 10
Chor
Statisterie

Ebert was saddled with *Martha*, better forgotten, but his *Ariadne auf Naxos* was a jewel, polished and gleaming. The lovely baroque sets and costumes were by Oliver Messel, who was not unknown to the Metropolitan. He had come to New York with the Sadler's Wells (now Royal) Ballet in 1949. His *Sleeping Beauty* with Margot Fonteyn opened their first American season, also the first time America had experienced a full evening ballet. Ariadne's blue-and-crimson, silver-trimmed costume was like the Madonna on some baroque church altar. When she and Bacchus, vine leaves in his hair, launched into the closing duet and the stars appeared in the dark sky, you really were carried with them to the heavens.

Günther Rennert, former general manager of the Hamburg State Opera and later general manager of the Bavarian State Opera in Munich, made his debut here with the first Metropolitan production of *Nabucco.* He later directed half a dozen Metropolitan Opera productions and *La Cenerentola* for the National Company. Dr. Rennert died a few days after he staged *Der Rosenkavalier* at the Salzburg Festival of 1978.

Nathaniel Merrill (above) blocks out stage action for Irene Dalis and an assistant, Nikolaus Lehnhoff, in a C-level rehearsal room at the new Opera House. The director earned his wings with the Metropolitan, starting as an assistant himself, meriting promotion to full credit in 1960 with a new production of L'Elisir d'Amore, *which was designed by his most frequent collaborator, Robert O'Hearn. This team has given the company eight productions:* Die Meistersinger, *1962;* Aida, *1963;* Samson et Dalila, *1964;* Die Frau ohne Schatten, *1966;* Hansel and Gretel, *1967;* Der Rosenkavalier, *1969; and* Parsifal, *1970. Working with other scenic artists, Merrill has directed other new productions:* Turandot, *1961;* Adriana Lecouvreur, *1963;* Luisa Miller, *1968;* Il Trovatore, *1969; and* Les Troyens, *1973*

Robert O'Hearn (above right) in his studio with the scale model of Hans Sachs' cobbler's shop, seen in Act II of Die Meistersinger von Nürnberg, *the designer's 1962 joint production with Nathaniel Merrill. In addition to many productions he has done with Merrill, O'Hearn has been engaged by the Metropolitan Opera to work with two other régisseurs. During the 1965–66 season, the last in the old Opera House, he collaborated with director Henry Butler, creating settings and costumes for Tchaikovsky's* Pique-Dame, *which had been absent from the repertory for over half a century. In the fall of 1975, for a new production of Mozart's* Le Nozze di Figaro, *O'Hearn's talent was paired with that of German director Günther Rennert. Outside the Metropolitan Opera, he has done* La Sylphide *for American Ballet Theatre*

His finale of the first act of *La Cenerentola* had the gentlemen of the chorus perform in animated cartoon choreography in identical green-satin tailcoats that you would have sworn were inspired by an old-time minstrel show, if Rennert and Beni Montresor, the designer had ever been exposed to this indigenous American art form. Besides being in demand in the major opera houses of the world, this gifted man worked in a factory in Bridgeport. His father was in the steel business.

The team of Nathaniel Merrill and Robert O'Hearn made their bow with *L'Elisir d'Amore* the season of 1960–61. They since have seven more productions to their credit. Their *Meistersinger* is the last word on that work to date.

The church the curtain sweeps up on is not the actual church of the Mastersingers. St. Katherine's was bombed and not rebuilt, so Merrill and O'Hearn went to two other beautiful churches of the same period. The columns are from St. Sebald. Veit Stoss breathtaking polychrome medallion of the Annunciation—*Englische Grüss*, "Angelic greeting," is the sweet German phrase—is copied to the last detail. The original in St. Lorenz is thirteen feet high; ours is eleven. The impression is startling. When the chorale takes over from the prelude and the action begins to unfold, you *are* in Nuremberg.

For the scene change in the last act a curtain falls, which is a blowup of a 1516 panorama of the town, which you can see today in the Germanisches National-Museum. Once the lovely interlude is over and the drums roll, the curtain turns out to be a scrim. It dissolves, and the now three-dimensional scene is behind it. To have the Mastersingers parade in identical robes and hats of dull-rose velvet is the final inspiration.

Merrill has directed five works with other designers. When Aoyama fell ill and could not come for *Turandot*, Merrill took over. Cecil Beaton's scenery and costumes take flight into fantasy. The first performance of the new *Turandot* was the occasion of one of those horrendous occurrences that make permanent retirement from the theater a happy prospect. The opening act is illuminated only by what the text calls the "funereal light" of a pale moon. Beaton's colors here are appropriately all blue and green, violet and gray. On opening night there appeared in the middle of these subdued hues a chorus lady in flaming orange—her costume for the second act, when everything is bright and blazing as midday.

Beaton shot from his place in the fourth row of the stalls as though a bayonet had come up through the chair. He catapulted backstage. By that mysterious radar of the theater the stage manager lured the lady into the wings, where Beaton, almost in view of the audience, literally tore the clothes from her body.

You don't have to have union regulations to guard against such assaults as this, and at the first opportunity, which was the first intermission, there was a little committee meeting. Mr. Bing sought out his fellow-Britisher. "You like this opera, Cecil?" he queried. "Yes," Beaton replied in his thin, dry voice. "You like this production?" By now Beaton was getting worried. "You want to see the second act?" Bing went on. "Well, you'd better get back there and apologize."

Now how, you may ask, can a thing like that happen? The story was the poor girl had had a virus, missed the dress rehearsal, and simply got into the wrong costume. How can it happen, you may further inquire, somebody didn't catch it? She had got past her colleagues in the chorus, wardrobe people, stage managers, and onto the stage. Such are the concentration and tension and terror of an opening night. "I wish," Noël Coward remarked later, "just one critic had said, 'That dot of orange in the first act! What inspiration! How it pulled the whole scene together!' "

Franco Zeffirelli had done *Falstaff* in practically every civilized country of the world, including Israel, when he was engaged to design and direct it for the Metropolitan. In fact he wanted to sue one major opera house whose settings showed his influence, he felt, a little too obviously. In his and Bernstein's deft hands Sir John and all the others—the Merry Wives, Anne, Fenton—came to life as fresh as they sprang from the imagination of Shakespeare and Verdi.

The opening scene reeked of stale ale. Ford's garden, reminiscent of Anne Hathaway's, looked like a blowup of one of Queen Mary's Christmas cards, but the picture was far from static. The stalks of the hollyhocks behaved like the real thing, not something from Woolworth's. When the

A new staging of Puccini's final opera, Turandot, *came into the Metropolitan Opera's repertory on February 24, 1961. During one of the final rehearsals, general manager Rudolf Bing posed in the orchestra pit with four of the production's mainsprings: Cecil Beaton, the designer, with one hand resting on his head; the director, Nathaniel Merrill; the conductor, Leopold Stokowski, on the podium; and, costumed as Calaf, the Unknown Prince, Franco Corelli (below). The first act of Puccini's musical fable unfolds outside a mysterious palace in Peking, a fearful populace awaiting a nighttime execution (top right). Act II, Scene 2, by contrast, takes place in a brightly lit public square, where on an immense staircase Birgit Nilsson refulgently sailed through Princess Turandot's murderous narrative, "In questa reggia," without so much as a tremor, while her aged father, sung by the veteran character tenor Alessio De Paolis as the Emperor Altoum, sat in attendance high on a throne behind her (bottom right)*

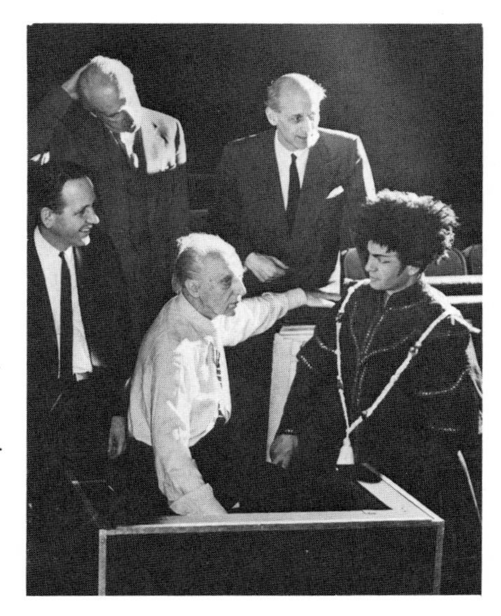

1965

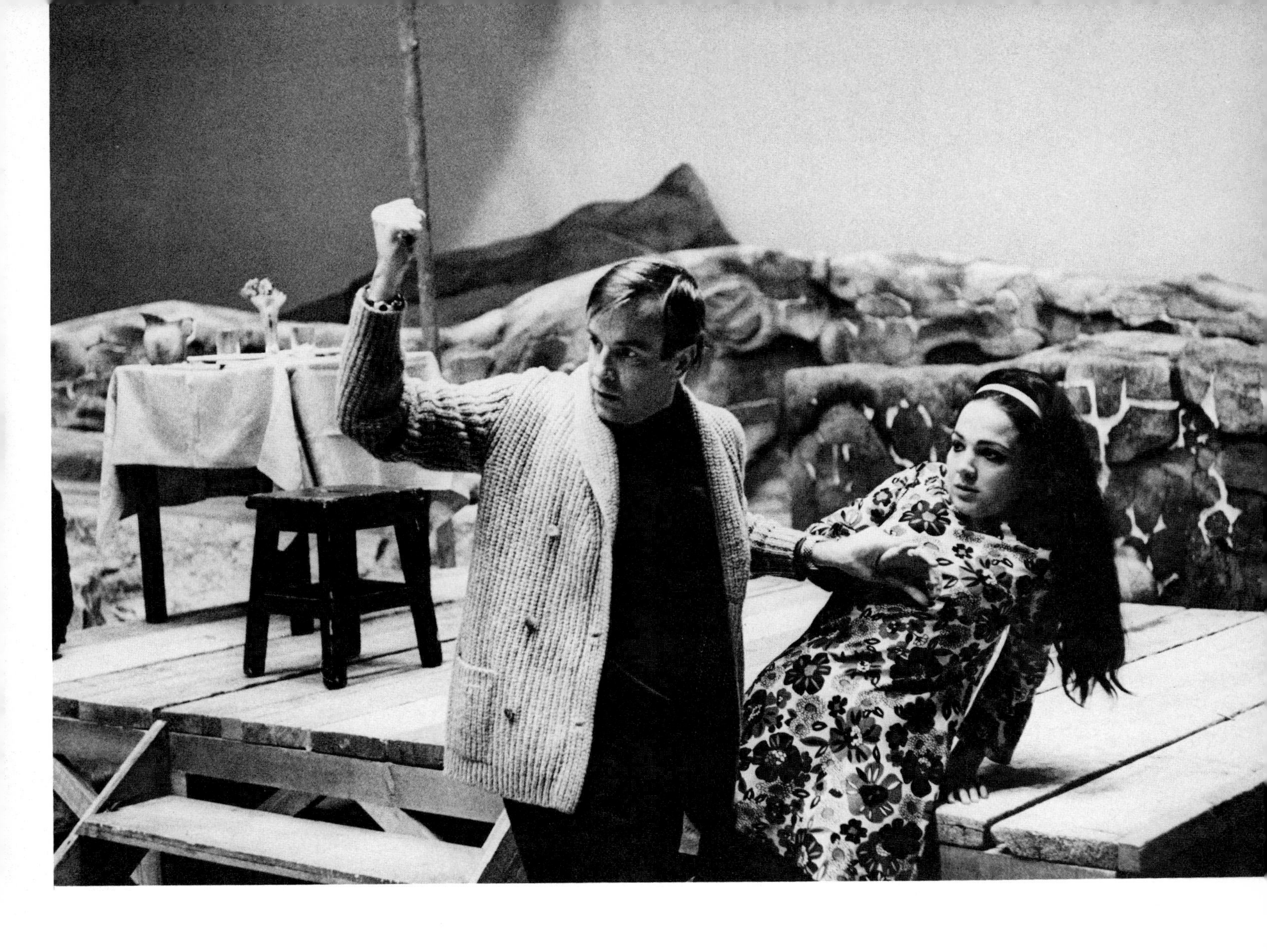

Franco Zeffirelli has been a triple threat at the Metropolitan Opera—stage director, designer of settings and costumes, and librettist for the opera that opened the new theater, Antony and Cleopatra. *In late 1969, during a stage rehearsal for his new productions of* Cavalleria Rusticana *and* Pagliacci, *he grasped Canio's knife to show his Nedda, Teresa Stratas, how to react to the maddened clown during her death struggle (above). Among Zeffirelli's finest scenic designs for the theater are those he created in 1964 for the Metropolitan's production of* Falstaff *(top left, Act III, Scene 1, outside the Garter Inn), one of the great nights in the old Opera House, bringing the debuts of both Zeffirelli and conductor Leonard Bernstein. Of another beauty is a costume painting the Tuscan artist did in 1966 showing the recumbent Cleopatra (bottom left). Zeffirelli has also staged* Otello *at the Opera House, which like his* Cav/Pag *has been telecast by PBS on its "Live from the Met" series*

men hid behind them and parted them to peep through, they reacted. Falstaff's wooing was genius at work, particularly when he disdainfully tossed an enormous bouquet out of a giant vase and replaced it with his own tiny nosegay.

And Zeffirelli's lighting. For the first time we saw real sunlight on a stage, several sunlights in fact, for they were different, as they are in nature. The pale sun through the cobwebs of the Garter Inn was as different from midday in the garden as that was from the slanted glow of late afternoon when Falstaff comes dripping from the Thames. Judith Raskin and Luigi Alva, as the young lovers, were part and parcel of the magic of Windsor Park Forest, and when the entire company —Anselmo Colzani, Regina Resnik, Mario Sereni, Rosalind Elias and Gabriella Tucci among the principals—comes down to the footlights for the finale, the big fugue—*"Tutto nel mondo e burlà,"* Everything in the world is a joke—that is the theater as it was in the beginning, it now, and ever shall be.

Franz Werfel tells us opera is a preposterous art. "Is it not truly preposterous," he asks, "for a dying man to assert in a melting G-flat that death cannot part him from his beloved, whereupon the beloved, in the same tone and tune, despairingly maintains the contrary, until at length both repeat their contradictory statements and identical tunes, finally starving (as the old theatrical joke has it) on a sustained B-flat?" Yet this very preposterousness, Werfel goes on, "is connected with the most delicate ecstasies man is capable of, the sense of the unreality of all things and the featherweight joy of irony. . . ." The dots are Werfel's. And so at the end of Verdi's last opera the old man reminds us that everything on earth is a jest. In this mood Franco Zeffirelli for a time contemplated having the scenery fly out of sight and having the company peel out of its wigs and costumes, but he thought better of it.

Henry Butler, himself a beguiling actor, showed he could handle such contrasting works as *La Sonnambula* and *Pique-Dame.* He first came to the Metropolitan Opera in 1961, staging an opening night performance of *La Fanciulla del West* starring Leontyne Price and Richard Tucker as the barmaid and bandit. In 1967 Butler distinguished himself as librettist of Marvin David Levy's *Mourning Becomes Electra,* adapted from the O'Neill tragedy and given its world premiere at the new Opera House.

Margherita Wallmann's debut with Attilio Colonnello in *Lucia di Lammermoor* at the old house was less successful than her *Gioconda* the second night at the new with Montresor. "Venice is a place," Madame Wallmann said, "where pigeons walk and lions fly," and that was the spirit of the production. This important director had begun life as a dancer. Her production of Gluck's *Orfeo* with Ted Shawn in the title role for the German Dance Congress of 1930 became the model for that masterpiece, whether she staged it herself or not.

Margherita Wallmann (above) has staged operas by Donizetti and Ponchielli at the Metropolitan. Jean-Louis Barrault (below) exercised his abilities on a pair of French works, Faust *and* Carmen. *The five men behind* Mourning Becomes Electra *in 1967 (right)—the designer, Boris Aronson; the composer, Marvin David Levy; the director, Michael Cacoyannis; the conductor, Zubin Mehta; the librettist, Henry Butler. A folio of current scenic artists and directors follows (next two pages): Peter Wexler, designer of* Les Troyens *(top left); Desmond Heeley, designer of* Don Pasquale *(bottom left); Beverly Sills and Justino Díaz rehearse* L'Assedio di Corinto *with the director, Sandro Sequi (top center); Otto Schenk stages* Fidelio *with Giorgio Tozzi, Walter Berry and Leonie Rysanek (bottom center); Günther Schneider-Siemssen, who designed six Wagner works for the Metropolitan (top right); and the régisseur-designer Jean-Pierre Ponnelle, adept in both Rossini comedy and Wagner tragedy*

Faust opened the last season in the old house, as it had the first. The new production by Jean-Louis Barrault and Jacques Dupont was so successful it was duplicated at La Scala, except they had Siébel sung by a tenor, Luigi Alva, instead of a mezzo.

The entire action takes place on a round, sharply raked stage. "The tree of life?" Claudia Cassidy queried. Could be. And the action unfolds, flows, logically and beautifully. A statue is brought in and placed in the center of the bare stage to create the town square for the "Soldier's Chorus." This gives way to a headman's block and finally to a tall, slender, gleaming cross, which Marguerite merely slowly approaches and reaches up heartbreakingly to touch as the sign of her redemption.

Great people can make mistakes on a scale corresponding with their accomplishments, and Barrault's and Dupont's *Carmen* in the new house is a case in point. The attempt to put the whole thing in a unit set resembling the interior of the bull ring was simply too arty.

Wieland Wagner was to have come for a new production of *Lohengrin* in 1966–67. His untimely death deprived us of his presence, but his plans were carried out by his gifted assistant Peter Lehmann. It was strictly in the postwar Bayreuth style, more Greek than Nordic, but highly effective. The chorus remained immobile, except when a few fainted from time to time, on three semicircular steps. The blue backdrop was like stained glass.

Rudolf Heinrich's death at the age of fifty is still mourned. He did the two Strauss shockers for us, *Salome* and *Elektra*, a *Tosca* with all three sets, particularly the dome of St. Peter's in the last act, to scale, and a truly beautiful *Werther*, Massenet's opera revived after sixty years for Franco Corelli. Heinrich both directed and designed *Der Freischütz.*

Werther was staged by Paul-Émile Deiber, France's greatest actor after Barrault. He is probably the finest Cyrano de Bergerac since Coquelin, and his production of *Le Cid* for the Comédie Française has been acclaimed throughout the civilized world. Deiber's wife, Christa Ludwig, was Charlotte. This remarkable artist has scrambled the mezzo and soprano roles in the dozen she has sung at the Metropolitan. She has done both Octavian and the Marschallin, Cherubino, Amneris, Brangäne, the Dyer's Wife, Ortrud, Fricka, Kundry, Leonore in *Fidelio*, and Berlioz' Dido. Deiber had directed

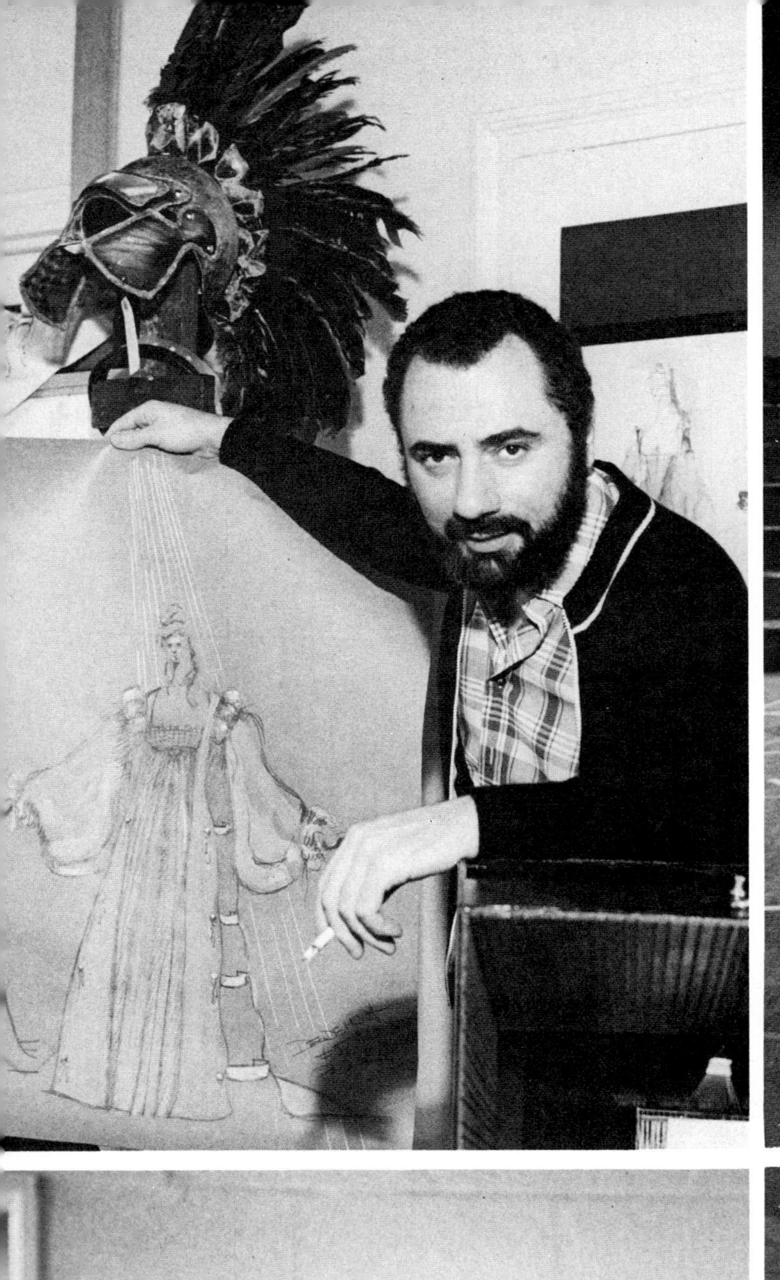

The German director August Everding and the Chinese designer Ming Cho Lee (above) have combined forces for new investitures of Boris Godunov *and* Lohengrin *at the Metropolitan Opera*

Overseeing all that happens onstage at the Opera House is the company's director of production, John Dexter (left), working out his own staging of Rigoletto *with James Atherton in the rear as Borsa and Robert Goodloe as Marullo. Gil Wechsler (below) is now the resident lighting designer of the Metropolitan Opera*

Norma with scenery by Desmond Heeley. These two were also responsible for *Pelléas et Mélisande.* His debut had been *Roméo et Juliette*. Heeley is a regular at Stratford, Ontario; designed *The Merry Widow* for Margot Fonteyn, and a lovely *Don Pasquale* for Beverly Sills's farewell to the Metropolitan.

Formerly general manager of the Hamburg Opera and now general manager in Munich, August Everding began in the legitimate theater. He started in opera with *La Traviata* in Munich and was then invited to direct *Tristan und Isolde* in Vienna. He was the first postwar director in Bayreuth outside the Wagner family, and his production of *Der Fliegende Holländer* there, with Josef Svoboda as designer, was a sensation.

Jean-Pierre Ponnelle's set for *L'Italiana in Algeri* was like alabaster, luminous as the interior of the Taj Mahal, and his staging was impish. The chorus line of eunuchs is surely one of the funniest sights ever seen on any stage. In stark contrast is his evocative *Fliegende Holländer*, on loan from San Francisco and played in a single act.

Nicola Benois, who designed the scenery and costumes for *L'Assedio di Corinto*, is the son of Alexander Benois, who created the first production of *Petrouchka* for Diaghilev. Invited by Toscanini to mount *Boris Godunov* and *Khovanshchina*, Nicola Benois became the chief designer for La Scala for three decades. Certain of the décors for *L'Assedio* are reminiscent of some other Russian ballet scenery, Bakst's for *Scheherazade*, which is a compliment to all concerned.

The director of *L'Assedio di Corinto*, Sandro Sequi, was known to New York before his hilarious *Fille du Régiment* starring Joan Sutherland and Luciano Pavarotti was brought over from Covent Garden. His production of Rossini's *Otello* was a highlight of the Rome Opera's visit to the Lincoln Center Festival in 1968. He did *L'Assedio di Corinto* at La Scala, which served as the vehicle for Beverly Sills's debut there as well as at the Metropolitan. In New York he was reunited with Miss Sutherland and Pavarotti for *I Puritani*, bel canto and bel veduto.

There is another kind of design, and that is with light. Since the season of 1976–77 the Metropolitan has had its own lighting designer. Gil Wechsler came to us from Lyric Opera of Chicago, where he held the corresponding post for five years.

He was born in Brooklyn, and his stockbroker father insisted he do something more—is practical the word?—than the theater, so he studied physics for three years at Rensselaer Polytechnic Institute in Troy, but his first love won out, and he took his B.S. degree in theater at New York University and later an M.F.A. degree at Yale, where he studied under Herman Krawitz, Eddie Kook of Century Lighting Company, and Donald Oenslager, who designed the *Otello* that served the Metropolitan through the late thirties and forties.

Wechsler was with the Harkness Ballet for two years and the Stratford, Ontario, Festival for nine. He was Desmond Heeley's associate on *Pelléas et Mélisande* and went with the production to Chicago when Lyric Opera borrowed it, which was his introduction there.

There is no more exciting work done in the theater today than John Dexter's. His credits are catalogued in a previous chapter. George Cehanovsky said of him, "He is twenty years ahead of his time." Fortunate we are to have him now.

ORCHESTRA, CHORUS, BALLET

The first opera was composed by Jacopo Peri, 1561–1633. The first genius of opera came close on his heels—Claudio Monteverdi, 1567–1643. Monteverdi did for opera what Aeschylus had done for drama 2,000 years before. Regarded as the father of European drama, Aeschylus introduced the second actor. Until his time, the tragedy was carried forward by the chorus and one actor, who emerged from the chorus line or circle to center stage. The second actor made for greater freedom, for greater development of plot and character.

When Monteverdi produced his first opera, *Orfeo*, in 1607, the art of opera was exactly ten years old. It had introduced multiple characters in a given work, but each voice had sung alone. It remained for Monteverdi in *Orfeo* to create the first operatic duet. Think of what this meant to the development of the new art form. The most striking thing that opera possesses, setting it apart from any other art, is its power to lay bare the emotions of two or more characters, often with conflicting emotions, simultaneously.

Suzanne Laurence and Eugenia Hoeflin of the ballet warm up (above); musicians in the pit (below) and the ladies of the chorus ready for Otello, *Act III (right)*

Monteverdi was as much an innovator in his day as Wagner was in his. The single sustained note in the prelude of *Orfeo* has been compared with the prelude to *Das Rheingold.* Monteverdi introduced violins to the orchestra—an appropriate move, since he was born in Cremona and a virtuoso of the instrument—and he raised the orchestra to the unheard-of magnitude of thirty-six players. He was also responsible for the novelty of the tremolo, which the musicians at first refused to play, to describe the agitation of a duel scene, and pizzicato to depict sword thrusts, effects still used in dramatic music.

The very words *orchestra* and *chorus* have their origins in the Greek theater, and it was in their attempt to restore classic tragedy that the young noblemen of Florence stumbled on opera. In the ancient theater the orchestra was the space in front of the stage allotted to the chorus, and in the Greek plays the chorus danced as well as sang or chanted. The word ballet comes later.

In the chapter on conductors we have seen that the quality of the orchestra has always been of first importance with the Metropolitan. *Opera News* says, "The soul of the Metropolitan Opera House is the orchestra pit." The chorus and ballet also carry their load in the scheme of things. Mr. Gatti and Maestro Toscanini brought their chorus master with them, Giulio Setti, and he is the conductor on a number of fine records where the chorus was involved, such as Ponselle's *Norma*, Martinelli's *Trovatore*, and Tibbett's *Tosca.* Rosina Galli, our prima ballerina and later ballet mistress, was Gatti's second wife. He used to plead with Howard Taubman, the leading reporter on music and later critic of the *Times,* "Say anything you please about my singers, but let the ballet alone." It is worthy of note that the Metropolitan Opera Ballet did perform *Petrouchka* and other works from the Diaghilev repertory.

For three years, Edward Johnson had George Balanchine and the American Ballet in the house. Bing brought Antony Tudor, and there was talk of making Ballet Theatre the resident company. The company is now fixed in the house as we shall see in a later chapter. Neither plan worked, but no one can say for lack of effort or expense.

Much of today's administration of the orchestra is in the hands of Abe Marcus, the personnel manager, who is also the first percussionist. The door of his office on A level is never closed to the ninety regular musicians and twenty-odd extra players. In fact they have to come in before each performance to see where they are sitting. Marcus has an enormous board with magnetized badges bearing each man's name. It's like consulting the seating plan before a formal dinner. The conductors check this board too.

Marcus describes the procedure for auditions. "They are usually held in the orchestra's rehearsal room on C level or in List Hall, and behind screens. Every other precaution is taken to preserve anonymity. The order is by drawing lots. If a candidate knows someone on the jury, he can't tip the judge off as to when in the sequence he will be playing."

The judges are the conductors who may be in residence, the first-chair men or in fact the entire section, and the judges are not allowed to talk to one another. Decisions are as free of prejudice as is possible. Quality is the only standard.

For a recent pair of vacancies in the flute section there were a hundred applications. They come from everywhere, even from Europe. No matter

Members of the Metropolitan Opera Orchestra at work in its C-level rehearsal room, with second violin Albert Weintraub (above) and tuba Herbert Wekselblatt (below). Also shown in detail are French horns E. Scott Brubaker and Howard T. Howard (top left); trumpet Melvyn Broiles (top right); clarinet Herbert Blayman (top center left); flute Trudy Kane and oboe Alfred Genovese (top center right); second violin Magdalena Golczewski, with Placido Domingo (bottom center left); cello Richard Kay (bottom center right); bassoon Paul Cammarota (bottom left); and double bass Georges André (bottom right). James Levine, the Metropolitan Opera's music director, says, "We have the most remarkable opera orchestra in the world because of the excellent standard it maintains despite an incessant performance and rehearsal schedule."

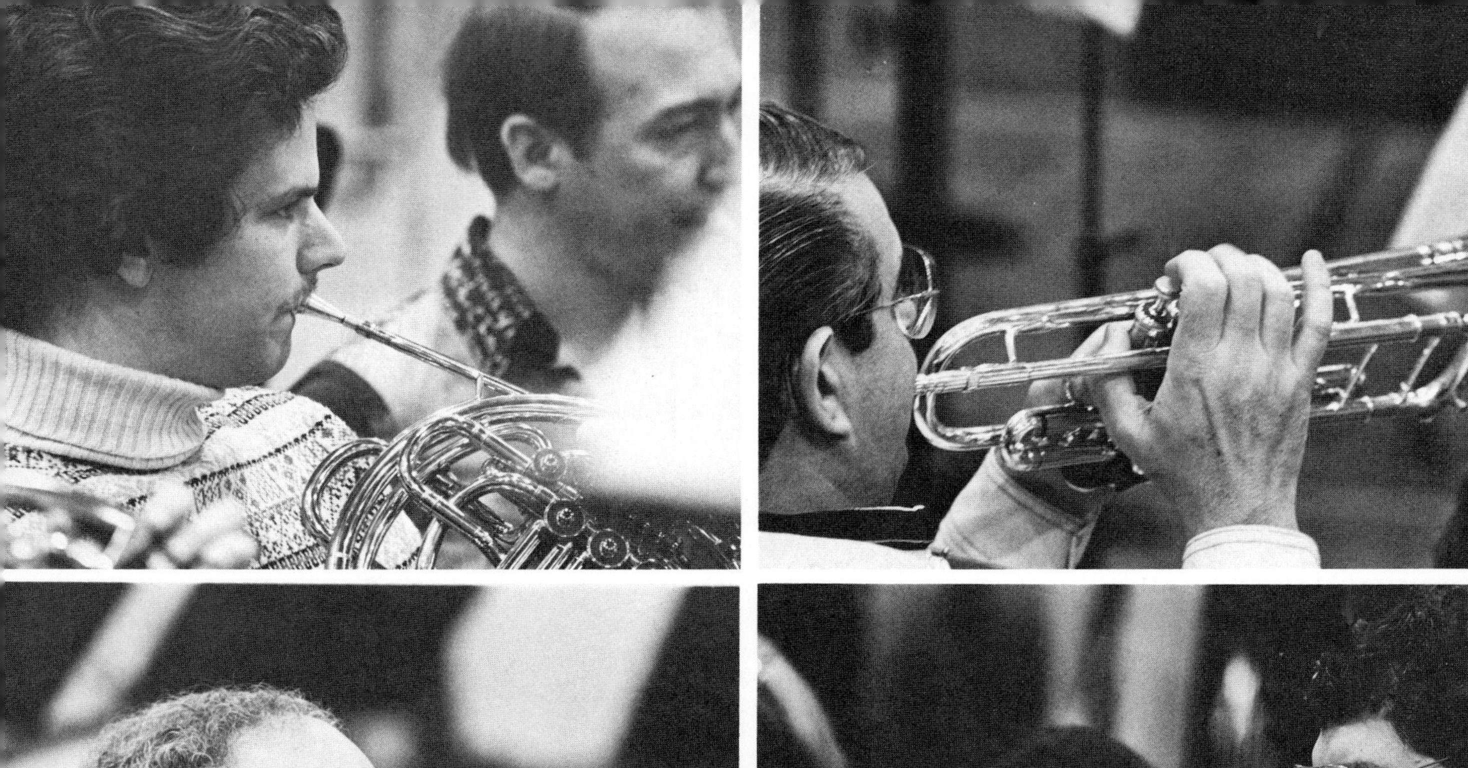

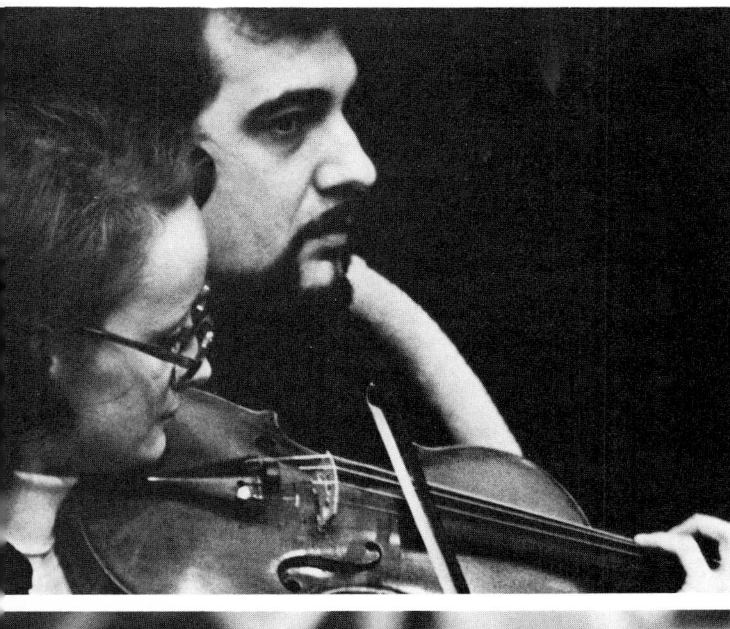

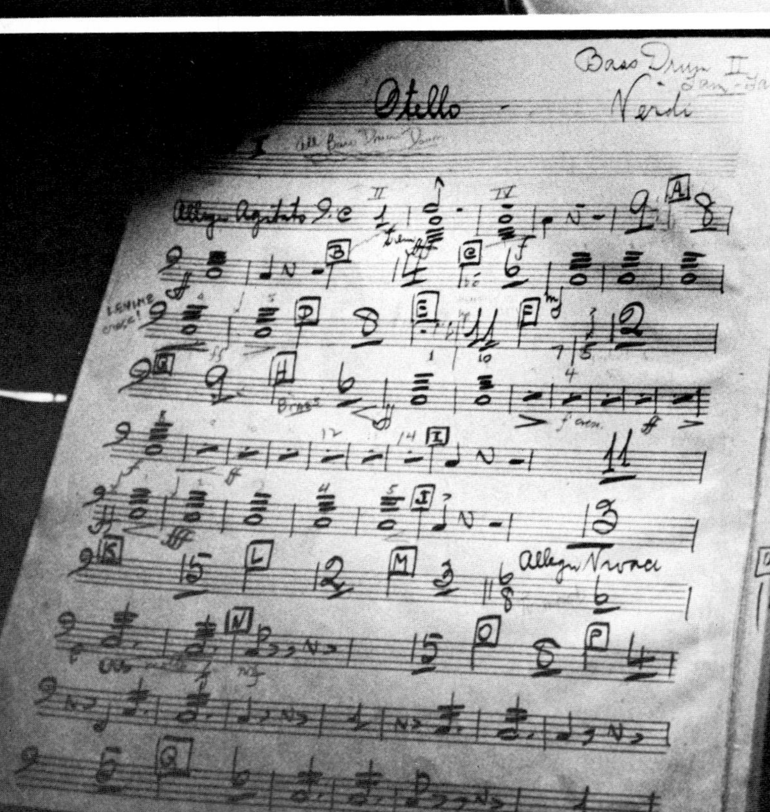

Otello
Verdi
27
G. VERDI
PROPERTY OF
METROPOLITAN OPERA ASSOCIATION, Inc.
OTELLO
GRAN CASSA

The orchestra as it sees the auditorium from music stands in the pit just before the house lights dim for a performance (above). Principal players in the percussion section include harp Reinhardt Elster (top right) and timpani Richard Horowitz (bottom right). The players feel the excitement of an outstanding performance tremendously and admit that they get chills when they hear an ovation on a great night, such as when they first did Die Frau ohne Schatten, Les Troyens, Lulu *and* Billy Budd. *At full force the orchestra numbers 101 players—ninety-one regulars and ten extras. Their work load is staggering because of the subscription system. With seven performances each week, every player is obliged to render nine services, that is, play five performances (as long as four hours) and do four rehearsals (a two-and-a-half-hour minimum). Everything beyond is overtime, making it one of the world's highest paid orchestras*

Before a performance: double bass Charles Urbont and French horn Arthur Sussman (above); bassoon Patricia Rogers with first violin Eugene Campione (top left); percussion Scott Stevens warming up in his instrument storeroom below the stage (top right)

Concertmaster Raymond Gniewek helping his wife, Judith Blegen, get ready to go onstage as Adina in L'Elisir d'Amore *(bottom left); second violin Leslie Dreyer enjoying a game of chess in a locker room despite the quips of cello Jascha Silberstein (bottom right); and trombone experts Hal Janks and David Langlitz, a principal (below)*

how badly a candidate may perform, he is asked to play the entire audition. There were six excerpts for the flute tests—the lovely Entr'acte before Act III of *Carmen*, the graceful solo before the Italian singer's aria from *Der Rosenkavalier*, the gavotte from *Manon Lescaut* and excerpts from *Così Fan Tutte*, *Falstaff*, the Nile Scene from *Aida*, *Salome*, *Il Barbiere di Siviglia* and *Die Meistersinger*—all schools and periods.

To represent the orchestra two contrasts come to mind, a beginner and a seasoned player, a girl and a man. The Metropolitan Opera is the first regular job Patricia Rogers has ever had. In the woodwinds it is customary at the Met to have two principals, and Miss Rogers is co-principal bassoon with Richard Hebert.

Blond, pretty as a picture, she won this important post when she was only twenty-two and fresh out of the Cincinnati College-Conservatory of Music. She answered the Metropolitan's advertisement in *The Instrumentalist*, the magazine of the American Federation of Musicians, in December 1976, and after two auditions in as many days she was notified she had the job.

She was born in Owingsville, Kentucky, but the family moved to Greencastle, Pennsylvania, when she was very young. Her father is a farmer, and she is the only musical member of the family.

At twelve she joined the school orchestra. Why did she choose bassoon? They needed a bassoon player. Serge Koussevitzky used to say the reason he played double bass was it was the only scholarship open at the Moscow Conservatory when he came along.

The Metropolitan isn't Miss Rogers' first experience playing under its music director. As a substitute with the Cincinnati Symphony she played under Maestro Levine in his home town.

In contrast to a newcomer like Miss Rogers is Eugene Campione, who though still a young man has been a member of the orchestra for more than twenty years. As assistant concertmaster, he calls his post the hot seat. When he occupies the place left of the concertmaster, Raymond Gniewek, the associate concertmaster, Edmund Jacobsen, is sitting behind him. Gene Campione seems to bear up.

He was born in St. Louis where his father was a double bass player in the St. Louis Symphony. The summer of his fourteenth year, Gene went to the International Music Camp at Interlochen, Michigan. Josef Hofmann was one of the judges and recommended him to his colleague at the Curtis Institute of Music, Efrem Zimbalist. He studied with Zimbalist for three years.

After a year and a half with the St. Louis Symphony, he was drafted. He continued in music for a time in the Army, but when the invasions began the bands were dissolved and sent to the infantry. Gene made such a high mark on his rhythm test he was sent to radar school at Camp Chanute, Illinois, and became an operator. For the remainder of his four years in uniform he guided crippled planes back to the U.S. through the Bahamas.

Since the war he has been concertmaster of the Farbman Quartet and the Columbia Concerts Symphonietta. For a time he was with the Little Orchestra Society and associate concertmaster of Radio City Music Hall.

The Campiones live in Westchester, where Mrs. Campione teaches clarinet. She also plays concerts. Their three sons are musical—trombone, trumpet, and clarinet—but "are not going into it." When Gene can find time

from his duties at the Metropolitan and his fifteen students, he plays a good game of golf.

Abe Marcus was born in Poland but came to this country at the age of three months. Not only did he not come of a musical family but his mother was tone-deaf. Never mind, that boy had to have violin lessons. He got into percussion through jazz and says he "grew up" with Buddy Rich and Gene Krupa. A scholarship to Juilliard brought him to Saul Goodman, long the New York Philharmonic percussionist and a famous teacher. Goodman asked him to play an A and accepted him.

Before he got so busy at the Metropolitan, Marcus did a wonderful program in the city's public schools, demonstrating the entire range of his section. As the finale he took youngsters and had them playing rhythms that would have been the envy of Stravinsky.

It is difficult to describe, impossible to evaluate the virtuosity of the Metropolitan Opera Orchestra. Once on tour, for example, a world-famous soprano, who was never known to make a musical mistake in her life, ran into difficulty with the repeats in the final scene of *Aida* and jumped about ten bars. Now in that split second there is no way for the conductor to indicate just where in the score the musicians are to pick up. It didn't matter.

Abraham Marcus, personnel manager of the Metropolitan Opera Orchestra, at his desk with assistant Edgardo Sodero (above) and costumed for the stage band used in Andrea Chénier *(below)*

Assistant music librarian Joseph Ortiz and his chief, John Grande, in the stacks (above), where scores for the Metropolitan's entire repertory can be found

They gallantly followed the lady, and you would have to know *Aida* pretty well to realize anything had gone wrong.

Another time in the old house Pietro Cimara, the conductor, had a stroke during the first act of *La Forza del Destino.* Walter Hagen, first desk of the second violins, caught him and began to beat time with his right hand while holding Maestro Cimara up with his left. Finally Cimara was carried out, Hagen mounted the podium and carried on without a hitch.

Before we leave the orchestra, a word about the library. There was a time when we rented our scores. Now we own 4,000 vocal scores of eighty works and full sets of orchestra parts for sixty operas—the entire standard repertory. Erich Leinsdorf once figured the repertory rests on about sixty works. Not many have made it in the 400 years since Jacopo Peri.

John Grande, the Metropolitan's music librarian, began studying clarinet at the age of nine. His father—born in Bari, the town Licia Albanese comes from—also played clarinet. John's sister wanted to be a concert pianist, his brother plays saxophone, and his wife is a soprano.

He studied at Juilliard and says two summers at Tanglewood, where he was student librarian, were invaluable experience. He also worked with the late Harry G. Schumer, the Metropolitan's librarian for over thirty years.

The Metropolitan Opera Chorus has been revivified by David Stivender, who first came to the Metropolitan as assistant chorus master to Kurt Adler in 1965 and advanced to the top post in 1973. He has conducted *Trovatore*, *Rigoletto*, and *Aida.* You can't be with him very long before you catch his eagerness for the job and opera in general.

"I never wanted anything but opera," he says. Born in Milwaukee, he came across the *Victor Book of the Opera* in the Milwaukee Public Library when he was twelve. That did it. There wasn't an opera score in that library he didn't devour. When he was sixteen or seventeen, he says, he became acquainted with *Esclarmonde*, little dreaming that one day he would be preparing the Metropolitan Opera Chorus for a production of it.

At Northwestern he was assistant director of the opera workshop in his junior year. After earning his B.A. degree there, he served a stretch in the Navy, conducting the Bluejackets Choir at Great Lakes. Then he won a Fulbright Scholarship, enabling him to study two years in Rome with the venerable Luigi Ricci, mentor of Leonard Warren and other greats. He put in two years at Spoleto and also worked with Lyric Opera of Chicago. His first professional job was with the Opera Arts Association in Atlanta, which was run by Ralph Errolle, a former Metropolitan Opera tenor, who gave many a young singer his first hearing.

Chorus Master David Stivender (left) takes his singers through their paces at a rehearsal in List Hall (above right). Chorus delegates to the management Edward Ghazal and Lorraine Keane (below), both of whom have pursued rewarding vocal careers beyond the confines of the Opera House. They are in costume for the third act of Otello

Stivender's enthusiasm for James Levine knows no bounds. "It's plus, it's positive," he says of the new dispensation. Stivender says his own biggest headache is time. "I'll work for no money," he declares, "but time . . . you have time to teach the notes, but the sound . . . that can only be done by drill." The triple meters are the tricky ones, and *Le Nozze di Figaro* is harder than *Boris* or *Tannhäuser*, he says.

On tour Stivender haunts old bookshops and has amassed a formidable library. There being no biography of Mascagni in English, he has put together an "autobiography" out of the writings and statements of the composer of *Cavalleria Rusticana.*

Lorraine Keane and Edward Ghazal have served as delegates of the chorus to the management and may be regarded as typical.

Both Miss Keane's mother and father were professional singers in concert, church, and radio. Her first appearance was at age four or five in a show her mother staged. Born in Winthrop outside Boston, she attended New England Conservatory and studied with Marie Sundelius, a Metropolitan Opera soprano for eleven seasons, who was also the teacher of Mildred Miller. She went to Europe for further study and concertized in Europe through the American Forces Network.

Back in this country she sang all the mezzo roles—Carmen, Amneris, Azucena, Ulrica, Dorabella—with smaller companies. She came to the

Metropolitan in 1962 and lives at the Ansonia Hotel, where Bidù Sayão, Fausto Cleva, and so many others of the Metropolitan roster made their homes.

Ghazal is a New Yorker, and he too was a church soloist, in Brooklyn. Later he became soloist with the glee club of Alexander Hamilton High School and the All-City High School Chorus under Peter Wilhousky, who prepared the children's choruses for Toscanini.

At Westminster Choir College, where he earned an M.A. degree, he studied with the founder, Dr. John Finley Williamson. In the Army he was a chaplain's assistant, which meant everything from duets with the major to conducting a hillside of GIs. He spent two years in France. Our forces were only seven miles into Normandie when he crossed the English Channel in an LST. He sometimes assisted at nine services seven days a week. They had to be conducted in gunpits because of antiaircraft, and twenty was a good-sized congregation.

He was at Radio City Music Hall for a year, and for a wild time he sang in the choruses of both the Metropolitan and the New York City Opera, which sometimes meant racing from a performance at the Old City Center on Fifty-fifth Street in time for the last act at Broadway and Thirty-ninth.

He has been director of the choir of the Lutheran Church of the Good Shepherd in Brooklyn and of the choirs of St. Nicholas and St. Mary's Antiochan Orthodox Cathedrals. Of Lebanese descent, he knows Arabic and has reclaimed a lot of music by giving it the proper liturgical texts, which the publishers had not bothered to do.

The gentlemen of the chorus (top left) ready to go onstage for Tchaikovsky's Eugene Onegin. *Thomas Powell (below), a chorus delegate to the management, works on his schedule during a break. A chorister who has enjoyed great success as soprano soloist, Elinor Harper (right), puts on the final touches of her makeup for the mighty third-act ensemble in Verdi's* Otello

mineral oil

Norbert Vesak (below), director of the Metropolitan Opera Ballet, demonstrates a combination of steps during one of the company's daily classes. Floor work by gentlemen of the ensemble—Jack Hertzog, Jacques Cesbron, Dave Roeger, Marcus Bugler (top left)—and bar work by ladies of the ensemble—Pauline Andrey, Antoniette Peloso, Eugenia Hoeflin, Suzanne Laurence (bottom left). The 1978–79 roster of dancers included (next two pages) Kimberly Graves, Miss Peloso, Michael Gleason, Naomi Marritt, Miss Hoeflin, Mr. Roeger, Ricardo Costa, Diana Levy, Ellen Rievman, Nadine Tomlinson, Carey Dresser, Mr. Bugler, Miss Laurence, Lucia Sciorsci, Christopher Stocker, Mr. Hertzog, Patricia Heyes, Vicki Fisera and Virgil Pearson-Smith.

Norbert Vesak, director of the Metropolitan Opera Ballet, was resident choreographer of the Royal Winnipeg Ballet and artistic director of the ballet of the Deutsche Oper. He has also been connected with the Eglevsky Ballet, the Atlanta Ballet, and Joffrey II.

For three years he was director of the ballet and resident of the San Francisco Opera. His "Bacchanale" for the recent *Tannhäuser* is appropriately orgiastic. He has also choreographed *Fledermaus Variations* to music of Johann and Josef Strauss, *Once for the Birth of . . .* to Rachmaninoff music, and *Belong*, a rock piece, for the Metropolitan Opera Ballet Ensemble. Vancouver-born, Vesak is the great-grandson of a painter. As a child he used to listen to the Saturday matinee broadcasts of the Metropolitan. Train up a child in the way he should go.

Audrey Keane, the ballet administrator, is a former leading dancer with the company, 1946–50 and 1955–62. She took time out to get married and start a family. Her husband is Orrin Hill, who was also a dancer in the company. Before that he played football for Carnegie Tech and now is production director for the opera companies of Dayton and Toledo.

As a solo dancer with the company Miss Keane performed in *Aida*, *La Traviata*, *La Gioconda*, *Samson et Dalila*, *Tannhäuser*, *Manon*, *Louise*, and *Faust.* Before that she was in the ballet company of Mia Slavenska and on Broadway in *Show Boat* and *Courtin' Time*, and for a while she had her own concert company. She became ballet mistress in 1963, advancing to administrator, where she remained through the season of 1978-79.

Ivan Allen (left), former ballet captain for the Metropolitan Opera and a member of the company from 1964, rehearses Alicia Markova's choreography for "The Judgment of Paris" episode in Francesco Cilèa's Adriana Lecouvreur

Captains of the ballet have included Ivan Allen and Diana Levy. Allen says being captain can involve anything from ordering new shoes (the life of a dancer's shoes is only about ten performances, in the case of the girls' toe shoes only three) to maintaining order in the dressing room, to seeing they don't overapply the makeup. There is a story of a Broadway stage manager who once said to one of his dancers, "Marge, peel off some of that makeup. Where do you think you are, in the audience?"

Diana Levy defines her job as den mother, looking after dressing room needs, and she sometimes conducts the all-important class. Every dancer, from the tiniest pupil to Baryshnikov, takes class. The routines of warming up, stretching, and generally keeping in trim is a never-ending imperative. Paderewski once said, "If I go a day without practicing I notice it, if I go two days the critics notice it, if I go three days the public notices it."

Ivan Allen came to the Metropolitan from the American Ballet Theatre, where he was a principal dancer. His roles were Prince Siegfried in *Swan Lake,* the boy in green in *Les Patineurs*, and the solo male roles in *Combat* and *Les Sylphides.* His blond good looks stand him in good stead for the romantic ballets.

He was born in Detroit, where his father, who didn't like the idea of his son's being a dancer, was in the steel business. His mother wasn't much more sympathetic. "The only thing I can really say"—he quotes his mother—"is you did it by yourself."

"I always wanted to be a movie star," Allen says. He was an ice skater and one day went with a girl friend to dancing class. When they came to the leaps, he said, "I can do that." They didn't believe him, but he showed them a trick or two. "I was sort of pushed into it," he says of his career.

If you think all dancers are impractical, you had better do a little reviewing. Allen owns two brownstones in the West Seventies. "They take all my extra time," he says. "I like working with good workmen. Plumbing is the only thing I am not good at." Does he live in one of his houses? No, he has an apartment in a ten-year-old building on East Fifty-sixth Street.

A folio of rehearsals at the Metropolitan Opera: James Levine (right) working with the orchestra on C level in 1979 during preparation for the new production of Don Carlo; *the same rehearsal room during 1972–73, when* Carmen *was due to open the season (next two pages), with the full forces of orchestra, chorus and soloists under the command of Leonard Bernstein (top left); ladies of the chorus voicing the cigarette chorus (bottom left); James McCracken poetically shaping the music of Don José (top right); Maestro Bernstein giving a cue (bottom center); and Marilyn Horne putting full emphasis on one of Carmen's low-lying passages (bottom right)*

Diana Levy was born in Brooklyn but as a child was taken to Los Angeles where her father, a stagehand, worked in the movie studios. At fifteen she enrolled in the studio of David Lichine and Tatiana Riabouchinska. Only those of us who were around at the time can tell you what this pair was to the ballet. They were members of the first company of Colonel de Basil's Ballet Russe de Monte Carlo, which brought the art of ballet back to life after the death of Diaghileff.

Lichine was the first dancer after Nijinsky to undertake *L'Après-midi d'un Faune*. The girl who became his wife was one of the three baby ballerinas Basil discovered in the Paris studios, the other two being Irina Baronova and Tamara Toumanova. Riabouchinska was the ingénue, pale and ethereal. When she lured Massine from Danilova and the two of them went off into their waltz in *Le Beau Danube*, it left one of the memories of a lifetime.

These were the influences that shaped the career of Diana Levy. Her teachers got her into the Australian Ballet at the time it boasted Margot Fonetyn. They taught her the dance of the Top in *Jeux d'Enfants*. "They were special teachers," Diana says. "They made you dance one at a time. They placed you in companies, and their dancers always did well."

After two years in Australia and New Zealand, Diana returned to this country. With the American Ballet Theatre she was one of the three girl leads in *Fancy Free* and a soloist in *Pillar of Fire* and *Lilac Garden*. Diana's little daughter, Ingrid Kessler, was a member of our children's chorus. "She's the only seven-year-old I know who has listened to *Wozzeck* with earphones," Diana says.

In his *Dramatic Essays* T. S. Eliot says that the lowliest dancer has been through a regimen, a school, that the biggest stars in the theater know nothing about. Agnes de Mille said it in one of her brilliant television documentaries on dance. The cool, aloof profile was in the foreground to the side of the screen, while at center stage a girl was going through a back-breaking *port de bras*. "It takes dedication," Miss de Mille said quietly, "to do that."

But what reward! A late poet laureate put it best. In 1938 John Masefield turned from the sea and occasional verses in honor of a royal anniversary to publish a big and handsome book called *Tribute to Ballet*. Here is the third and last stanza of the first poem:

> But what are you to us, O radiant dancers?
> After the Winter of our prose and sickness,
> The bones of old belief and news of murder,
> You bring together all that makes men happy,
> Colour and lovely movement and sweet music,
> Old fable breathed upon to make new beauty,
> The grace and elegance of gentle women,
> The power and the courtesy of knighthood.

The Metropolitan Opera Ballet in rehearsal: Ivan Allen and Naomi Marritt by a mirror (top left); the choreographer Alvin Ailey guiding a practice session for Carmen *(top right); and Norbert Vesak and Audrey Keane, the director of ballet and the ballet administrator, discuss new projects for the dancers after a company class (bottom left). Diana Levy, formerly the women's ballet captain, with Miss Keane (below), who retired from the Metropolitan at the close of the 1978–79 season*

THE UNSEEN ARMY

In *Puccini Among Friends* Vincent Seligman writes of "the vast army of labourers, most of them unseen and many even unsuspected, who assist at the birth of an opera." At the Metropolitan the army is bigger than in any other opera house in the world. It may be unseen, but it is not unsung.

Ninety-five percent of what you see on our stage is built right under our own roof. The more conspicuous exceptions are shoes, gloves, and arms. Of our full-time 700 employees, our shops account for eighty-three. These break down as follows: scenic, twelve; carpenter, twenty-five; electric, three; property, six; costume, thirty-four; wig, three.

Actual work on a new production can begin as long as a year ahead. By having its own shops and its own people manning them, the Metropolitan can bring in a new production at far less than the prevailing costs on Broadway. The mere saving of the transfer bill from a builder is considerable.

Come on a trip through this world of wonder. It is new every time you see it. The fifth floor is a good place to begin. Walking down is easier than walking up, and by not having to wait for the elevator between floors you can do it in an hour. There is also logic to starting on the fifth floor. This is the scenic shop, and once the designs leave the artist's studio, here is where it all begins.

The first door is the design office of Stanley Cappiello, scenic artist. As guideposts for visitors (the Gish sisters always referred to non-theatrical folk as "private people"), Cappiello has devised handsome lettered signs explaining just what everything is—and does.

"Creative starting point for new productions," the design office is identified.

"Translation of designs into practical drawings for all departments.

"Creating three-dimensional models of concepts to scale.

"Preparation and selection of material to develop designers' models to full size.

"Coordination of concepts with practical needs of Met's repertory staging."

That tells you about all, doesn't it, and in the fewest and clearest possible words?

When Herbert von Karajan was advised that his original plan for *Die Walküre* wouldn't work at the Metropolitan, that we simply couldn't get it off the stage and the night show on if it were a matinee or, reversing, we couldn't get it on after the matinee of some other work if it were the Saturday evening attraction, he was dumfounded. He had worked under festival conditions for so long he had lost sight of anyone else's problems.

But the Metropolitan is a repertory house, six different works each weekday evening and another on Saturday afternoon. No other theater in the world holds to such a schedule. One appears for premieres in Italy on, say, a Monday to be told, "Sorry, folks. We won't be ready until Thursday," by which time you might be in another city or another country. It would be nice to perform when you feel like it, but that is a luxury the Metropolitan has never been able to afford and never will be. The hard facts and figures dictate otherwise.

Stanley Cappiello studied at the Art Students League and Pratt Institute. The Army got him before Pearl Harbor. He was released, only to be summoned back, and was not free again until he emerged as a first lieutenant in the corps of engineers in 1946. He had served in Alaska, the Philippines, and Japan. As though that weren't enough, he was called back into the Korean war.

His father came from Sorrento and had studied painting. His son, just out of Lynchburg College, is a sculptor, so there is decidedly a strong artistic strain in the family. Stanley apprenticed at Alliance Studios, which doesn't exist any more but at one time did a land-office business on big Broadway shows. His baptism was *South Pacific*, *The King and I*, and other Rodgers and Hammerstein musicals. By happy coincidence he worked on *Ring Around the Moon* and was surprised to find some of his handiwork on the Dufy murals at the Top of the Met.

His first work for the Met was in the early fifties on the Rolf Gérard-designed productions. For a time he forsook us for films and television, but he came back in 1974.

If there is anything more beguiling than a miniature set of *Boris* or some other great work, I don't know it. It is the quickest restorer—or preserver—of youth, and we all become children in F. A. O. Schwartz' again. The gilt will never wear off the gingerbread. The models are endlessly fascinating, and if the music began and the action started, you wouldn't be surprised. There was once a Danish restaurant in Chicago where the propri-

Previous two pages: during an afternoon rehearsal, seen from a vantage point high above the stage (right), stagehands wait to clear a skeleton set to get on with the business of putting the evening's show in place. The performers dispersed, some of the crew roll up an unneeded ground cloth under the supervision of theatrical veteran Mark Antonio Licameli (bottom left). Elsewhere, other workers, Edward B. Ford and Harold Lauckner, station outsize fans that will billow the sails of Otello's giant vessel as it majestically pulls into port (top right)

Design office's Robert Winkler (below) perfects a transparency to be projected on a cyclorama during Die Frau ohne Schatten. *The scenic artist Stanley Cappiello (top right) at his drafting table labors on a projected revival of* Boris Godunov. *Also shown (bottom right) are pieces to detailed scale models for the settings of* Rigoletto *and* Boris

mosaics, painting

etor, Fred Chramer (an opera-lover, needless to say), gave full-length puppet performances of the standard repertory. Sometimes that was the only opera Chicago had. The food was good, too.

Beyond the design office is a space forty-three by seventy-one feet. Painters usually are at work here on a big piece stretched over the entire floor or on detail pieces.

"Prepares full-scale pattern for carpentry shop, prop shop, electric shop," the next sign reads.

"Creates the finished look of all visual elements that appear onstage.

"Finish treatment of properties, furniture, hand props, etc.

"Final treatment of costumes. This involves toning, distressing, painting, dyeing."

How do they go about "distressing" a costume? The answer might be an inventory of a sergeant's desk of the homicide squad—"razor blades, knives, cheese graters." Costumes mustn't look too new. When Lucrezia Bori sang her first performance with the Metropolitan—it was *Manon Lescaut* in Paris, not in New York—she had bought her own costumes, and they cost a fortune. Puccini came backstage after the dress rehearsal. In one hand was the ever present cigarette, in the other a cup of coffee. "Everything was fine," he said, "only in the last act, where Manon is starving and penniless, your costume is too clean," and he tossed the contents of his cup on her dress. That is "distressing" a costume.

Scenic artists are in most cases designers and painters. Our dozen have had exhibitions in the house at Christmastime of their work, very impressive. Rollers with cut texture patterns and feather dusters dispense special texture effects—"shlepishka" is the word, onomatopoetic we would call it if that adjective applied to sight as well as sound.

In 1965 artists of the scenic department faced the awesome task of translating Marc Chagall's multicolored drawings for Die Zauberflöte *(above) into canvas drops that would fill the huge expanses of the Metropolitan Opera's stage. Under the guidance of Vladimir Odinokov (right, holding design), artists Elizabeth Matta, Robert Winkler and Mary Ann Reppa lost not a detail, amazing and delighting Chagall himself when he arrived to put the finishing touches on his production, which remains one of the glories of the theater*

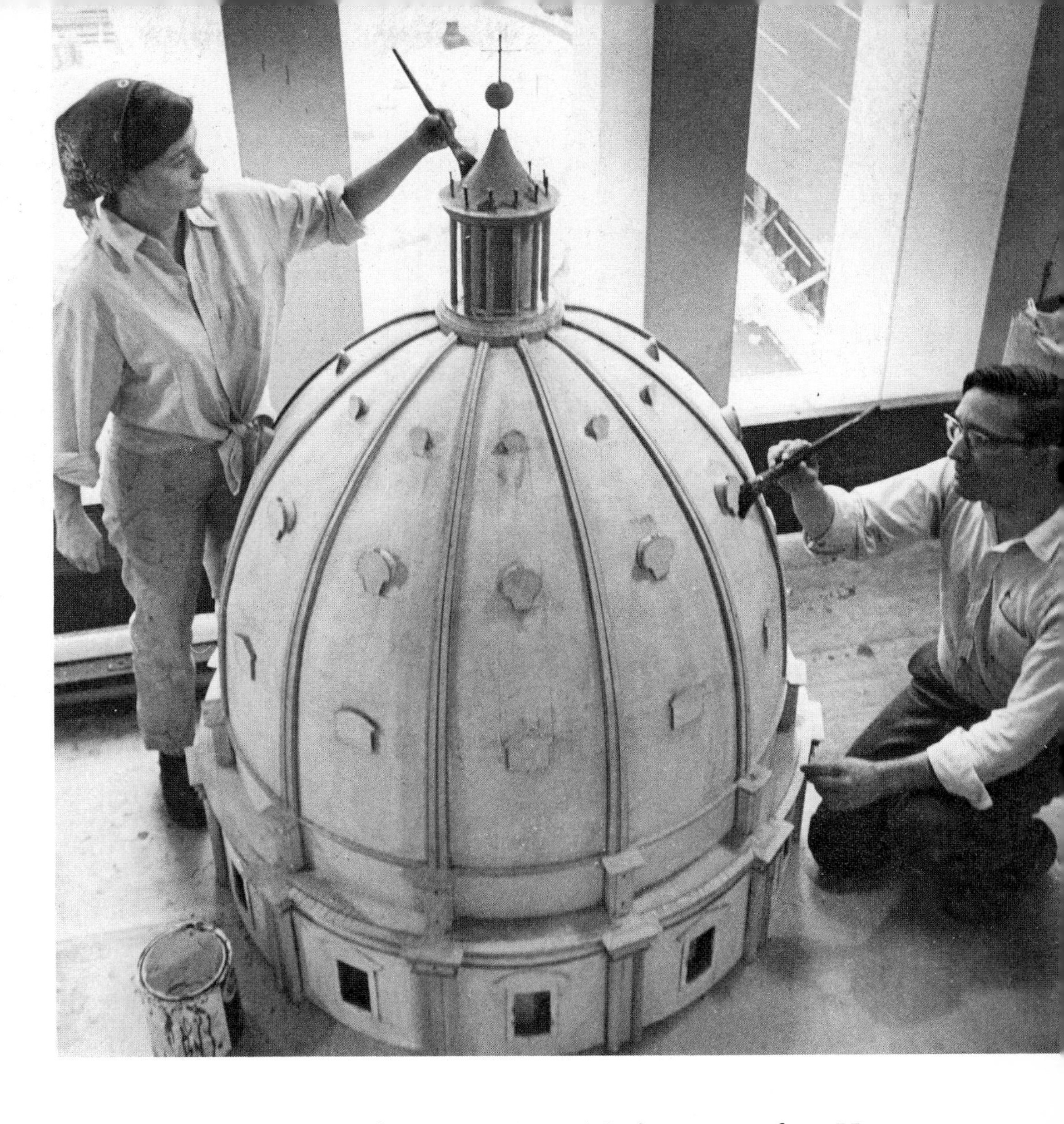

The Metropolitan Opera has facilities to paint settings vertically as well as horizontally. On the fifth-floor paint bridge (top left), David Reppa, the resident scenic designer, checks the progress of the backdrop of Florence for his production of Gianni Schicchi *as associates Vladimir Odinokov and Paul Goranson confer. Reppa's wife, Mary Ann, is also a familiar hand in the scenic shop, shown here at work on the huge cannons to be used in* Billy Budd *(bottom left) and, aided by Edward Haynes, painting a replica of the dome of St. Peter's Basilica, utilized in* Tosca *(above right)*

Now we come to the big space, sixty-eight by seventy feet. Here occurs perhaps the major miracle in this world of miracles. How can these people expand an artist's sketch of sixteen by twenty inches to a backdrop or ground cloth seventy feet wide? There are, to be sure, those guiding squares, but that's not enough. Edward Johnson, who was a leading tenor at the Metropolitan before he became general manager, used to say, "Opera is a world where when you wink your eye you shake your head." The twenty-eighth row has to see it, and here on the fifth floor you watch these wonderful craftsmen laying something with a mop or a broom which from the front appears to be only a hair line and their margin of error is almost nil. In the biblical phrase, what is written stays written. There is almost no correction.

You would think they would prefer to paint on a frame, vertical instead of flat. Vertical, you can stand back and gauge your effects, but the Italians particularly seem to prefer the floor. There are two up-and-down frames, however, sixty-seven by fifty-six feet, a few steps up from the fifth floor, going down through an opening to the fourth and on thence to the stage.

Next we come to the office of David Reppa and Gil Wechsler. Reppa's wife, Mary Ann, a fine scenic painter, keeps right up with the men, but her blue slacks, pullover sweater, and bandanna do not conceal her gender.

David hails from East Chicago, Indiana, where his father was a judge. Mary Ann comes from Rockford, Illinois—not far away, but they met at the Metropolitan. One December day they asked their boss for a little longer lunch hour, during which they went down to the Municipal Building and got married. When they returned, the first company Christmas party in the new house was in full swing, so their wedding reception (catered) cost neither them nor their parents anything.

The carpentry shop on the fourth floor is Richard Hauser's domain. There is nothing so expensive as the smell of fresh lumber. Chanel No. 5 isn't in it, and our supply is on an epic scale. The week before the house opened, I took Tony Randall through. At the carpentry shop he gasped, "There isn't anything at M-G-M like this," and he was quite right. That was as high as he could go.

The carpenter shop is a comparatively new assignment for Hauser. He joined the Metropolitan in 1954 and was for twenty-three years in the property department. Like the Reppas', his marriage was made at the Met. The former Judy Rogers, Mrs. Hauser was a member of our ballet, and two of the four daughters are literally following in their mother's footsteps. The oldest, Lauren, is in the New York City Ballet, and Susan, the youngest, is in the school of American Ballet Theatre. In between, Caroline gave up modeling to go to Rutgers, and Christine goes in for jumping horses.

"I am a constructive person," Dick Hauser says. "I like to build and watch things built." He and his family live in Teaneck, New Jersey, but he says, "the Metropolitan gets to be your first home, and where you live is your second home." It was nothing for him in the old days to arrive at the theater at eight o'clock in the morning and get home at one or two the next.

"Each day is different, poses a new problem," he says. "There are so many productions, when you go right down to the wire." The new *Lohengrin* was "ticklish," *Frau* "had its moments." Behind his desk are Eugene Berman's sketches for Desdemona's mirror and a torch in *Otello*.

The buzz of saws and the pounding of hammers fill the air of the Metropolitan's carpentry shop (these pages), housed on the fourth floor in the rear of the Opera House. Photographed during construction of the settings for Billy Budd, *this department is under the supervision of Richard Hauser (below). Also seen are carpenters Thomas De Santis and Harry Bakst (right)*

As you come from the stairway or through the locked cage door from the elevator to the third floor, the first thing you see is a metal chest of thin drawers like the old spool trays from ancient dry goods stores, now collectors' items. There are samples to indicate the colors of the gelatines inside. No. 17, Surprise Pink, is said to have been invented by David Belasco and guaranteed to smooth out wrinkles as well as restore color to the cheeks. There was a spotlight called "Baby Belasco," and Geraldine Farrar used to ask for two on her, one on either side of the prompter's box, during "Vissi d'arte."

Further on there is another steel chest of drawers with even more fascinating labels. "Smoke clouds," "fleecy clouds," "storm clouds," "*Otello* clouds," "*Rheingold* clouds," "fire," "ghost ride," "rain of fire," "ordinary rain," etc. These are projections and produce, on the height and width of the proscenium, just what they claim.

Unlike other departments back of the curtain line, the electric shop covers the entire theater. "We are responsible for the wall-to-wall activities of the house," says Bruce Katzman, who is responsible for the maintenance of the building and stage. "The only thing we don't do is the telephones."

The master control room at the back of the auditorium we call Cape Canaveral. Very few, even members of the company, have had a good look at it, even through the two thicknesses of glass at the front, and its door is one of the only three in the house that do not open to the master pass key. Think of having the massive stage wagons and platforms at your beck and call from a hundred feet away. The switchboard covers three walls and is hand-operated, but it is a ten-preset thyristor. That is, each light can be preset for ten scenes.

Bruce Katzman was twenty-two and just out of the Navy when he came to the Metropolitan in 1955. He went to Jersey City State College and taught English, but electronics at the naval training school at Great Lakes prepared him for his real career. His biggest headache is keeping the bulky machinery of the stage running and keeping the performances going as smoothly as possible. "There is always a problem when a technical type like myself deals with an aesthetic type," he says, and he hasn't forgotten the nightmare of the early weeks in the house, when Act III of *La Traviata* with its three levels wouldn't come into place, but he stoically carries on.

The electric shop's James Sweeney, Sr., and Bruce Katzman (above) iron out a technical problem by the switchboard used on tour. Meanwhile, a young electrician, Joseph Baer, repairs a prop candelabra needed for a performance that night (below). Among other effects this department provides are smoke, steam and fog—all handily dispensed by automation (right), as demonstrated by James Connolly of the staff

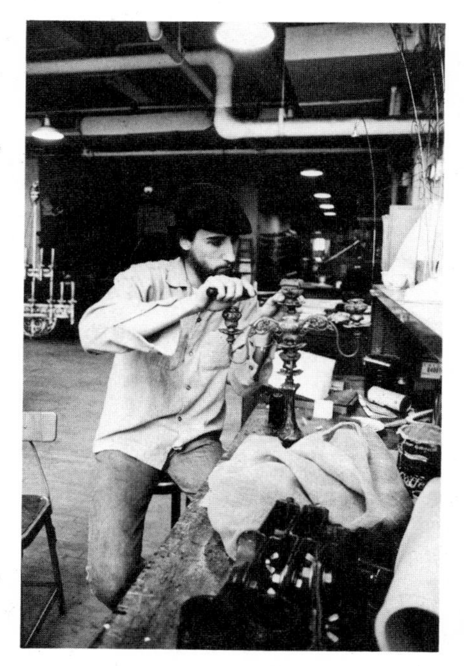

One of the largest constructions ever built by the Metropolitan Opera's prop shop was the sphinx head for Antony and Cleopatra *(left). This beautiful sculpture was later attached to the full body of the monster and rolled about the stage by a group of stagehands who were hidden inside, something like the Greek soldiers in the legendary Trojan Horse. Masks are another specialty of props, those shown under construction by Edward Haynes (below) for the witches in* Macbeth. *Two mainstays of the Metropolitan are Ralph Piccone of the prop shop and his son Jack of the night crew and a stage carpenter (above right). They are part of a long-standing backstage tradition at the Opera House—members of a family working together. Those who wonder how human hands could have built the pyramids should watch the Metropolitan Opera's crew move Franco Zeffirelli's mammoth production of* Otello *into position (next two pages). It is an amazing sight, and the job is accomplished by these miracle workers in only a few hours*

On the same floor with the electrics is properties construction, and the man here is Richard Graham. "If you can work on the Met stage, you can work anyplace," he says. "Everything here is unique. It's the first time." He first worked on the stage, came into the prop shop in 1955 and has been head of it since 1964. He had an offer from the Pittsburgh Pirates and tried it for a while but said he was "too old!"

That revolving sphinx in *Antony and Cleopatra* he says was his biggest and most difficult job. Plastics and heat have revolutionized his craft, and incredible things come from his oven. Fiberglas, butarine, and polystyrene (thermal plaster sheets) have liberated theater props. Dick Graham and his crew can reproduce just about anything you bring in or have in your imagination. The first days in the new house the "alabaster" goblets were out for the shipboard revel in *Antony and Cleopatra.* On the same table were the hollow-stem crystal champagnes for Act I of *La Traviata*—a span of 2,000 years in drinking habits.

The horse from the Royal Hunt and Storm of *Les Troyens* still hangs above, and walking through the prop shop can be as surrealistic as something out of a Fellini movie—an elongated, gnarled hand in plaster, a Tudor lute, a cherub's head, a breastplate of classic armor.

"You are only as good as the people you have," Dick graciously says of his colleagues. One of his hearties is Ralph Piccone, who says with no bravado whatever, "No job is hard." Ralph and his son Jack, who is younger and better-looking than Sylvester Stallone, are one of those family teams with which the Metropolitan backstage seems to abound. It is not just a family but *the* family. After Xavier High School and a year at Manhattan College, Jack came into the property department in 1969. He is now in the night crew of the carpenter department.

The second floor is the area that lady visitors never want to leave—wardrobe, wigs, and makeup. In the wardrobe, men work on men's costumes and women on women's. It has nothing to do with modesty or morality, though some of the gentlemen of our chorus were a little squeamish in Paris when they found their dressers were women instead of men. It just seems to make for a different feeling in the product. This is the province of Peter J. Hall, head of the costume shop, and Charles Caine, resident costume designer. The chief cutters are man and wife Dick Wagner and Gisela Scharf.

The costume shop in the new Metropolitan Opera House is divided between the ladies' workroom (top left), where the former directress, Maureen Ting Klein, is shown checking a measurement with a seamstress, and the men's workroom (bottom left), where sewing machines hum the season long. Key members of the department's current staff are resident costume designer Charles Caine, who has done new garb for Don Pasquale *and* Luisa Miller, *and the new shop head Peter J. Hall (top right), who has created costumes for productions of* Otello, Aida, Un Ballo in Maschera, I Puritani, Boris Godunov *and* Lohengrin. *Other central figures involved with operations are Dick and Gisela Wagner (below), who are seen with the former shop head, Ray Diffen, costume designer of* Don Carlo, *going over sketches for* The Bartered Bride

Dick started at the Metropolitan with the new house. All his training was from his father. "He was a tough boss," Dick says. "The son had to do everything better than the father." The elder Wagner, Nick, had learned his business at the Dresden State Opera, one of the more respected houses in the world and the site Richard Strauss favored above all others for his premieres.

"It's hard to keep the standard high when you are always fighting the budget," Dick Wagner says. The wardrobe department turns out between 1,600 and 1,700 costumes a year. "If things get tough, we can always call Father," he smiles.

The outfits for the children masquerading as tree stumps in *Hansel and Gretel* and the foam rubber armor for *Les Troyens* are the toughest assignments his department has had to bring off, Wagner says. The armor was in layers and was "a carving job, not a tailoring job. That was something you do only once," he adds with relief.

"The greatest satisfaction is when you are involved with something for months and with every detail. It comes out of your hand, and when you see it at dress rehearsal it gives you a great sense of accomplishment. That's why I'm still here. Brooks"—the costumer, not the classic men's store—"offered me more money, but it isn't the same. You have to be able to be proud of your work."

Gisela Wagner came from Essen in 1959 and three weeks later started at the Metropolitan. She was an apprentice for three years. "It wasn't much of a costume department then," she says, "two old ladies sitting there doing alteration." Most of the costumes were done by Karinska or Eaves in those days.

Her favorite of the costumes she has done is Leontyne Price's for the final act of *Antony and Cleopatra.* Both Wagners are "besieged" with requests from the artists to make their personal costumes.

Adjoining the women's side of the costume shop is the wig department. Nina Lawson, a Scottish lass, is the hair stylist. It is amazing to think that she and two assistants take care of the hair requirements of the entire company. There was a time when we rented our wigs. Now we not only own them; we make them.

Brought up on her grandfather's farm, Nina got the cattle ready for showing. From the age of four or five she was taught to take strong soap and water to their tails and then braid them. This may not seem preparation for the handling of Mélisande's blond tresses or Salome's feathered hairdo, but Nina says, "I was fascinated by hair as long as I can remember." After hairdressing school in Glasgow, she got to know Rudolf Bing when Glyndebourne gave the world premiere of *The Rape of Lucretia.* She later worked for Sadler's Wells, the Carl Rosa Opera Company, and the Stratford, Ontario, Festival.

The wig department, which shares the second floor of the Opera House with the costume and makeup shops, takes care of everything theatrical pertaining to hair. Sarolta and Magda Szayer, a mother and daughter, have long been on the staff to assist the wig and hair stylist, Nina Lawson (right)

Her assistants are mother and daughter, Sarolta Magyar and Magda Szayer. In their native Budapest, Mrs. Magyar had her own business. Her son, now an engineer, was an usher in the old house. That family again. Tom Prideaux, the drama editor of *Life* magazine, once wrote that the Metropolitan Opera House is "a house, a place where people live. It is because the Metropolitan Opera House through the years has had so many characteristics of a family home, including its faults and feuds, that it has meant so much to American people."

Victor Callegari, the makeup artist, is a wizard with his paints and powders and brushes. He has done live demonstrations on television around the circuit and is in great demand at the colleges in our ports of call. He has given classes at New England Conservatory of Music and the University of Minnesota, and he is a regular in July at the American Institute of Musical Studies in Graz, Austria.

It was during the last year in the old house that Victor joined the Metropolitan. Just out of the Army, he was attending New York University and heard there was a vacancy. "I ran down like a nut," he says. He was interviewed by Nina Lawson, Charles Riecker, and George Shindhelm, the former head of the makeup department. "The only reason they hired me is because I spoke Italian." There was more to it than that. His rise from apprentice was rapid.

"I study painting and the history of painting," he says. He studied at the Art Students League for two years and spends a lot of time at museums in New York and on tour. "Everybody thinks I am there to chase girls, but it's not true. I am serious about paintings."

Born in Brooklyn, he now shares an apartment with his brother on Broadway and Eighty-second Street. Arthur Callegari has been head of the Metropolitan's libretto department for five years. More family.

Tom Prideaux wanted Jennie Cervini, then already retired as wardrobe mistress of the Metropolitan, to be his guest at the gala farewell in the old house, but Jennie had already been invited to occupy a place of honor just offstage in the wings. Kirsten Flagstad told me she went through the ordeal of her postwar return to the Metropolitan without an emotion—no joy or satisfaction, no anger, bitterness, or rancor, nothing—until she saw Jennie. Then the tears came. How many performances must that sweet-faced woman and her two successors, both relatives, have saved or, if they didn't need saving, made better?

When Jennie retired, her sister, Rose Calamari, took over. The week before the 1977 spring tour, Rose suffered a heart attack and died a few days later. She had been with us fifty-two years.

Rose's daughter-in-law, Chrissie Calamari, stepped in, and things went without a hitch. "The people who are important aren't here any more," Chrissie says. "They made the place." Her performance of her knotty task denies that, but her modesty and loyalty are refreshing as they are rare. Chrissie is proof that important people are still here.

Backstage, the wardrobe department's Christina Calamari must scurry from costume rack to dressing room to garb the prima donnas in her charge (below). She is shown pinning up Mignon Dunn as the Nurse in Die Frau ohne Schatten *while the mezzo-soprano's conductor-husband, Kurt Klippstatter, beams. A folio on makeup follows (next two pages): Katia Ricciarelli touches up her lip liner before an entrance as Desdemona in* Otello *(top left); Mario Sereni dons pancake and eyebrow pencil to give added character to Sergeant Belcore in* L'Elisir d'Amore *(bottom left); on another floor, in a communal dressing room, a group of supers excitedly puts on greasepaint for another performance, of which they are an important element (top center); the makeup artist Victor Callegari painstakingly works with Cornell MacNeil, who is being transformed into Count Di Luna in* Il Trovatore *(bottom center); Marilyn Horne adjusts her hat for the first act of* L'Italiana in Algeri *under the watchful eye of Nina Lawson (top right); and José Carreras, costumed and made up, sits ready to go onstage to sing Nemorino in* L'Elisir d'Amore *(bottom right)*

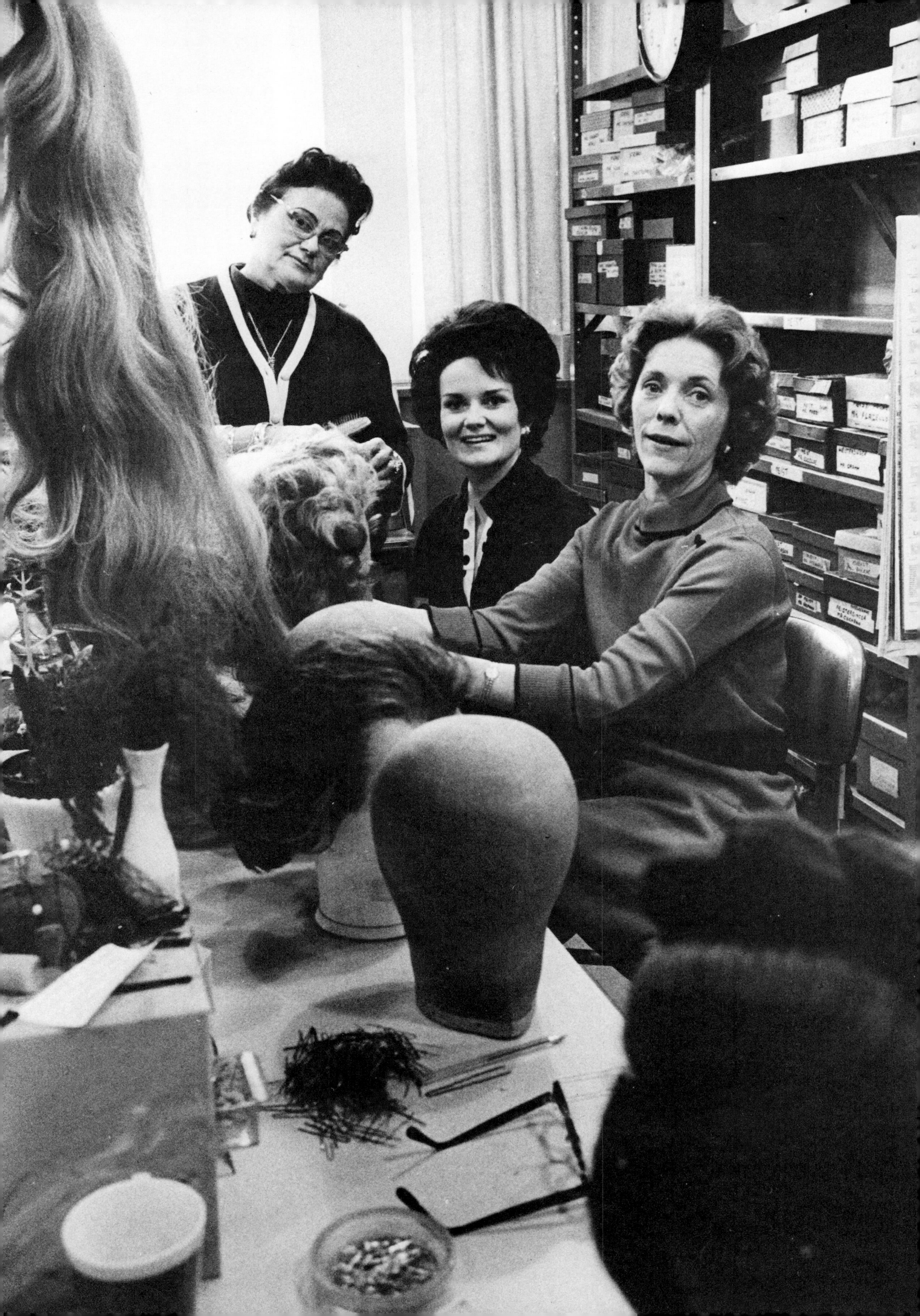

KLIEGL

Rudolph Kuntner (top left), who oversaw stage operations at the Metropolitan until 1977, with two Kliegl lights made by the firm with which he was associated before joining the staff of the Metropolitan in 1951. During the construction of the Opera House he was involved with all technical plans with Herman E. Krawitz and Wallace K. Harrison. When Kuntner left the Metropolitan, he was given an award by the United States Institute of Theater Technology in recognition of his long, dedicated career in the performing arts

Mrs. John DeWitt Peltz (bottom left) at her desk in the Metropolitan Opera Archives, which she founded in 1957, creating order out of chaos from the company's three-quarters-of-a-century accumulation of correspondence, contracts, receipts, production plans, documents, programs, photographs, memorabilia, etc. Before accomplishing this task, Mrs. Peltz founded and for twenty-two years edited Opera News, *the magazine of the Metropolitan Opera Guild. A lecturer of quality, she is one of the best-known voices heard during the Saturday broadcasts from the Opera House*

On the men's side of the wardrobe department is John Casamassa, son of the late Angelo, who had the job until his death in 1964. Angelo was with us forty-four years. His first season was Caruso's last. Oh to have heard that Christmas Eve *La Juive.*

As a boy John took violin. "My father hoped someday I would be playing in the Met orchestra," he recalls. "I was never good at it. I could never see myself there. You know when you are good." It was Depression time, and Angelo took "anything I could grab," a job in the post office. "I learned to repair, and my father took me into the shop. 'I can teach you as we go along,' he said." Sounds easy, but when the graduates of Smith or Vassar used to write Alexander Woollcott, as regularly as June came, to ask how to get into the theater, the Town Crier would reply, "Choose as your grandmother a star of a generation ago."

One of the important people who, in the words of Chrissie Calamari, "made the place" is Rudolph Kuntner. Until 1977 he was director of stage operations. Lighting was his specialty, and he began at the Metropolitan as first assistant to Jacob Buchter, our chief electrician for forty-five years. It was Buchter who used to train those Baby Belascos on Miss Farrar.

Before Rudy Kuntner came to the Metropolitan, he was chief electrician at the Forty-sixth Street Theatre, and before that he had been foreman of the theatrical division of Kliegl Brothers, the firm whose name became a common noun—klieg lights.

He was born in Vienna but came to this country at the age of ten. His father worked for another Viennese, Joseph Urban. The famous designer gave him a letter to Florenz Ziegfeld, who was just producing *Show Boat.*

Five feet six and weighing in at 205 pounds, Rudy Kuntner is built like a Greek wrestler. He was on the U.S. soccer team in the 1928 Olympics and is in the Olympics Hall of Fame.

His professional honors are equally distinguished. He is a member of the Illuminating Engineers Society of North America and of the Theatre, Television, and Film Lighting Symposium. "Whatever is on that stage, I put it there," he says with justifiable pride, and then he adds, "You never know when the lamp may go out."

In *Das Rheingold* there were photoflash bulbs strung behind a masking to create the lightning that Donner's hammer releases. On opening night, not one went off. Blood must have been on the floor, but no one in the audience seemed to notice it, and not one critic mentioned it.

His memories of twenty-six years at the Metropolitan? "The first act of *Butterfly* is too beautiful. That's a story by itself. I thought cherry blossoms were pink. It took that to inform me they are white in Japan!"

The various levels backstage at the opera house are numbered European-style. The floor above the stage is not the second but the first. The theater was planned and opened in the days before Women's Lib. Even if it hadn't been, I fancy we would have been old school enough to favor the ladies. Herman Krawitz' official guide book says, "It will be noted that the slogan 'Ladies First' has been observed as far as possible." Accordingly, the dressing rooms for the ladies of the chorus and ballet are on stage level. The gentlemen must go up one flight, and that is the first floor.

Under stage level, the house goes three floors underground; in fact, we struck water during excavation. On A level are the conductor's room, locker rooms, a lounge for the musicians and gargantuan stage machinery. There are also locker rooms and lounges for carpenters, electricians, and property

men. B level is more stage machinery, the music library, a big room used by box office and subscription during peak work loads, and archives. Mrs. John DeWitt Peltz, the archivist, was the first editor of *Opera News.* Before that she was Deems Taylor's assistant on the *World,* and when she was appointed to her present post she went to Smith College for a course in archiving. Though she is now in her eighties, few members of the Metropolitan family are so thorough or capable, none more devoted.

On C level, way below sea level, there are three rehearsal stages practically the size of the main stage. All are equipped with barre and mirrors, but the ballet soon found its own space, an inviting room with deep-blue walls and a special floor very conducive to work—lucky, in view of the hard labor that is the dancer's lot.

The rehearsal stage assigned to the orchestra has black velvet curtains which, to avoid distraction, can be drawn over the one mirrored wall. Opposite this is a high platform which in a pinch could accommodate the entire chorus, but they have their own elegant quarters in List Hall.

The rear stage of the Opera House, looking toward the proscenium opening and into the auditorium (above). To the right is one of the side stages that have the capacity to slide into position at center stage on the push of a button, bringing a totally different setting into the audience's view. There is a similar stage to the left. In addition, the floor at center stage may in fact become the roof of a huge elevated stage (above right), which raised to full height, lifts yet another new set before the public. The center stage is also in seven sections which may be raised independently to any level. All told, if the specific opera demanded, four different sets could be jockeyed into center stage in a matter of minutes. The production that comes closest to such needs is Die Frau ohne Schatten. *One of the stage's great cycloramas being hung for a performance follows (next two pages)*

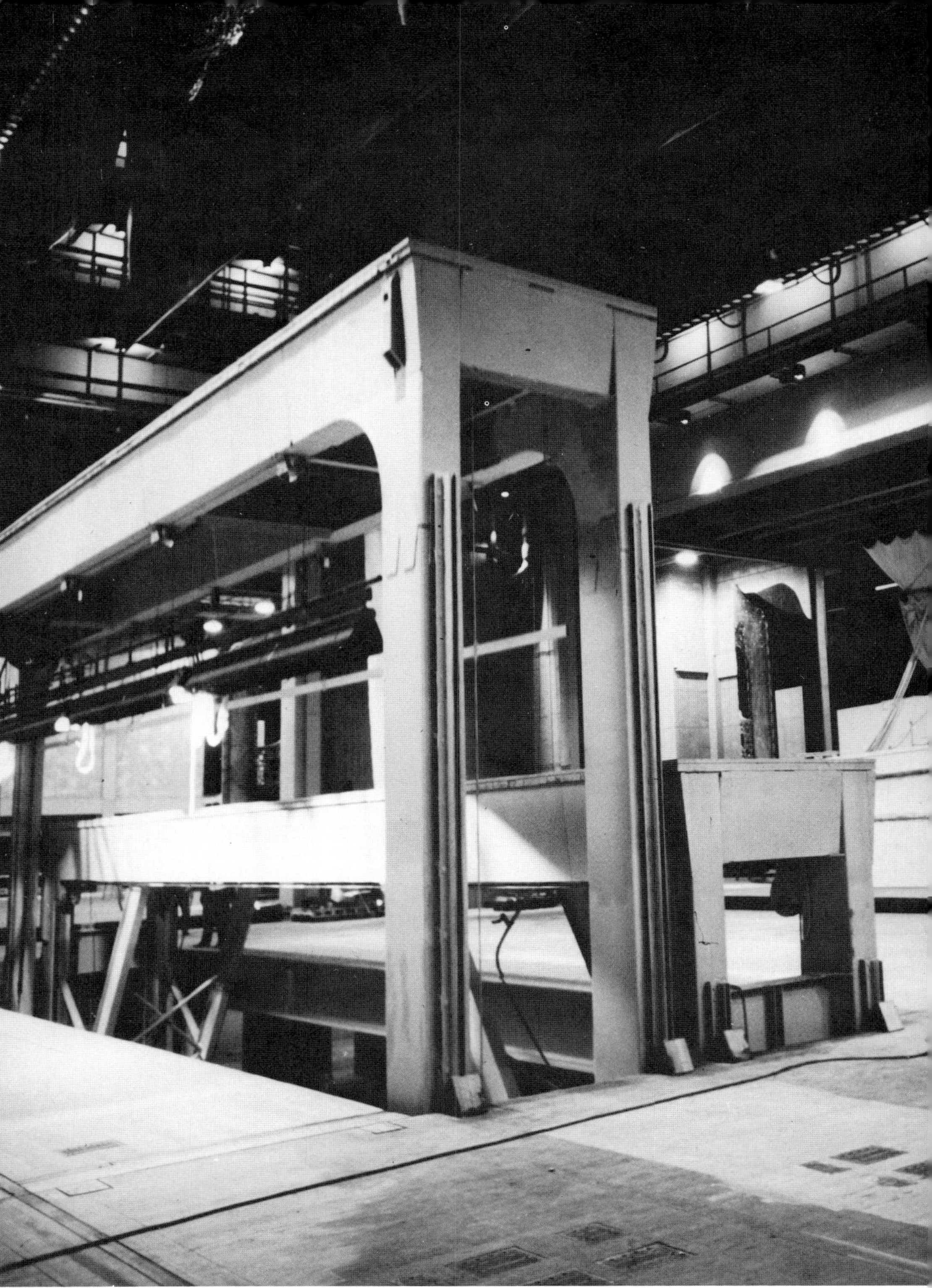

Opposite the press office off the south lounge, List Hall is a separate little theater with its own foyer and an outside entrance and exit.

The orchestra room has another of the Raoul Dufy curtains, this one appropriately of the Avenue de l'Opéra, with the Paris Opera resplendent in the background. Practical as well as decorative, it conceals acoustic material. The room has been treated for sound, with the side walls and ceiling in broken planes, and it is a marvel. It has the properties of the auditorium, and the conductor may feel safe with the volume and balance he has established in rehearsal here, as Karajan proved with *Die Walküre*. The third rehearsal stage, which has still another Dufy, is devoted to staging and usually has platforms and stairs from the actual production for the singers to get used to.

The underground space to the rear of the building is the storage area, three clear stories high. It can take anything we build, even a twenty-eight-foot flat. There is an enormous elevator, twenty-seven by twenty-five feet, to the stage. When we moved to Lincoln Center, we hoped to have storage

Joseph Volpe, technical administrator of the Metropolitan Opera

space for the season's repertory. In no time we outgrew that and we can now accommodate about half. Each designer wanted to show what he could do with the new toy. In the interest of artistic results, not to mention economy, that urge has been somewhat subdued lately, but we still have to resort to three warehouses, one an old car barn of 35,000 square feet at 129th Street and Amsterdam Avenue, another the size of an airplane hangar, 38,000 square feet, which the Metropolitan built in 1964 at Maspeth, Long Island, and the third in the Bronx at 135th Street and Third Avenue. There was a disastrous fire in the Bronx warehouse in November of 1973, and the costumes of forty-two productions were destroyed, 6,572 in all. More than half have been replaced, a Herculean task.

The Metropolitan Opera stage is the biggest and best-equipped in the world. In fact it is four stages. The proscenium opening is fifty-four by fifty-four feet, but the space back of it is more than twice as high, 110 feet, and more than four times as wide, 234 feet. You could set a fourteen story building on the main stage and it wouldn't scrape the rigging loft.

The main stage is in seven sections, sixty feet wide and eighty feet deep, any one of which can be raised or lowered hydraulically to any level. These move individually or can be locked together in any combination. Six of them are double-decked. One set of scenery can be in use while another is waiting in readiness on the top deck. At stage right there is an auxiliary stage, which can come in in sections or in toto. At stage left there is another auxiliary stage, which can be broken up like its mate. These stage wagons can move at a speed of ninety feet per minute.

The stage at the back of the main stage carries the turntable. Fifty-seven feet in diameter, it can revolve in either direction at the speed of 180 feet per minute at the perimeter.

Two cycloramas rolled up on either side at the corners of the main stage measure 207 by 109 and are the biggest curtains ever made. The white is for day, the blue for night. They can be calm or stormy, according to the script or those cloud slides in the electrical department.

Offstage right, down near the curtain line, is the stage manager's console. He has closed-circuit television on the conductor and on the stage at all times. His prompt book is a musical score that has been interleaved: between each pair of pages a blank sheet has been bound, on which he makes diagrams and notes, a permanent record of each production. Beside him sits his assistant, with a microphone to the dressing rooms, from which he calls the artists, chorus, and ballet.

In the old house, an assistant conductor had to watch the maestro through a hole in the scenery and relay the beat to the offstage chorus or stage band. Now he has a small closed-circuit television screen, but he still has to anticipate the conductor the fraction of a beat, because of the distance the sound has to travel from backstage to auditorium. In other words, when you are together you aren't. There is a little lag.

On the left auxiliary stage is the organ, an Aeolian Skinner. The two-manual console is in the pit, but the pipes are backstage in a big black box the size of a house.

To the rear are the principals' dressing rooms, dreams of luxury compared with the old house. It was within the memory of living men that running water was introduced to the soloists' quarters on Broadway and Thirty-ninth. We won't even think about the chorus and ballet. Imagine

The turntable at the back of center stage which gave way during rehearsals for Antony and Cleopatra *in 1966, before the theater even opened (left). It was not repaired until 1970 (below), when it had its baptism with the new production of* Norma. *Since then the turntable has enhanced a number of productions, most charmingly perhaps during the curtain calls for* The Bartered Bride, *when it makes the circus carousel revolve*

after an *Aida* or *Samson*, which require body makeup. There is a story that one of the old-time Russian ballet companies slept in its warpaint.

Each artist's room has a piano, a loudspeaker from the stage, telephone, toilet, and shower. Except for one small opening in the executive director's office, a concession to Rudolf Bing, the windows on Amsterdam Avenue in the dressing rooms are the only windows in the opera house that open. Usually the vents are heavily covered with boards and blankets. Between pollution and air-conditioning, singers will take pollution every time.

The stage is the realm of Stephen Diaz, master mechanic. He began life as a longshoreman but grew weary of the strikes every October. "We faithfully looked forward to them," he says. In 1962 he joined the night crew. His brother, Eddie, came in in 1966 and is now head of the night crew, which arrives at midnight and clears the stage for the next day's rehearsal or matinee.

Master of properties is Arthur Ashenden, known affectionately as Kayo. He was a fighter, trained for the Golden Gloves, but says that has nothing to do with his nickname. He was only eighteen when he joined the night crew in 1955; then he left us for a while for City Center. It is good to have him back.

Sander Hacker, master electrician, is an electrical engineer. He graduated from Syracuse and did graduate work at Columbia. For Infra Electronics Corporation he did research and design until they fired a friend of his and he quit. That tells you a lot about the man. When he found his secretary was making more than he was, he quit engineering altogether.

Walter Taussig, the associate conductor (below), aided by a TV monitor on a side stage, keeps perfect time with Karl Böhm in the orchestra pit while giving musical cues to Gildo Di Nunzio at the keyboard and the Voices of the Unborn Children in Die Frau ohne Schatten, *sung via microphone by Shirley Love, Jean Kraft, Isola Jones, Alma Jean Smith and Betsy Norden. Costumes and wigs (right): Gisela Wagner works on a garment in the costume shop (top left); Beverly Sills at a fitting for* L'Assedio di Corinto, *aided by Charles Caine and Maureen Ting Klein (top right); tailors cutting fabric for costumes in* La Gioconda *(center left); Magda Szayer making a new wig (bottom left); and the late Rose Calamari with John Casamassa in the wardrobe holding Turandot's costume (bottom right). A drawing that shows a cross section of the entire backstage area follows (next two pages). The artist, Donald A. Mackay, who did the rendering in 1966 for The New York* Times, *gives a view of the audience in the auditorium, the sets of* La Gioconda *on various stages, glimpses into dressing rooms, practice quarters, storage and loading areas and, upstairs, the various construction and maintenance shops—capturing the complexity of putting on opera at the Metropolitan*

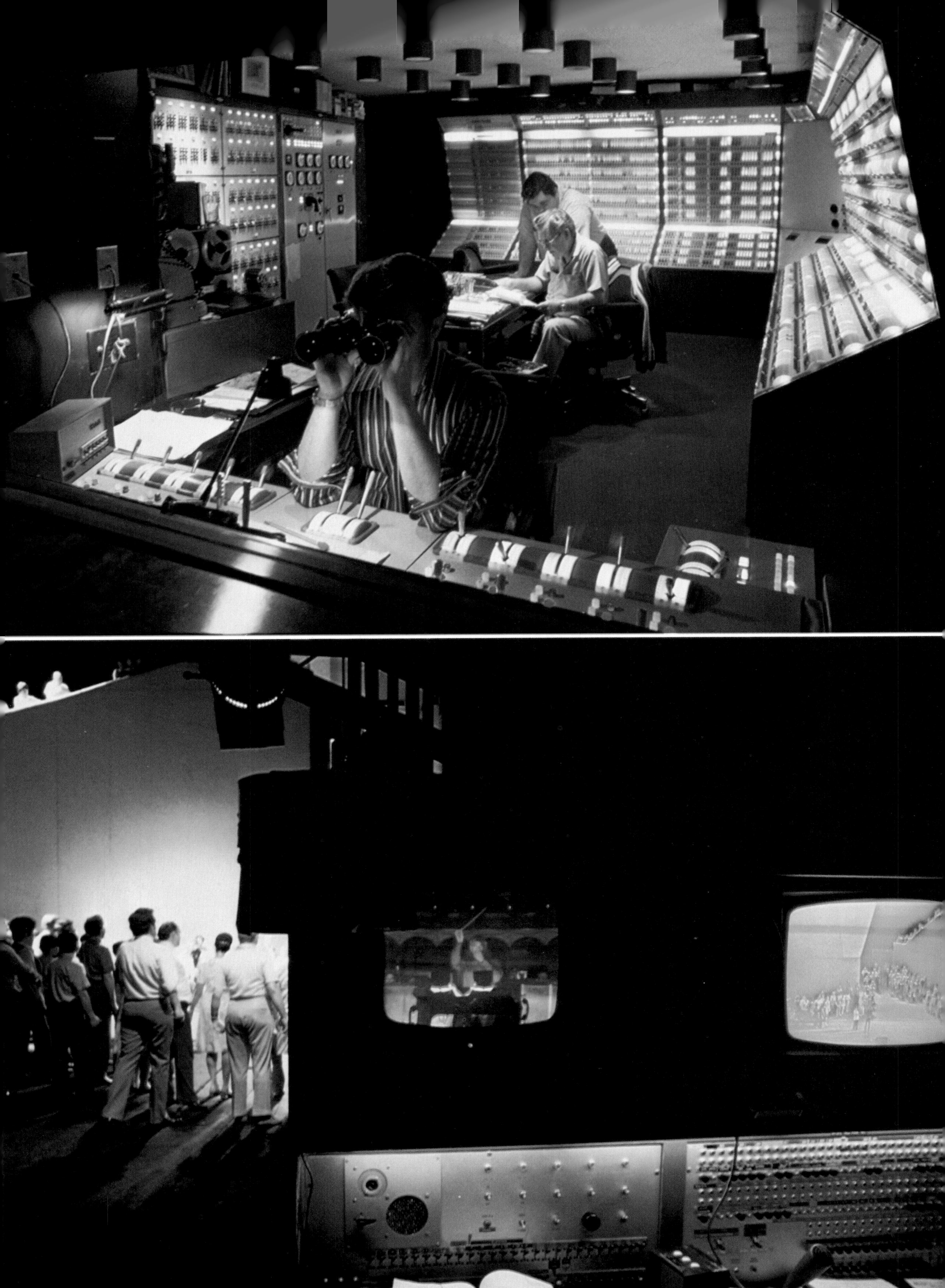

The central light control booth (top left), located at the rear of the auditorium with a full view of the stage; the executive stage manager's desk on the south side of the stage (bottom left); master mechanic Stephen Diaz with his brother Edward Diaz, head of the night crew (bottom left); and Arthur Ashenden, master of properties (bottom right)

His first job in the theater was assistant carpenter on *The Girl in Pink Tights.* He has also worked as a property man and he has 150 shows to his credit. Brooklyn-born, his father worked at the old Metropolitan Opera House, and he remembers programs and pictures dating back to 1903, the latter showing the horse-drawn wagons that transported the scenery to and from the warehouse.

He and Mrs. Hacker make their home in Nutley, New Jersey. They have three sons and a daughter. The oldest son graduated from Norwich University and works for City Corporation, the next is studying veterinary medicine at Ohio State, and the youngest is still in high school. The girl is studying nursing at the University of Rhode Island.

Presiding with admirable cool over all this frantic activity (Alfred Lunt used to say the Metropolitan was "organized chaos") is Joe Volpe, technical director. He had worked at Peter Fellers, a house that supplies all kinds of theatrical material, at the Radio City Music Hall, on Broadway, and at the World's Fair when he joined us the year of the latter, 1964. The shops in the new house were just being set up, so he got in on the ground floor. Eight years he put in as master mechanic, and for a time he was head of the carpenter shop, where he started as an apprentice. He had a sideline, an interest in a baseball-throwing machine used by the leagues and in amusement parks. Maybe there's a connection.

Wandering Dante-like through this forest of the Metropolitan's backstage, you are amazed at all this reality going full tilt to create unreality. And then the old Pirandello problem raises its head: what is reality?

TOUR

In a world where "The show must go on" is law, the record of the Metropolitan Opera is unique. The only time it ever missed a performance on tour, it lost the rest of the engagement, and for a very sound reason—the San Francisco earthquake and fire. Opera was ever larger than life. That is perhaps its most immediately arresting property.

The season of 1978–79 was the Metropolitan's ninety-fourth. The tour that spring was its ninety-second. That doesn't mean the company has taken to the road every year of its history except two. In some war and depression years the tour was a casualty, but in the earlier seasons there were sometimes tours in the autumn as well as in the spring. No other opera company in the world can point to such activity off home base.

Seven cities are now regular ports of call—Boston, Cleveland, Atlanta, Memphis, Dallas, Minneapolis, and Detroit. All are one-week stands except Memphis and Dallas, which share the fourth week. There is also a post-tour week in June at Wolf Trap Farm Park outside Washington, D.C., and in 1978 we played a three-night engagement at Robin Hood Dell in Philadelphia, which we hope will expand to a full week. With the New York season at thirty weeks, this means the tour represents in time alone more than 20 percent of the Metropolitan's entire operation.

Because of the bigger houses on tour—Public Auditorium in Cleveland has a capacity of 9,000—the percentage outside New York of the Metropolitan's total public is even higher. The Metropolitan plays to about 700,000 persons during the season at Lincoln Center. On tour it's about 250,000, or 26 percent of the 950,000 who make up the Metropolitan's paying public.

Francis Robinson (above), tour director for the Metropolitan Opera, who first went on the road with the company over three decades ago. One of the most visited cities, and among the most hospitable, is Atlanta, where the performances formerly took place in the ornate Fox Theater, a movie palace (right). Faced with a veritable caravan of productions, some such as Boris Godunov *of extraordinary complexity and weight, the craftsmen of the carpenter shop must invent all kinds of custom-made dollies and the like to get the show rolling (below)*

METROPOLITAN OPERA
TONIGHT 8:PM

The Metropolitan Opera has been a traveler since its very first season, 1883–84, when it interrupted its New York run to play a New Year's fortnight in Boston. That visit brought the company's initial performance of Carmen, *so from the beginning, tour cities have been privy to some special events, on occasion scooping the home audience in New York. Sometimes a star singer will appear in a role on tour that only later he repeats at the Opera House, a case in point being Adelina Patti's Martha (right), heard when the Flotow romance was given in Boston during an 1891–92 visit. Patti always traveled in a luxuriously furnished private pullman comparable to a suite in one of Europe's grand hotels, with no comfort lacking. The rest of the company made do with the best of normal quarters, enjoying those moments when the train would halt and they could descend from their coaches to stretch out in the grass like the Gay Nineties group shown here (below). By occupation singers must be tourists, and they often indulge in the kind of pastime all travelers enjoy during a trip to an exotic locale. For example, when the Metropolitan Opera played a season in Buffalo during 1896—a three-day stand consisting of* Faust, Roméo et Juliette, Aida *and* Falstaff*—seven distinguished members of the troupe—Jean de Reszke, Pol Plançon, Edouard de Reszke, Maurice Grau, Willy Schütz, Victor Capoul and Fred Rullman—did not pass up the opportunity to gather for a souvenir photo, showing the group in a formal pose superimposed on a rock with the full magnificence of Niagara Falls as fake backdrop (left)*

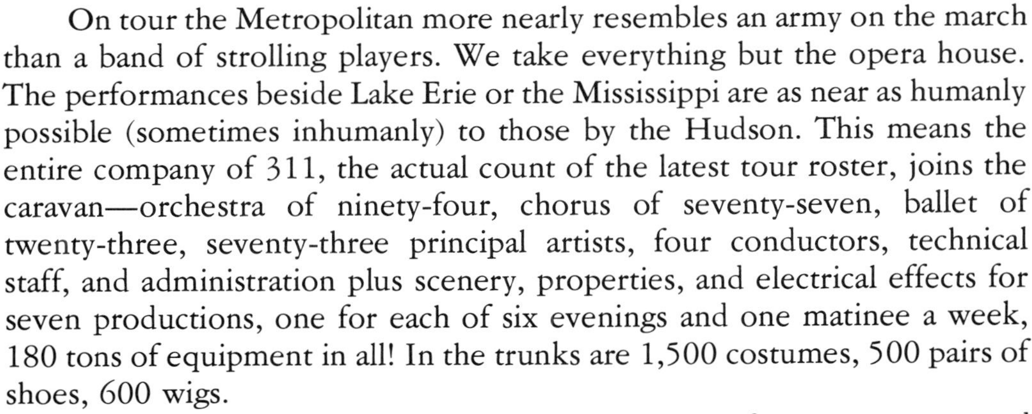

On tour the Metropolitan more nearly resembles an army on the march than a band of strolling players. We take everything but the opera house. The performances beside Lake Erie or the Mississippi are as near as humanly possible (sometimes inhumanly) to those by the Hudson. This means the entire company of 311, the actual count of the latest tour roster, joins the caravan—orchestra of ninety-four, chorus of seventy-seven, ballet of twenty-three, seventy-three principal artists, four conductors, technical staff, and administration plus scenery, properties, and electrical effects for seven productions, one for each of six evenings and one matinee a week, 180 tons of equipment in all! In the trunks are 1,500 costumes, 500 pairs of shoes, 600 wigs.

To transport all this requires two charter planes for the company and their personal baggage, twenty-five to thirty trucks, an entire year of planning, the strength of Hercules and the patience of Job. Until 1968 we went by rail. That required two special trains, a total of eighteen sleeping cars and twenty-two baggage cars.

Before the New York season expanded, the tours were longer. We even played one-night stands. The tour of 1948 was longest—fifteen cities in nine weeks over a distance of nearly 9,000 miles. But there is nothing so costly as pulling this big company into and out of a town, so we have had to limit ourselves to engagements of a full week.

In an operation so vast there are bound to be mishaps on a corresponding scale, but miraculously San Francisco in 1906 remains the Metropolitan's only cancellation on tour. Caruso was shaken out of bed in the Palace Hotel and so frightened he swore never to sing on the West Coast again, an odd reaction for someone born in Naples, practically in the crater of a volcano—but then again, perhaps not so odd. He knew what nature could do. He kept his vow, which may have everything to do with the fact that the Metropolitan Opera did not cross the Rockies again for forty-two years, not until 1948.

The company had opened in San Francisco the evening of April 16, 1906, with what must have been an indifferent performance of an indifferent opera. Goldmark's *Königin von Saba*, unperformed today. In any event it was not too well received. Next night was a different story—Caruso and Olive Fremstad in *Carmen.* Caruso probably made a late night of it. At a little past five the next morning the earth began to move. "Give me Vesuvius!" Caruso shouted.

He was next sighted in Union Square, the park beside the St. Francis Hotel, several blocks from the Palace, fully clothed with a towel around his head and clutching a signed photograph of President Theodore Roosevelt. He seemed to think it would be his passport to safety, and in a way it turned out to be. Martial law was immediately clamped on the city. Barricades had been set up, and at one point Caruso flashed his sole salvaged possession to a confused guard. "O.K.," the soldier said, "any friend of T. R. . . ."

In spite of the loss of everything—scenery, costumes, musical instruments—there was fortunately no loss of life. The first thing the company did on its return home was to stage a mammoth benefit for victims of the disaster.

An act of God dealt a heavy blow to the Metropolitan Opera in 1906 during a trek to the West Coast. The second night of the season, in San Francisco, was a Carmen *starring Enrico Caruso (above left, with Mrs. Lionel Mapelson, wife of the company's music librarian) and Marcel Journet as Escamillo (above). Not many hours after the performance, the great earthquake and fire took their grim toll, all but leveling the city and with it the settings and costumes on tour with the Metropolitan. Citizens, fearful for their lives, fled to the outskirts (top right) and Caruso, who was a gifted cartoonist, drew a memento of his own ignoble escape by wagon (below). Among the refugees who made it safely home (bottom right) were the conductor Nahan Franko, Edyth Walker, Robert Blass, Marcella Sembrich, Bella Alten, Ernest Goerlitz and Caruso himself (bottom right). Miraculously there had been no injury or loss of life among the members of the company, but the Metropolitan did not return to California for over four decades*

APRIL 18,

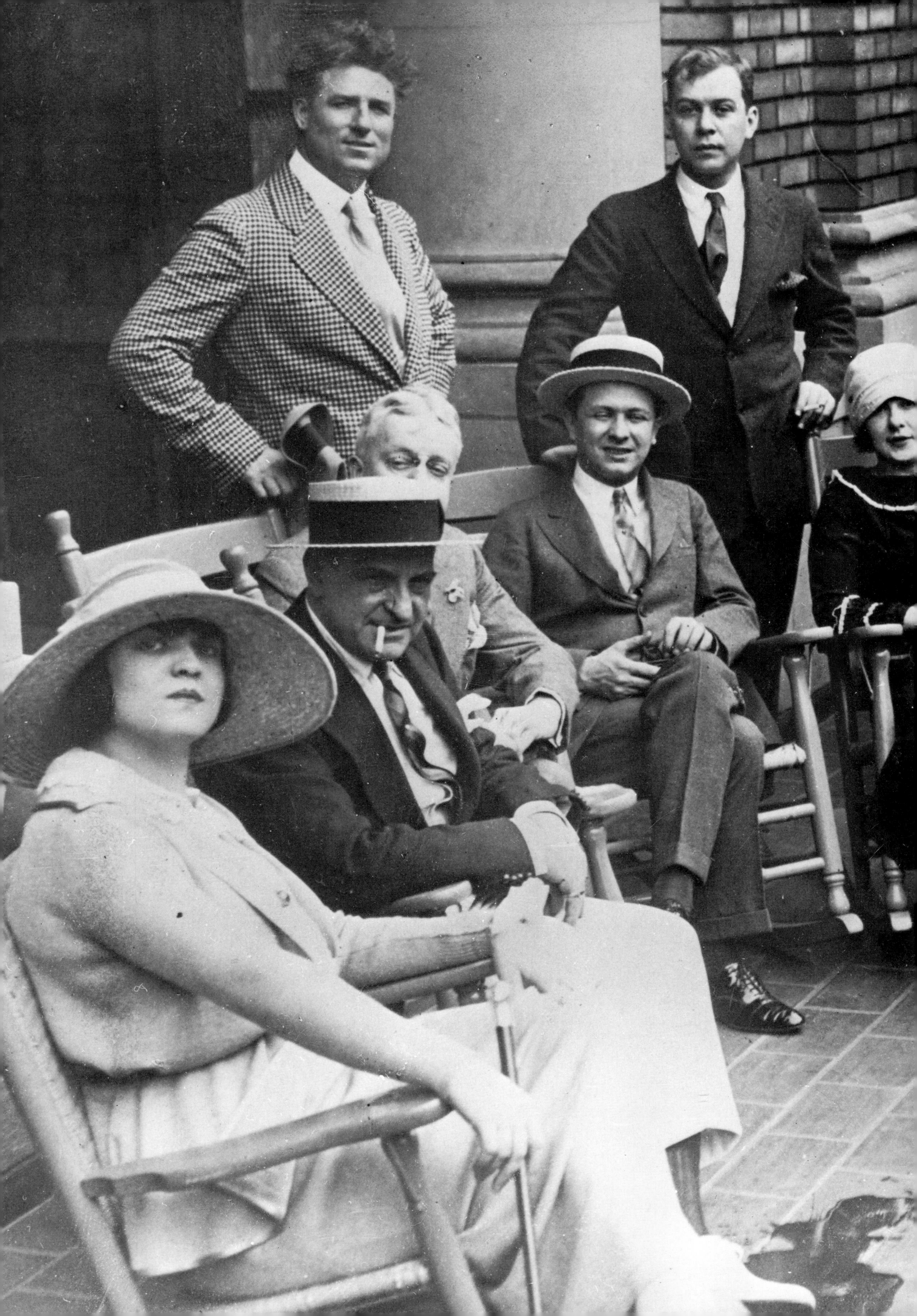

OPERA
NEWS

METROPOLITAN OPERA
1948
SPRING
TOUR

Previous two pages: barnstorming songbirds and some associates during a visit to Atlanta in the spring of 1923—Rosa Ponselle; Antonio Scotti; the assistant general manager, Edward Ziegler; Giovanni Martinelli; the conductors Giuseppe Bamboschek and Wilfrid Pelletier; Miss Ponselle's secretary, Edith Prilik; Léon Rothier; the assistant conductor and photographer Carlo Edwards; Maestro Gennaro Papi; Giuseppe Danise; and Lucrezia Bori. The man behind Edwards is unidentified

The wording of our tour contracts is strange and wonderful. Among the eventualities cited as reason for non-performance are "epidemic, fire, acts of the elements, labor disputes, governmental or court orders, acts of God, civil commotion or any other cause constituting an act of force majeure." Those final two words are usually whispered.

The closest the company came to missing a performance since San Francisco was on that tour of 1948. Spring rains had washed out the tracks on the main line between Richmond and Atlanta. Our second train did not arrive until 6:30 P.M. for an eight o'clock curtain—not time enough to notify the public there would be a delay. Looking as only he could in white tie and tails, Edward Johnson came in front of the curtain and begged the indulgence of the audience.

In the shuffle some of the baggage didn't reach the theater. Risë Stevens had brought her costumes with her, but the company trunks hadn't arrived. The result was a costumeless *Carmen*—in street clothes, not in the nude—which began at 10 P.M. and didn't come down until one the next morning. Many old-timers said it was the most exciting *Carmen* they ever witnessed. The story made front pages around the world. "You give a hundred perfect performances," Mr. Johnson said ruefully, "and nobody pays any attention to you."

Two years before had been strike year—rail and coal. Johnson once observed that John L. Lewis must have timed his movements to ours. If the railroad strike of 1946 had come off as scheduled, it would have caught us in Dallas, our most distant point from home that season. A week's delay found the company at zero hour compressed into one train at four o'clock on a lovely May afternoon, moseying through the Virginia countryside after the final performance of the tour in Chattanooga the night before. We pulled into Washington about six-thirty.

Not a locomotive was moving. Most of the tracks were deserted. It was as though an atom bomb had fallen. That great Union Station, so big and bustling in those years, lay empty and silent. By some dispensation never explained and certainly never questioned, the special was miraculously allowed to go through. Perhaps the crew wanted to get home; otherwise there might have been some tuba-tooting pickets around the White House. On the station platform the gentlemen of the chorus sang the prayer from *Tannhäuser* and the prisoners' chorus from *Fidelio*, and away we went.

Despite wartime exigencies, the Metropolitan Opera continued to take to the road during the 1940s, traveling as much as the government would permit. Shown here in Pennsylvania Station, during a wait for their train to depart, are Irra Petina, the assistant conductor Antonio Dell'Orefice, Risë Stevens, Nino Martini and Ezio Pinza, passing the time by reading the latest issue of Opera News *(top left). In the spring of 1948 the company returned to the West Coast for the first time in forty-two years with a two-week engagement in Los Angeles (bottom left). On the platform of the observation car are Martha Lipton, Désiré Defrère, Dorothy Kirsten, Frances Greer, Hertha Glaz, Alessio De Paolis, Irene Jessner, Mario Berini, Marks Levine and Mae Frohman. Standing on the tracks below are Dezso Ernster, Frank St. Leger, Edward Johnson, Jan Peerce, Gerhard Pechner, Giacomo Vaghi and the tour director, Francis Robinson. Many honors are awarded the company as it wends its way from state to state. Edward Johnson (above right) reads one such citation to proud members of the chorus, a document from the state of Georgia commemorating the artistic contributions of the Metropolitan Opera during its visits to Atlanta, the first of which was in 1901*

A few weeks earlier, the coal strike of 1946 had left Chicago with two weeks' supply of coal. After that, nothing. A curfew was immediately slapped on the city, restricting lights in public buildings from 2 to 6 P.M.

We heard this in Minneapolis on a Thursday before we were to open in Chicago the following Monday. I was dispatched to Chicago to see what could be done.

I pleaded with the commission, quite eloquently I thought, to give us our four hours from 8 P.M. until midnight. Three thousand people in the Chicago Opera House burning one set of lights, I argued, was better than all those people at home playing bridge or listening to the radio (TV was then only a fantasy) or, who knows, perhaps even reading. The commission was unmoved.

It was the Navy rather than the Marines to the rescue. Jack Manley, a former Navy officer later with the port authority in Chicago, told us about six maritime ships that had been completed just at the war's end and never used. They were tied up at the Twelfth Street docks. Why not lease one of them from the Maritime Commission, bring her up the river, tie her alongside the opera house, and use her motors for our power?

In some of the fastest red-tape cutting on record, that is exactly what we did. The Maritime Commission exacted a deposit of $25,000 subject to overcall, but the gun was in the ribs. We were in no position to bargain. It was a bright, brisk Sunday morning when we brought the *Mainsheet Eye*—I can never forget her name—up the river. All that was lacking was a calliope playing arias from *La Traviata.* Now Chicago isn't known as the Windy City for nothing, and the windiest part of a city is around the skyscrapers. By the time a forty-five-miles-per-hour wind swept down the forty-six stories of Mr. Insull's opera house, it must have been about a ninety-mile gale. A negligent crew took care of the rest. Leaving only one man aboard and only one line out, they went ashore for coffee. That line snapped like a silk thread, and a 325-foot ocean-going vessel was adrift in the Chicago River. Her stern jammed the *Daily News* building on the opposite bank, inflicting $10,000 damage.

I had gone back to my hotel to write the ads for next day's papers. By the time I got to the wreckage, the *Mainsheet Eye*'s stern had smashed into the Washington Street Bridge, making such sounds as I never heard outside a horror movie. The Chicago River is a federal waterway, and if that bridge hadn't gone up, we might have all gone to jail. At that point it seemed a welcome possibility.

Unlike most opera plots, the story has a happy ending. The unruly ship was brought back under control, and the Metropolitan Opera was the only attraction playing in America's second largest city that week. "We glory in tribulation," St. Paul says, "knowing that tribulation worketh experience and experience hope." Many a time since, when the going has been tough, we have remembered that boat and known we would get through.

Houston was a near casualty in 1947. The Texas City explosion, which took 512 lives, had filled Houston's City Auditorium with evacuees. A week before our engagement, no one could say whether they would be out or not. Mercifully they were, and the hall made ready. What did the company do the Sunday evening before but give a benefit in Dallas for the dispossessed survivors? "There's no business like show business," and there's no show business like opera.

The Mainsheet Eye *(above) provided both power and headaches for the Metropolitan Opera in Chicago during a national energy crisis in 1946. Lily Pons (right) takes a curtain call after the second act of* Lucia di Lammermoor *with John Brownlee, John Carter, Thelma Votipka and Jan Peerce at Fair Park Auditorium in Dallas, 1942. In time, the coloratura grew so enchanted with the Texas city and its public that she decided to make her home there. For the Metropolitan's wardrobe department, packing and unpacking costumes is a daily chore during tours. The indefatigable Jennie Cervini (far right) did this task for nearly half a century, much of that time aided by John Casamassa. The 9,000-seat Public Auditorium in Cleveland (next two pages) is the biggest hall the Metropolitan plays. Cleveland visits began in another house in 1886 with Wagner's* Rienzi

M11

During the 1960s, the Metropolitan abandoned rail travel (top left) for its personnel in favor of the airplane; sets and costumes now travel by truck. In 1965, between its last season in the old Opera House and its first in the new, the company made a whirlwind flight to Paris (bottom left), playing two works based on comedies by Beaumarchais—Mozart's Le Nozze di Figaro *and Rossini's* Il Barbiere di Siviglia*—at the charming Odeon Théâtre, where the world premiere of Beaumarchais's* Le Barbier de Séville *had taken place. It was the Metropolitan's second visit to Paris, where in 1910 it gave nineteen performances, with Bori, Caruso and Toscanini among the luminaries*

A folio of classic works in the repertory of the Metropolitan Opera: Gluck's Orfeo ed Euridice *in the 1970 Sparemblek/Gérard production, showing the dance of the Furies (top right) and the Elysian Fields, with Gabriella Tucci as Euridice being reunited with Grace Bumbry as Orfeo; the Rennert/Chagall production of Mozart's* Die Zauberflöte *(next two pages), with Jerome Hines as Sarastro in the final scene (top left), the two Papagenos, Theodor Uppman, who sang the role in English (bottom left), and Hermann Prey, who sang it in German (bottom center), Edda Moser as the Queen of the Night (top right) and Rosalind Elias, Jean Fenn and Ruza Baldani as her Three Ladies discovering the prostrate Tamino, Nicolai Gedda (bottom right); the Rennert/O'Hearn production of Mozart's* Le Nozze di Figaro *follows (subsequent two pages), showing Justino Díaz as Figaro with Frederica von Stade as Cherubino (top left), Judith Blegen as Susanna with Evelyn Lear as Countess Almaviva (bottom left), Miss Lear as the Countess with Miss von Stade as the disguised Cherubino (top right) and the quartet of Andrew Foldi as Dr. Bartolo, Wolfgang Brendl as Count Almaviva, Jean Kraft as Marcellina and Andrea Velis as Don Basilio (bottom right)*

HANSEL AND GRETEL

Two German classics in the repertory of the Metropolitan Opera: Humperdinck's Hansel and Gretel *in the magical 1967–68 Merrill/O'Hearn production, with Teresa Stratas as Gretel and Rosalind Elias as Hansel (top left), Karl Dönch as the Witch stoking her fire (top right), and the gingerbread and candy house with the children freed from an enchanted spell after the Witch explodes in her oven (bottom left); and Beethoven's* Fidelio *(previous two pages) in the moving Schenk/Aronson re-creation of 1970–71, which commemorated the bicentenary of the composer's birth—Judith Blegen as Marzelline (top left), Leonie Rysanek as Leonore—alias Fidelio—with Giorgio Tozzi as Rocco (bottom left), the haunting chorus of the prisoners (top right) and the joyous finale in which the populace rejoices in Leonore's victory over tyranny, Miss Rysanek as Leonore and Jon Vickers as Florestan, the husband she liberates from unjust imprisonment (bottom right)*

One night in Philadelphia the worst thing occurred that can happen in a theater. There was a puff of smoke from the wings and to a man the audience was on its feet. The orchestra, led by the conductor, was halfway to Broad Street Station when Edward Johnson, again immaculate in white tie and tails, appeared before the curtain. "Ladies and gentlemen," he said in the voice that never lost its tenor ring, "It's only a blown fuse or a burnt gelatine. If you will take your places, the performance will resume immediately." When the orchestra finally got back into the pit, it did.

Next morning Mr. Johnson summoned Gennaro Papi to his office. "That needn't have happened last night, Maestro," he began firmly. "There might have been a panic; there might have been loss of life. Nothing would have happened if you had remained on the podium." By now he was waxing eloquent. "The band on the *Titanic* played as the ship was going down, but you . . ." Maestro Papi was a little squint-eyed Neapolitan. The Italians are realistic, and none so realistic as the Neapolitans. Finally he had had enough. *"Signor direttore,"* he said, "you engaged me to be a conductor, not a hero."

No two places on tour are alike. In Minneapolis people come from twenty-seven states and two provinces, from Regina, Saskatchewan, a thousand miles away. The big space under the Cleveland Public Auditorium is converted into a pavilion. When the opera is not in town, it houses trade shows, and during the circus, the animals. One remembers a Boston critic's line when the Metropolitan followed the horse show into Mechanics' Hall. "With Madame Nordica's first note," the gallant scribe recorded, "all traces of the previous week's occupants vanished."

But the foregoing is only setting the scene. Cleveland's Pavilion during Opera Week is all glamour, trimmed by the city's best decorator, fountains playing, walls and columns hung with what looks for all the world like chiffon. The point of all this is we might not be in Cleveland if were it not for the Pavilion. Distances in the Ohio metropolis are second only to those in Detroit and Los Angeles. The nearest subscriber is miles away. To get home from work, get dressed, and get back to town for an eight o'clock curtain—who needs it? Our sponsors had the divine inspiration to offer dinner—and a good one, again from the town's leading caterer—right on the premises in the most congenial surroundings. And after the opening night performance our sponsors throw a party for the entire company, all 311 of us.

Jerome Hines (below), who in 1979–80 tied Antonio Scotti's thirty-four-year record with the Metropolitan Opera, studies a book late at night in a railway car during the 1960 spring tour

The Atlanta Opera Guild gives a Sunday afternoon party the day before our opening to which the entire company is invited. After the closing performance in Memphis, our sponsors there, Arts Appreciation, have a party right in the auditorium, with drinks, supper, plus a rock band for the entire company, Southern hospitality at its warmest. Opening night in Memphis, Mr. and Mrs. Dayton Smith give a party at the splendid restaurant that bears Mrs. Smith's name, Justine's. At the end of a street, the old mansion looks like a stage setting. The gardens and interior are even more magical.

Atlanta has a great tradition as regards the Metropolitan. Except for those war and Depression years, the company has journeyed there each spring since 1910, the longest it has gone continuously anywhere. What Mardi Gras is to New Orleans, we are to Atlanta. "Work has stopped, sleep has stopped," moaned Rudolf Bing on his first visit to the Georgia capital, but like everybody else he loved it. Apparently it's a two-way street. The chairman of our committee there once gasped, "You people play to kill."

Scenes from the Metropolitan Opera's tour to Japan during the spring of 1975, when the company presented eighteen performances divided between Tokyo, Nagoya and Osaka: Luciano Pavarotti, who sang three Rodolfos in La Bohème, *visiting the sights in Nikko (top left); Loretta Di Franco making new friends (top right); Lucine Amara, one of the Micaelas in* Carmen, *enjoying the beauty of Kyoto (bottom left); Dorothy Kirsten, who appeared four times as Mimi, with James McCracken, Don José of all five* Carmens *(center right); and the trio of John Reardon, three times the Marcello of* La Bohème, *Shirley Love, the constant Mercédès of* Carmen, *and Nedda Casei posing by a historic bridge in Kyoto (bottom right). For television, Joan Sutherland did forty minutes of excerpts from* La Traviata. *Also shown here are Japanese stagehands scrambling to load a truck with pieces of the* Carmen *production (above) and a bilingual cast sheet for a performance of* Carmen *(below)*

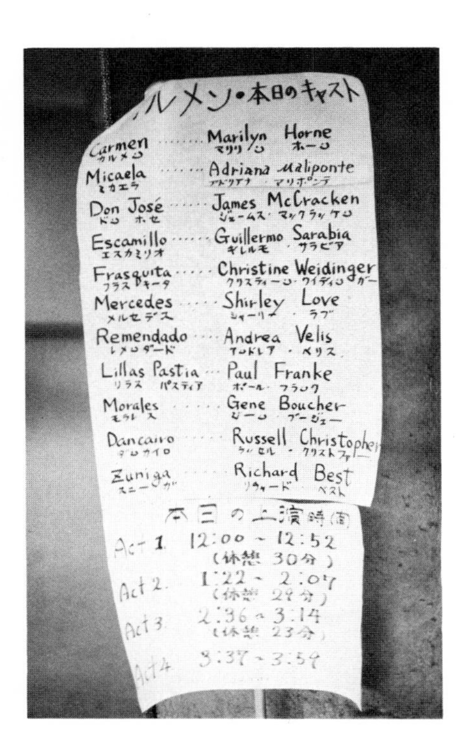

After a particularly gaudy night Maestro Serafin once scolded his baggy-eyed forces at rehearsal: "Remember, we are also here to sing!"

But there is no doubt about it—the biggest event in our lives was the historic visit to Japan in 1975. The epic venture was sponsored by Chubu Nippon, the independent broadcasting network of Japan, to celebrate its twenty-fifth anniversary. Even with a scale of admission prices from 7,000 to 16,000 yen, about twenty-four to fifty-five dollars by that year's exchange, there was a sizable deficit. Our hosts seemed to bear it gladly. To save transportation, they copied exactly, minutely, our productions of *La Traviata* and *La Bohème.* We brought *Carmen* and the costumes for all three.

Our first Japanese review was in *Yomiuri Shimbun* and began, "The Metropolitan Opera of New York . . . should be known as the Metropolitan Opera of the world" and then went on, "We have in the past encountered numerous opera companies of varying dimensions, from Italy, Germany, France, the Soviet Union and elsewhere, but it is truly an historic event of astounding proportions that the Met, which is said to have the most international character of them all, has moved to Japan in its entirety, including chorus, orchestra, and ballet."

Ruth St. Denis used to say, "I tried to bring to the exuberance of the West some of the quiet of the East," and our Japanese friends gave us in return things that cannot be measured but will never be forgotten. Along with the first sight from the plane of their jagged coastlines and blue two-dimensional mountains, looking exactly like their art (as why shouldn't they?), will remain the memory of a sea of happy faces and eager hands waving goodbye as our buses left the hall after the final performance in Tokyo. That is gold only a singer or an actor or a musician knows.

The Japanese might not like to shake hands, but presents turn up everywhere and from everybody. They also give of that most precious thing, themselves. As an example of their hospitality and their desire to help a visitor, a man they had never seen before walked ten minutes out of his way to escort Georges André, then our first double bass, and his wife to a bus stop. When they tried to convey their concern that he might be inconveniencing himself, their guide said, "My wife can wait. She's not American."

Another time Harold Traub, whose wife, Dorothy, is a member of our chorus, was looking in the window of a camera store. A man came up and asked if he had ever been on Guam. Thirty years before the man had been a prisoner on the island while Traub was stationed there.

Commodore Perry wasn't in it. The Japanese will never be the same. Neither, for that matter, will we.

ECONOMICS

Anthony Bliss said it was like turning the *Queen Mary* around in the East River, but a third of the way through the season of 1977–78 he was able to announce the Metropolitan Opera for the first time in eight years was meeting its expenses, and that the next season in New York would go from twenty-seven to thirty weeks.

The increased season ended with a surplus of $575,000, so the miracle happened two years running. Expenses for 1977–78 totaled $34,200,000. Operating revenues amounted to $22,300,000, resulting in an operating loss of $11,900,000. Contributions of $12,500,000 covered that with a small overage to go into our severely depleted working capital.

"We still have a long way to go and it will never be easy," Mr. Bliss said when announcing the results of 1977–78. "We are by no means out of the woods, but we have made a start.

"The management controls and economies we have instituted over the past several seasons have made it possible for us to operate without being under the cloud of crisis and constant struggle for survival that have been so much a part of the recent history of the company."

He attributed this dramatic change to tighter management and the increasing popularity of opera, spurred in part by live televised performances from the stage of the Metropolitan. "It has given us a whole new forum for fund-raising," he said of the telecasts.

The operatic facts of life, however, remain the same—only more so. The season of 1977–78 it cost $138,000 to raise the curtain on a Metropolitan performance. This is $7,000 more than the average cost per perfor-

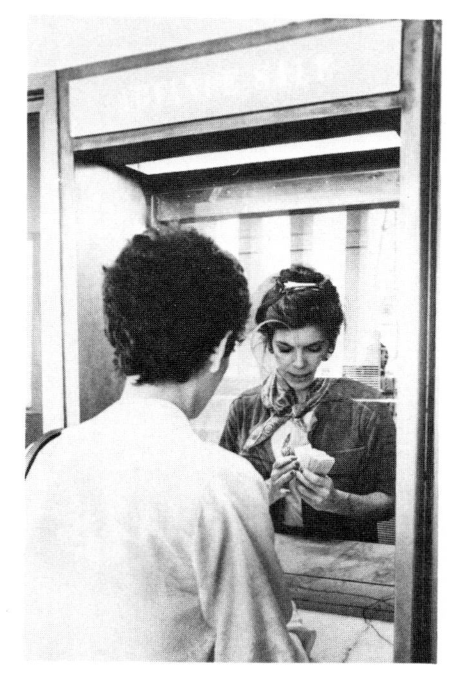

Ticket sales (above) account but for only a small percentage of the cost of operating the Metropolitan Opera. For several years a bazaar and auction were held at the theater (below), with three-sheets, records, books, food and all kind of related matter on sale, some items adorning Maillol's Summer *(right)*

MET

MADAMA BUTTERFLY
GIACOMO PUCCINI
METROPOLITAN OPERA
November 5, 8, 11, 17, 23, 26
December 2, 7, 10, 13, 17, April 8
Conductor: Giuseppe Patané
Production: Yoshio Aoyama
Set & Costume Designer: Motohiro Nagasaka
Supervisory Scenic Designer: Charles Elson
Supervisory Costume Designer: Ming Cho Lee
Stage Director: Patrick Tavernia
Renata Scotto/Gilda Cruz-Romo, Florence Quivar/Shirley Love, Veriano Luchetti/Giacomo Aragall/Gianfranco Pastine/Giuseppe Giacomini, Mario Sereni/ Allan Monk/ Ryan Edwards/ Theodor Uppman, James Atherton, Alma Jean Smith, Arthur Thompson/Gene Boucher, Russell Christopher, Richard Best, Fawayne Murphy, Gina Puleo
Metropolitan Opera
American Ballet Theatre stands alone.
At The Met
TOSCA

With the enormous increase in the number of performances at the new Opera House, the volume of ticket orders has grown accordingly, especially since the Metropolitan assumed sponsorship of outside attractions during spring and summer months. As a result, the staff of the ticket department works at full capacity the year round (above). Alfred A. Hubay is box office manager and Clare Moroney the subscription coordinator. Outside the theater, replacing the drab three-sheets of yore, which simply listed the title and cast of a work, the company now announces its repertory with beautifully designed posters that far more effectively catch the eye of a prospective ticket buyer (left), while dressing up Lincoln Center Plaza as a home of opera and ballet. Mastermind behind much of the modernization of the company's public image is marketing director Patrick L. Veitch (below)

mance the season before, an increase of 5.3 percent. With a box office take of $70,000 a night, that means the board of the Metropolitan must raise an average of $68,000 per performance to fill the gap between expenditures and income.

The cost of a season of Metropolitan Opera in 1976–77 was $31,175,-000, nearly double what it was ten years earlier; in 1967–68 the season cost $16,900,000. Though payroll costs have remained at approximately the same percentage of total costs, 76 percent in 1967–68 and 77 percent in 1976–77, box office receipts have not kept pace, since in 1967–68 they recouped 64 percent of costs, whereas in 1967–77 they recouped fifty percent of total costs. This situation has arisen even though attendance has remained at 96 percent and prices have been increased.

Those figures say a great deal for the product. They also reflect a massive, skillful, highly effective marketing campaign. Not so many years ago, Metropolitan Opera advertisements were single-column affairs in telephone-book-size type. All that changed, and full-page ads invited the public to "Strike a Blow for Civilization." The Metropolitan also went on the air in a big way for the first time to sell tickets, with some of the greatest moments in opera underscoring the announcements. The old block-letter three-sheets have given way to stylish posters in color devoted to the various works in the repertory.

Patrick L. Veitch is responsible for our advertising and marketing's leap into modern times. He joined the Metropolitan as advertising coordinator in 1973 and became its first marketing director in 1976.

Before that he was director of publications at Manhattan College, was corporate public relations counselor for Ketchum, MacLeod & Grove, and did systems analysis for Columbia University Libraries.

A native of Beaumont, Texas, he likes to point out Beaumont is also the birthplace of Texaco. It was our broadcasts sponsored by Texaco that gave him his first taste of opera and the Metropolitan. The first performance he heard live was in Dallas while he was a student at North Texas State University.

He did graduate study in non-profit management at Columbia and is frequently called to consult on marketing with opera companies throughout the United States, Canada, and Australia. He serves as a member of the board of the Opera Orchestra of New York.

There is nothing so costly as a dark theater. In the case of the Metropolitan, this is true a thousandfold. Our housekeeping costs run more than $3 million a year, nearly 10 percent of the annual budget. Our electric bill is more than $40,000 a month. Think of that next time you send your check to Con Edison.

As long as S. Hurok was alive, the Metropolitan never had any worry about the house off-season. For more than four decades, from the day we would go off on tour, Hurok rented the house, bringing a steady stream of attractions. He always said the real revival of ballet in this country was in its third season here when he was able to present Colonel W. de Basil's Ballet Russe de Monte Carlo at the Metropolitan Opera House. "Now for the first time," he said in his autobiography, *Impresario*, "New York really saw ballet."

Ballet troupes move into the Metropolitan Opera House the moment the resident company goes on tour—dance attractions sponsored by the Metropolitan itself. Among the artists who have appeared at the theater since 1977, when the company made its first step as dance impresario—Natalia Makarova and Erik Bruhn in American Ballet Theatre's production of The Firebird *(above); the legendary Alicia Alonso with her partner Jorge Esquivel in the ballerina's own staging of* Giselle *for her Ballet Nacional de Cuba (top right); Gelsey Kirkland and Mikhail Baryshnikov in his version of* The Nutcracker *for American Ballet Theatre (bottom right); and Rudolf Nureyev, one of today's undisputed superstars, who in the summer of 1978 sold out a two-week season dancing twenty-one times with the London Festival Ballet in his own production of* Romeo and Juliet *(below), Albrecht in* Giselle *and a triple bill of* Conservatoire, Le Spectre de la Rose *and* Scheherazade.

With the old man's death, his empire scattered. Contracts with the Bolshoi Opera and the Paris Opera were fulfilled posthumously, but what about the Bolshoi Ballet, the Kirov, the Royal Ballet, all the other great companies he had been importing?

The spring and summer of 1977 the Metropolitan turned impresario in the Hurok sense, presenting attractions other than its own product. There were ten weeks of American Ballet Theatre, three of the Stuttgart Ballet, and two of the National Ballet of Canada. American Ballet Theatre played a return engagement in September. It was all a howling success. We have been at it ever since.

American Ballet Theatre returned the spring of 1978 for eight weeks, followed by a fortnight of the National Ballet of Cuba, starring Alicia Alonso. The sensational announcement of the season was that the 150-member troupe of the People's Republic of China, the largest company ever to come out of China, would visit the United States for the first time under the auspices of the Metropolitan Opera and the National Committee on United States-China Relations. After ten days at the Metropolitan Opera House in New York, the company was to move on to Wolf Trap, Minneapolis, Los Angeles, and San Francisco. Martha Graham, the high priestess of contemporary dance, and her company had a one-week engagement in the house in June. In a recent interview a reporter asked Miss Graham, since she had been in the forefront of her art for more than half a century, what we could next expect in the dance. "Young man," Miss Graham declared, "if I knew, I would do it!"

Another attraction of the summer of 1978 was the London Festival Ballet with Rudolf Nureyev. This and the Cuban ballet were to be presented jointly by the Metropolitan and the John F. Kennedy Center for the Performing Arts in Washington. The dynamo behind these fantastic collaborations is Jane Hermann, whose title is director of presentations, but that tells only a small part of it. A former pupil of Alexandra Danilova, she truly knows ballet from the floor up.

A member of the board of directors of Eliot Feld's first company for three years, she later was co-director of the company. In the interim she was for two years audience development director of the Joffrey Ballet. She returned to the Joffrey as assistant general administrator. From that she came to the Metropolitan in 1976 as consultant on planning and was promoted to director of special projects the following year.

Other attractions have brought new audiences into the Metropolitan. During the fall of 1974, Vladimir Horowitz (top left) christened the auditorium as a concert hall, an afternoon recital for which thousands of music-lovers formed a line around the Opera House hoping to obtain tickets although those at the end knew the box office would sell out before they reached it. Jane Hermann (above) is the Metropolitan Opera's presentations director, booking the many outside attractions that play the theater. A single showing of Einstein on the Beach *(bottom left), an* avant-garde *piece by Robert Wilson and Philip Glass presented in 1976, proved so popular with its audience that it had to be encored a week later. On June 26, 1978, when the Martha Graham Dance Company made its debut at the Opera House, the octogenarian choreographer created a delightful new work for the occasion,* The Owl and the Pussycat, *narrated by Liza Minnelli (below). Miss Graham programed two other premieres during the season,* Ecuitorial *and* Flute of Pan

She attended Bennington College and was graduated from Barnard. Married to Dr. John S. Hermann, a prominent eye specialist, she has a grown son and daughter. Withal she keeps her dancer figure and is at home in Havana or Peking as she is in Lincoln Center.

We have always had rentals, such as Vladimir Horowitz, the first recital in the new house, and at the other end of the pole, *Tommy, the Who*, but on two consecutive Sundays in November 1976 the Metropolitan with the Byrd-Hoffman Foundation presented Robert Wilson and Philip Glass' *Einstein on the Beach*, attracting a new and interesting audience.

No possible avenue of fund-raising is left unexplored. The Met Marathon, a four-hour concert from the big stage, is relayed by radio station WQXR to fourteen other good-music stations across the country. In 1977 the Marathon raised $260,000—$80,000 more than the preceding year. The third annual auction and bazaar on the first Sunday in December brought in $143,000, not to mention a merry throng that was almost as surprised as we were to see Maillol's bronze ladies on the grand tier sporting bright red Met T-shirts. The gift shop in the north lobby purveys these T-shirts, books, records, greeting cards, jewelry, and prints. The Guild has a lively mail-order department parallel to this. Plans for expansion include an outdoor café, in addition to the three already operating in the opera house.

The Metropolitan is finally into television on a continuing scale. Costs again have delayed this: 400 people is a ruinous payroll, and three hours and a half is too long for prime commercial network time, so we turned to public broadcasting.

The first telecast of a Metropolitan Opera performance was *Otello* on the opening night of 1948–49. It was the handsome Donald Oenslager production and a great performance, but you couldn't tell it from the screen. Most of it came from one camera nailed down at the back of the auditorium of the old opera house. Color at that time was of course undreamed of.

The next year things were decidedly better—*Der Rosenkavalier* with Steber, Stevens, Berger, and Reiner conducting—better because there were camera angles and more closeups.

The opening scene of *Don Carlo*, Rudolf Bing's production for the opening night of his inaugural season, was a video disaster. That version of the opera began in the monastery of St. Just, with Philip II visiting the tomb of his father, Emperor Charles V. It was dark enough in the opera house. So careful was Margaret Webster, the stage director, that she had the lamps on the musicians' stands lighted at every rehearsal, whether the orchestra was in the pit or not, to determine just how much illumination was leaking to the stage.

The television people came swooping in, and you could have performed the most difficult surgical operation in the most remote corner of the stage. Miss Webster said, "Nothing doing. This is for the paying customers." As a result, the nationwide screen was dark for the entire first scene of *Don Carlo.* You could hear the sets clicking off. Things got better as the evening wore on for those who were still tuned in.

Opening night of 1954 went out closed circuit over Theatre Network Television, a gala made up of Leonard Warren singing the Prologue to *Pagliacci*; De los Angeles and Tucker in Act I of *La Bohème*; Peters, Valletti, Merrill, Madeira, De Paolis, Hines, and Corena in Act II of *Il Barbiere di Siviglia*; and Milanov, Thebom, Del Monaco, Warren, and Hines in three

scenes of *Aida*. There was another closed circuit into movie houses across the country of Stevens, Tucker, and Guarrera in the new Tyrone Guthrie production of *Carmen* with Reiner conducting, but the problems were simply too great to make many new friends for opera. Most of the evening Stevens looked as if she were walking on her knees.

The gala marking Sir Rudolf's farewell as general manager and Danny Kaye's "Look-ins" for young audiences were televised, but it was not until March 15, 1977, that a complete opera was telecast from the new house. It was *La Bohème*, with Scotto and Pavarotti, and it was an enormous success. The next season there were three telecasts from the house, the next, four.

There is money being made in recording, and the Metropolitan should be getting some of it. When we recorded the Gentele production of *Carmen* in 1972 with Marilyn Horne, James McCracken, Adriana Maliponte, and Tom Krause under Leonard Bernstein, we hadn't made a recording for thirteen years—not since *Macbeth* in 1959, with Leonard Warren and Leonie Rysanek. *Vanessa* was recorded in 1958 and four years earlier there had been a single disc of *Un Ballo in Maschera* with Marian Anderson and with one exception the cast of her debut.

The last three years of the 1940s the Metropolitan had a contract with Columbia Records, which produced one complete opera a year. These were later transferred to long-playing discs and most of them are still in the

Milton Cross (above) for forty-three years served as announcer and host for the Metropolitan Opera's Saturday matinee broadcasts, which since 1940 have been sponsored by Texaco Inc. Cross was with the series from its inception, a Hänsel und Gretel *in 1931. His warm greeting, "Good afternoon, ladies and gentlemen—Texaco presents the Metropolitan Opera," became a trademark, his voice as familiar and loved by the public as that of any of the great singers he described on the stage. When the broadcasts were transmitted from the old Opera House, Cross, his associates and their bulky equipment crowded into an antechamber to Box 44 on the Grand Tier, but from 1940 he operated from a nearby glass-closed box. The move to the new Opera House in 1966 provided far more comfortable working conditions—a roomy, up-to-date broadcast and control center on the Grand Tier level, with a full view of stage action through a soundproof window. Though as a young baritone Cross had to abandon his dream of a singing career, he nonetheless was the voice of the Metropolitan Opera until his death in 1975*

Intermission features make the Metropolitan's Saturday matinee broadcasts more informative and more fun. A veteran participant before the microphones is musicologist and author Edward Downes (top left), for many years quizmaster of "Texaco's Opera Quiz." Geraldine Souvaine, producer for intermission features since 1940, goes over a script at the keyboard with lecturer Boris Goldovsky (top right) for his usual first-interval slot, "Opera News *on the Air." Another popular feature is a panel discussion called "Singers' Roundtable" at which well-known guests—Robert Merrill, Zinka Milanov and Richard Tucker (above)—exchange career anecdotes and tell tales out of school. Mrs. Souvaine is of the old school herself and likes all features broadcast "live" with an audience present. The new Opera House provides an ideal setting for such programs, List Hall (next two pages), where a session of Texaco's "Opera Quiz" is seen in progress with a panel of experts made up of pianist Ivan Davis, critic Martin Bernheimer, author William Weaver and conductor Julius Rudel*

catalogue today. In the early Bing years, four more complete operas followed under the Columbia label, which are also current, and there was an arrangement with the Book-of-the-Month Club whereby excerpts were recorded and sold only on subscription. Nobody can say we haven't tried.

The Metropolitan Opera went on the air the first time with *Hansel and Gretel* Christmas Day, 1931. The announcer on that first broadcast was the beloved Milton Cross. He remained with us until his death, forty-three years later. He missed only two broadcasts, and that was when his wife died.

For the first few years the broadcasts were sustaining. Texaco assumed sponsorship in 1940 and has never failed us, a pioneering and a continuing example of corporate responsibility both laudable and unique. They sponsored the telecasts of Danny Kay's "Look-ins," the gala marking the retirement of Sir Rudolf and the transmissions of complete works beginning with *La Bohème* in 1977. The Saturday matinees live from the stage of the Metropolitan Opera House are the only long-term radio broadcasts of serious music left on a nationwide scale.

Another outstanding example of corporate support for the arts was Eastern Airlines' gift of half a million dollars toward the new production of *Der Ring des Nibelungen.* Our first corporate gift toward a new production was $135,000 from American Export and Isbrandtsen Lines for the *Aida* that opened the 1963–64 season.

The National Council of the Metropolitan has sponsored twelve new productions, two jointly with Mrs. Albert Lasker and two with Francis Goelet. The Metropolitan Opera Guild has its name on five.

The largest individual contributor of new productions was the late Mrs. John D. Rockefeller, Jr., nineteen in all. The Gramma Fisher Foundation and Francis Goelet each have been responsible for ten productions. J. William Fisher and Mr. Goelet are members of our board. Goelet's family have been benefactors of the Metropolitan since the beginning, and the grand staircase in the new opera house is their gift in memory of Robert Walton Goelet. Another generous member of the board is Mrs. Edgar Tobin, who has given three new productions. Mr. and Mrs. Samuel L. Tedlow and Mrs. DeWitt Wallace also contributed three each. The late Mrs. Izaak Walton Killam came forward with two. Mrs. Albert Lasker was co-sponsor of another, in addition to the two with the Council. The children of Otto Kahn gave two productions in the Bing era, and his daughter, Mrs. John Barry Ryan, was co-sponsor of a third. They sold a Rembrandt to pay for *Don Carlo*, the first production of the Bing regime. There's art serving art.

Eight times in thirty years the season has been threatened because of labor difficulties. In the summer of 1948 it was announced that the forthcoming semester would be canceled, but we opened almost on time, only three weeks late. There were similar announcements in 1956 and 1961. It was in 1961 that the President of the United States got into the act. John F. Kennedy summoned his Secretary of Labor, Arthur J. Goldberg, and simply told him to settle things. Goldberg "persuaded" the two parties to accept arbitration.

When that three-year agreement was up, the Metropolitan and the orchestra could not come to terms, and we began the season of 1964–65 with no contract with the musicians. Two years later we still had none, which meant that on opening night of the new opera house we were negotiating during the first intermission. We were told there would be no second night.

A folio of French and Russian works presented at the new Metropolitan Opera House: Marilyn Horne as Carmen and James McCracken as José in the 1972–73 Gentele/Svoboda/Walker production of Bizet's Carmen, *Act I (above left); Adriana Maliponte as Micaela with Mr. McCracken as José during the first-act letter duet (top left); Miss Horne as Carmen dancing with her castanets, Act II (top right); and the fatal confrontation between dishonored soldier and defiant gypsy, as portrayed by Mr. McCracken and Miss Horne, Act IV (bottom right). The 1973–74 Merrill/Wexler mounting of Berlioz'* Les Troyens *follows (next two pages)—the pageant of Part I,* La Prise de Troie *(top left), Jon Vickers as Aeneas (right), and Part II,* Les Troyens à Carthage, *with Shirley Verrett as Dido (bottom left). Then comes the 1974–75 Everding/Lee/Hall production of Mussorgsky's* Boris Godunov *(subsequent two pages) with Martti Talvela in the title role and Paul Offenkrantz as his son, Fyodor, Act I (left); the Coronation Scene with Mr. Offenkrantz as Fyodor, Mr. Talvela as the newly crowned Czar Boris and Betsy Norden as his daughter, Xenia (top right); and the Act III scene in the duma, where Paul Plishka as the aged, blind monk Pimen relates a miracle that finally topples the guilty Boris Godunov from his throne, with Mr. Talvela as the Czar (bottom right)*

A folio of two recent John Dexter productions at the Metropolitan Opera: his staging with designer William Dudley of Benjamin Britten's Billy Budd, *a work never before given at the theater, with the call to battle in Act II (top left)—on the bridge David Ward as Mr. Flint, Peter Pears as Captain Vere, Peter Glossop as Mr. Redburn and John Cheek as Lt. Ratcliffe, and below the bridge Robert Goodloe as Donald, Andrew Foldi as Dansker, Richard Stilwell as Billy Budd and Robert Nagy as Red Whiskers; Mr. Pears as Captain Vere conferring with James Morris as John Claggart, the master at arms (above right); and the opera's final moment, when Mr. Stilwell as Billy is executed (bottom left); Bedřich Smetana's beguiling human comedy* The Bartered Bride *(previous two pages) was televised coast-to-coast over PBS in a production staged by Mr. Dexter with settings by Josef Svoboda and costumes by Jan Skalicky. Here are Nicolai Gedda as Jenik and Teresa Stratas as Marenka during their first-act love duet (far left); Martti Talvela as the talkative marriage broker Kecal (top center); Miss Stratas as Marenka with Jon Vickers as her stuttering fiancé, Vasek, in Act II (top right); and the revolving carousel of the finale, with Mr. Vickers as Vasek huddled with some youngsters on its rim, Andrij Dobriansky as "Red Indian," Alan Crofoot as the burly Circus Barker and Colette Boky as the flirtatious dancer Esmeralda (bottom right)*

The eyes of the world were on us, and that couldn't be allowed to happen. Only at the second intermission was Mr. Bing able to announce that a settlement had been reached and the season would go forward. Such cliff hanging is hardly conducive to a creative atmosphere. Producing opera is hard enough at best, with everything running smoothly.

We lost almost half the season of 1969–70. The opening, scheduled for mid-September, did not take place until late December. We lost subscribers whom we are only now regaining. Subscriptions dropped almost 20 percent, from 75 percent of capacity at the time we left the old house to well below 60. Continuity is the first law of life.

The 1972 agreements expired the summer of 1975, but we got no new contract with the orchestra until little more than a half hour before curtain time on New Year's Eve. A jolly gala that would have been.

The summer of 1977 brought another crisis, but we opened on time. The board heroically committed itself to $40 million over the next three years to meet the annual deficit of more than $13 million.

Just as we have pursued every means of increasing income, we have introduced every possible economy. A big saving has been effected by calming down our productions wherever possible—less lumber and canvas onstage. A "five-act monster" like *Le Prophète* would have been impossible in these times of financial pressures if John Dexter and Peter Wexler had not devised a unit set that worked effectively. In *Dialogues of the Carmelites*, Dexter and David Reppa again proved that less is sometimes more. Scenery was reduced to the minimum but was highly atmospheric, underlining the psychological elements of the drama and the strong personal relationships of the characters. The nuns' habits were borrowed from *Suor Angelica* and the peasants' costumes later turned up in *Andrea Chénier*, with no damage to the stage pictures.

Some new productions are borrowed rather than built, notably *Esclarmonde*, *La Favorita*, *Thaïs*, and *Der Fliegende Holländer*, from San Francisco and *La Bohème* from Chicago. Those companies in turn have borrowed ours.

Edward Johnson used to say, "There is nothing wrong with the Metropolitan Opera that money won't cure," and Rudolf Bing, when practically commanded to mount a World's Fair season in 1964, countered, "My first question is an artistic one: who pays?"

Their predecessors were not so beleaguered. After Henry E. Abbey's disastrous first season of 1883–84, the Metropolitan sailed through its first half century free of financial woes. For half that time Otto Kahn picked up the tab. Everything was fine. Then came the Great Depression.

At the first meeting Mrs. August Belmont attended as the first woman member of the board, it was announced that if real money wasn't forthcoming within the month the closing notice would go up. Some initiation.

Mrs. Belmont shared a taxi uptown that afternoon with Cornelius N. Bliss and Allen Wardwell. That ride is as important in the annals of the Metropolitan as Paul Revere's is in the history of our nation. New York, the country without the Metropolitan? Unthinkable. Something had to be done.

Mrs. Belmont organized the first campaign for funds. They actually passed the hat in the theater. There was a famous *New Yorker* cartoon at the time of the Triumphal Scene of *Aida.* Rethberg, Martinelli, Tibbett, and Pinza were all lined up, and the caption read, "The artists will pass among you with tin cups, and anything you care to contribute . . ." It wasn't quite that bad, but Lucrezia Bori did come in front of the gold curtain to beg, and Geraldine Farrar came out of retirement for the only time after her farewell eleven years before. It was a matinee of *Parsifal*, and her appeal went out over the air. She quoted the closing lines of *Die Meistersinger*, Hans Sachs' warning to the people should they lose their holy art.

With $300,000 in the till and the assurance the house would not close, Mrs. Belmont moved on to organize the Metropolitan Opera Guild. In less than four months she had 2,000 members. Today there are 105,000. Since its founding in 1935, the Guild has given the Metropolitan $12,800,000. It has sponsored 211 special matinee performances for students of high school age and under, to audiences totaling 828,750. Its magazine, *Opera News,* has the widest circulation of any periodical on opera in the world.

The next financial crisis came in 1940, when it became necessary for the Metropolitan Opera Association, the reorganization that grew out of the Depression, to buy the old house from the real estate company that had held title since 1883. The families who built and owned it and their descendants were dying off or scattering or just plain losing interest. The price was $1,400,000. One third of the money came from the surrender of bonds by sale or gift, another third from the Guild, which in five years had become a tower of strength, and a third from the radio audience. Without the continued loyalty and support of our nationwide audience, we very likely might not be in business today.

There was no general appeal for funds again until 1952–53, when we had to raise $1,250,000. During the late thirties the National Broadcasting Company had given us a weekly hour. One night Bidù Sayão and Armand Tokatyan were doing practically the entire first act of *La Bohème.* He sang the narrative, she in turn did "Mi chiamano Mimi," and together they were just launching into the duet when the music stopped dead. Milton Cross came on and in his famous pear-shaped tones said something to the effect, "Now you see what will happen if you don't send in your dollars." It worked so well that some genius remembered and thought it should be tried at an actual performance.

Eleanor Robson Belmont (above), who on December 13, 1978, celebrated her centenary, founded the Metropolitan Opera Guild in 1935 at the peak of the depression, banding together music-lovers—now over 105,000 in number—to the service of the Metropolitan Opera. The first woman in history to be elected to the Board of Directors, she arranged for dress rehearsals to be opened to Guild members, began the magazine Opera News, *which in 1979 spawned a sister publication,* Ballet News *(below), helped start the company's pension and welfare funds and, in 1952, invented the National Council. This far-sighted woman was among the first to champion the concept of a new Opera House, where a beautiful room on the Grand Tier now honors her name. Students at the old theater and new (top right) can follow scores at performances for a modest entrance fee, an outgrowth of special matinees for young people instituted by Mrs. Belmont in 1937. Student Look-ins followed in 1973 with Danny Kaye as host (bottom right), James Morris, Atsuko Azuma, Marcia Baldwin, Loretta Di Franco and Paul Plishka among the soloists he bantered with*

The Metropolitan Opera National Council came into being in 1952 at the behest of Eleanor Robson Belmont. Its many and varied programs do not overlap those of the Metropolitan Opera Guild, rather they complement them. The Council now has members in fifty states, Mexico, Canada and Australia. One of the major challenges on its work calendar is an annual Regional Auditions Program, which searches for outstanding vocal talent throughout the country, awarding cash prizes for study, with some winners going directly onto the roster of the Metropolitan Opera. One such singer was Justino Díaz (left), shown in 1963 receiving his contract from Mrs. Lewis E. Douglas of the Council, watched by fellow contestants Michael Trimble and Junetta Jones and four of that year's judges, John Gutman, Robert Herman, George Schick and Kurt Adler. The contest is a test of courage and ability for any young artist, as the expression of concentration on the face of one gifted entry, Debby Robert, reveals (below). Another important branch of the National Council is its Central Opera Service, a clearing house of information for opera-producing organizations. The COS publishes a news bulletin of interest to the professional and each year sponsors an annual conference at which leaders from regional opera companies gather to discuss problems and seek answers to solve them. The 1973 conference took place in New York at the Sheraton Hotel (top right), with all major opera directors of the nation involved. President of the National Council is Alexander Saunderson, shown at the 1973 conference with his wife and COS national chairman Elihu M. Hyndman (bottom right)

A worse moment couldn't have been picked—*Tristan und Isolde*, just as the curtain is about to rise on Act II. The radio audience didn't know whether Helen Traubel had fainted, Fritz Stiedry had collapsed, or what, and the scheme backfired. The switchboard was clogged with calls and telegrams, there were irate letters to the newspapers. Rudolf Bing's reaction was typical.

"Money-raising in this country is a special technique," he said. "This was recommended, and I felt I had to go along with it. My business is to spend money, not to raise it." He was also pretty good at the latter. He brought Mrs. Rockefeller, who before her marriage had been a successful concert pianist, more and more into the opera fold.

That same year Mrs. Belmont organized the National Council, which today boasts more than 856 members in fifty states. The Council sponsors and runs the national auditions, which begin in sixty-five districts of sixteen regions across the country and end with the finals in the Metropolitan Opera House each spring. Forty-five young singers have come to the Metropolitan through the auditions, among them Teresa Stratas and Justino Díaz, and as many more to other companies over the world.

The Central Opera Service, headed by Maria F. Rich, is also an arm of the National Council. It has records on 936 opera-producing units in this country and can give you the word on any one of them. This of course runs all the way from two performances a year with two pianos in the church basement to the big companies. Bruno Walter said, "The roots must be greater than the foliage." The COS can tell you where to get anything from a backdrop for *La Traviata* to the orchestra parts of *Amahl and the Night Visitors.*

The financial crunch in the wake of the move to the new house amounted to an additional deficit of $6 million. "Like moving from a cottage to a castle," said our director of finance at the time. Just as the cost of the house itself and Lincoln Center had run into increases nobody could have foreseen, there were unbudgeted jolts in the operation. Ticket prices were raised in midseason, slashes were effected in expenditures wherever possible, and we made it.

Ten years later, the season of 1976–77, it became necessary to raise $4,110,000 more than the $8,700,000 we had raised the previous season, an increase of nearly 50 percent. Again it was done. "There is an added cost to excellence," says Richard J. Clavell, our director of finance. His statement is

Richard J. Clavell (above), financial director of the Metropolitan Opera, and Marilyn Shapiro (below), the company's development and public affairs director. Despite an enormous annual deficit, the Metropolitan Opera recognizes a deep responsibility to its home community. One way the company has found to serve the public at large is an annual series of free concert-opera performances in New York City parks. The first took place on June 24, 1967, at Crocheron Park, Queens, with an audience of over 35,000 seated on the grass under the stars to hear Anna Moffo as Mimi and Sándor Kónya as Rodolfo in La Bohème. *Six subsequent events that summer at other parks in other boroughs set the general pattern, maintained to this day. The repertory has been varied, including* Don Giovanni, Fidelio, Fledermaus, Lucia di Lammermoor, Rigoletto, La Traviata, Il Trovatore, Aida, Cavalleria Rusticana, Pagliacci, Tosca, Madama Butterfly, Turandot, Carmen, Faust *and* Samson et Dalila. *Some of the most celebrated names on the roster have participated—Tucker, Scotto, Arroyo, MacNeil, Corelli, Merrill, Resnik, Peerce, Kirsten, Stratas, Cruz-Romo, Tozzi, Peters, and Dunn*

based on knowledge and experience. Before joining the Metropolitan, he was business manager for the Corporation for Public Broadcasting, and prior to that audit manager for Price Waterhouse & Company, for many years the Metropolitan's auditors. "It is impossible to perform opera in half time, or to use half the people called for by the score. As it is, we are operating on the minimum to satisfy the composer's intention as laid down in the music."

Mr. Clavell is a native of Bristol, England, but served in our Army from 1954 to 1956. After graduation from Hofstra College he took his master's degree in business administration from New York University. He plays a tough game of tennis and is a member of the board of governors and secretary of the West Side Tennis Club. He is a member of the executive committee and treasurer of the National Institute of Social Sciences.

The Metropolitan's improved fiscal health is due in large measure to Marilyn Shapiro, development and public affairs officer since 1977. She brought a wide range of experience to her Metropolitan responsibilities. For a year and a half she worked on the Rockefeller Brothers Fund Study for the Performing Arts. For three years she was assistant to Mayor John V. Lindsay and for two years research assistant to Alvin Toffler, author of *The Cultural Consumers,* which chronicled the cultural explosion of the sixties.

Miss Shapiro's most recent post before she joined the Metropolitan was administrative assistant to Representative Elizabeth Holtzman, which she filled for three years.

Graduating with highest honors in political science from Wellesley College, she had been elected to Phi Beta Kappa in her junior year. She won a Woodrow Wilson Fellowship from Columbia University and received her M.A. degree there. She has fulfilled all requirements for the Ph.D. degree except her dissertation.

Gifts from foundations amount to about 8 percent of the Metropolitan's budget, government support to a little more than six. In 1976–77 the Rockefeller Brothers Fund made us a grant of $1,500,000. Other foundations generous with us have been the Louis Calder, Mary Flagler Cary, Doherty, Ford, Andrew W. Mellon, Ambrose Monell, and Edward John Noble.

The most significant increase in contributions, however, has come from the government. In 1977 the $1,500,000 in funds to be matched was the largest single grant the National Endowment for the Arts had ever made, just as the million dollars it gave us in 1974 was the biggest up to that time. In 1977–78 the New York State Council on the Arts came through with $850,000 and the New York City Department of Cultural Affairs with $130,000.

The chancellor of a great university once said, "We have only what our friends give us." The same is true of the Metropolitan. An annual gift of $1,250 or more carries membership in the Patrons of the Metropolitan Opera and the appertaining privileges. We now have 700 patrons, whose average gifts a year come to $2,200 each. In all there are 155,000 individual contributors. The average gift is $25 each. They make up 19.1 percent of our expenses, corporations 2.9 percent. Truly the Metropolitan belongs to all America, and at the time of the 1974 grant from the National Endowment the New York *Times* paid the Metropolitan a unique compliment. An editorial hailed the company as "This national treasure"—an honor but also an awesome responsibility and a sacred trust.

AUDIENCE AND FUTURE

Julius Rudel on more than one occasion has made the surprising statement "I don't want everyone to like opera." Before you have picked yourself up off the floor from that one, the former director of the New York City Opera goes on to explain, "Art is not and never has been for everyone. It is for an elite. The wonder, the miracle of America is that such an elite exists, ready for discovery, in every class, race, religion, ethnic group, and even sex."

Once past the shock of Mr. Rudel's initial remark, my reaction was: he's lucky. Most emphatically not everyone likes opera. What's more, the time will never come when everyone does. We all have things we would rather die than have to face. Opera to some people heads the list. Most Presidents of the United States seem to have been in this category. When Rudolf Bing ever so deftly suggested to President Johnson he would like to see him at the opera—he didn't even phrase it as an invitation but as a question something like, "When may we hope . . ." etc.—L.B.J. literally laughed in his face. President Eisenhower attended a Washington opening, and President Ford two at Wolf Trap, but the first president to have heard a performance in the Metropolitan Opera House is Jimmy Carter.

I won't say with Mr. Rudel I don't want everyone to like opera. The facts take care of that. But I will say I want everyone at least to have the opportunity of choosing for himself. Once exposed, I have observed, few can resist what Franz Werfel calls the seductive muse.

The opening-night audience at the new Metropolitan Opera House, September 16, 1966 (right), and the entrance to the theater during the holiday season of 1978 (below). The two photographs span over a dozen years, a period that brought many problems and many changes to the company. In a recent report, Anthony A. Bliss, the Metropolitan Opera's executive director, wrote: "Strengthened quality of our artistic product and encouraging progress toward financial stability are the major achievements of the Metropolitan Opera. It is a warming affirmation to the entire company that efforts to improve our musical and dramatic values are appreciated by the audience. We look forward to new challenges, confident in our ability and resolve to lead the Metropolitan Opera successfully into its second century. Morale has never been higher. The company as a whole has responded to the excitement of new artistic directions. Everyone is putting forth the immense effort needed to maintain the highest performance standards in the world. The audience of the Metropolitan Opera expects, and deserves, no less."

Audiences for the future have been sought, groomed and developed since 1937, when the Metropolitan Opera Guild organized the first student performance at the old Opera House, an Aida *starring the renowned Elisabeth Rethberg. During the 1978–79 season the Guild's education department sponsored four other such performances*—Don Pasquale—*publishing a comprehensive Teacher's Guide about Donizetti and his comedy so that proper classroom study could precede the visit to the Opera House. Young people from neighboring schools also attended fifteen dress rehearsals of other works and director's rehearsals of four new productions. Combined, these programs brought more than 30,000 children to the Metropolitan under Guild auspices, with the grand total since the program's inception nearing 3,000,000*

The Metropolitan had a friend and patron, Virginia Perry, who came to us almost by accident, perhaps literally by an accident. She was a beautiful creature and a superb horsewoman from that lovely horse country in Ohio. Laid low by an illness or a spill, she began to tune in on our broadcasts, became a devoted listener, a loyal friend, a generous supporter.

Right with her in all this was her husband, Seborn. A minister I know told of a member of his flock who would say, "My religion is in my wife's name." There are countless similar cases in the arts. The route doesn't matter, just so they come. The most promising young American tenor today told me his urge to sing came from listening to Elvis Presley!

Mrs. Perry's husband was a big industrialist down in North Carolina—lumber, furniture, textiles, name it. They had come to Atlanta for our week there. He and I met in front of our hotel one midday somewhat the worse for wear from a late party the night before. It was not of the revels we spoke but the glory of the performance that had preceded them, which had given us cause to want to celebrate.

Instructing young audiences has been approached on many fronts by the education department of the Metropolitan Opera Guild. Among its teaching aids are color filmstrips of over fifty works in the current repertory. Those dealing with a season's student performances are sent gratis to participating schools. Colorful posters, with pertinent information on the composer and an opera's background, are distributed free to schools nationwide in conjunction with the PBS "Live from the Met" telecasts. Teachers in the New York area can enroll in a two-semester introductory course on opera and attend workshops at the Opera House focusing on specific aspects of opera. These explore ideas for presentation to students, seeking to make a young person's visit to the Metropolitan Opera both more rewarding and more meaningful

Eyes slightly narrowed in the bright sunlight of a Georgia spring, he said something I have never forgotten and never will. "There are millions of people in the world hungry for music who don't know what's wrong with them."

"Better than tranquilizers," Geroge R. Marek, former vice president of RCA, author and authority on opera, puts it. Martha Graham has other ideas: art doesn't soothe, America's greatest dancer has said—it shakes you up. The great thing about it is it can do both.

More and more people are discovering these truths. Support of the Metropolitan, we have seen, is at an all-time high in both ticket sales and contributions. Our free concerts in the city parks of New York attract 310,000. With ballet audiences numbering more than 400,000 in the spring and autumn, the Metropolitan is host to more than 1,000,000 persons just in the opera house in New York. We have been on radio nearly half a century and are adding television—to reach tens of millions. Public Broadcasting Service, which carried the Metropolitan's first telecast of a full-length opera from the new house, says it was "viewed by the largest audience ever gathered for the performance of a single opera." Encouraging as all this is, the base must be wider yet. Telecasts will become more frequent. Cassettes, video discs, and perhaps as yet unknown forms will come.

Private and foundation backing are forthcoming as never before, but there must be more and more government support. It isn't enough to say, "Let them as like it pay for it." Suppose that were the point of view on schools and colleges, libraries, hospitals, and parks. The arts have always been the measure of a nation's true worth. When you think of Greece you think of the Parthenon. Martha Graham quotes a Greek historian writing about a lost civilization, "They had no poets, so they died."

As we have seen in the preceding chapter, it is costly business. In the effort to stem the tide, the New York season was shortened by four weeks. New productions were canceled and both old and new ones cut back, short of cheating the composer and the public. Economy in every conceivable area is the rule, and still the bills go up.

We have seen there has been drastic reorganization in the administration of the Metropolitan. The same is true of the board of directors. New blood has been brought in. For the first time in its history, the Metropolitan Opera has a president who, in the words of Donal Henahan of the New York *Times,* is "capable of sitting down with professional musicians and playing the keyboard part in a Brahms piano quartet."

Frank E. Taplin is former president of the Cleveland Orchestra and the Cleveland Institute of Music and first president of the Chamber Music Society of Lincoln Center. He has an office in the opera house. Three days a week he spends there, and the others he is available in Princeton, where he and Mrs. Taplin make their home.

Man with a Mission was the headline on Henahan's interview with Taplin a few weeks after the latter's election as president. The article dwelt on Taplin's concern for the survival of the Metropolitan in "a society numbed by mediocrity and commercialism."

That touches a point. For nearly a century the Metropolitan has been the operatic standard-bearer, the pace-setter, the taste-maker in this country, the one to which others here and the major houses abroad must inevitably be compared. Harold Schonberg wrote of our new *Rigoletto*, "Opera at the Metropolitan's best, which means the best there is anywhere." David Lloyd, director of the Lake George Opera, formerly a leading tenor at the New York City Opera and a former Navy man, summed it up when he called the Metropolitan "our flagship."

You often hear the charge that opera is moribund, that nothing is being written of lasting value. The works of recent years which hold the stage are conspicuously few, but Richard Strauss in the early thirties gave the New York *Times* an interview which takes care of that. He said if not another note were written in the opera form we still had enough of a treasury that the art would not die. Each generation views a masterpiece through its own eyes, and nobody goes to *Hamlet* to see how it ends. Just as there are ever new ways and means to reveal the glories of Shakespeare, so there is always something to discover in Mozart and Verdi, Wagner and Puccini. "We are entrusted," Rudolf Bing said, "with the masterpieces it has taken three hundred years of genius to create."

Before we left the old house, Leonard Bernstein did a telecast on the outstanding series called "Omnibus" that the Ford Foundation sponsored.

A report from Frank E. Taplin (above), president of the Metropolitan Opera Association, issued in the spring of 1979, stated, "We hope that within the next few years we shall see the Federal government contributing a greater share toward support of the arts—all the arts—and not just the Metropolitan. If the costs of operating the Opera House, for example, were absorbed by government sources as they now are for the Metropolitan Museum of Art, among other important arts institutions, the Metropolitan Opera would recover more than three million dollars currently spent in running the Opera House. In a recent study of government support of the arts, commissioned by the Twentieth Century Fund, Professor Dick Netzer of New York University concludes that the Metropolitan Opera cannot survive on ticket income and contributions from the private sector alone. He states that government support for the Metropolitan Opera is essential and should not be based on arguments such as education, building new audiences, or special projects, but on the sole fact of merit. It is clear, however, that private philanthropy—individual, foundation and corporate—will and must remain the heart of the Metropolitan's financial support. As we look ahead beyond the immediate needs and challenges of the coming year to the company's 100th anniversary, during the 1983–84 season, we are taking steps to ensure the Metropolitan Opera's long-range artistic and financial stability. With the help of our loyal public, we shall fulfill our commitments to the next generation of Metropolitan Opera audiences."

When the Metropolitan Opera plays to a full house, the audience now often reaches across the country. The company's weekly radio series began nearly a half-century ago, at the end of the 1978–79 season having achieved a grand total of 779 broadcasts from the stage of the Opera House and various stops on its annual spring tour. The inaugural telecast of La Bohème, *on March 15, 1977, proved a supreme test both for the Metropolitan Opera and for the Public Broadcasting Service. The response by the public and press was so overwhelming that many subsequent "Live from the Met" telecasts were scheduled, all of which were funded by a major grant from Texaco, Inc. with additional grants from the National Endowment for the Arts and the Charles E. Culpeper Foundation. Through the 1978–79 season there have been eight such telecasts:* La Bohème, Rigoletto, Don Giovanni, *the double bill of* Cavalleria Rusticana *and* Pagliacci, Otello, The Bartered Bride, Tosca *and* Luisa Miller. *Over the years the broadcasts and telecasts have managed to touch millions of people who have never seen a performance at the Opera House, indeed, some who have never had the opportunity to attend an opera. Between the acts of the telecasts viewers are invited backstage into the magic world of opera where they can see the scenery changed, enjoy personal interviews with the performing artists, learn from biographical sketches by Francis Robinson of composers and historic singers, and other educational commentary. The country's gratitude and interest have been reflected in thousands of postcards and letters, many of which have contained contributions. The Metropolitan Opera has been called a national treasure, and rightly so. Much of its glory, after all, is as free as the air*

This particular Sunday afternoon was on opera, and Bernstein with his unique turn of phrase called it "What Makes Opera Grand." The text is published with some of his other scripts in his book *The Joy of Music.*

For his final example of what makes opera grand he chose the third act of *La Bohème*, when they are out there in the snow. He took the quartet: he had actors read it, and it was a jumble. Then he had singers sing it, and it came out one lovely flow of sound and meant everything.

He wasn't the first to do this. On the intermissions of our broadcasts we have had actors read the quartet from *Rigoletto* or the sextet from *Lucia*, and it's chaos; but when the singers take over, it's glorious. The point is that opera is the only art that can give you more than one emotion, even conflicting emotions, in one experience.

By these demonstrations we prove that drama can't do it. "People just can't speak simultaneously," Lenny said—"that is, if they want to be heard. But music accomplishes the miracle, because notes are born to sound together as words are not."

You can't do it in a novel; you can't even do it in a painting. My old aesthetics professor used to take *The Last Supper* and point out to us how skillfully Leonardo grouped the apostles down the table, because you can't take it all in at once.

"You see," Lenny says, as much a master of words as he is of notes, "music is something terribly special. It doesn't have to pass through the censor of the brain . . . It goes directly to the heart. This is really the crowning delight of opera," he goes on, "that in the very same moment we can experience conflicting passions, contrasting moods and separate events." And since this thing of looking down and being able to get it all at once is possible only to the gods, in such a moment we are raised to their level and become one with the gods.

And he carried it further. He took Mimi's farewell, which precedes the quartet. An actress read it. It goes something like this:

> Gather up the few things I left. In the drawer are the little gold ring and my prayerbook. Wrap everything up in an apron, and I'll send the porter around. But under the pillow there's the pink bonnet you bought me that night we first met. Keep it, if you like, to remember our love. And now goodbye, and no bitterness.

To read it took thirty-six seconds. Then he had a singer sing it: it took 210 seconds, but what seconds! The 210 didn't seem any longer than the thirty-six. In them time stopped. It was "both a moment and an eternity," and we were lifted into a new and better world.

Without saying I rest my case, that is my brief for the future of opera. The questions persist. How can we go on in the face of runaway inflation and cruelly spiraling costs? We can because we must. What can we do about new works? Make it worthwhile for young composers to write operas. As it stands today, the costs of production have become so great their chances of getting a hearing make it hardly worth the effort. They have become discouraged and shy away from writing on a big scale. The output has shrunk almost to the few commissioned pieces and chamber works for reduced forces. How can we find the new audience without which we can't survive?

My answer is, there is always somebody hearing *La Bohème* for the first time.

GENERAL MANAGERS

of the resident company at the Metropolitan Opera House

SEASONS	
1883–1884	Henry E. Abbey
1884–1885	Leopold Damrosch *(died 2/15/85)*
1885–1891	Edmund C. Stanton
1891–1892	Henry E. Abbey Maurice Grau John B. Schoeffel
(1892–1893)	*(season omitted due to fire)*
1893–1897	Henry E. Abbey *(died 10/17/96)* Maurice Grau John B. Schoeffel
(1897–1898)	*(season omitted due to Abbey's death and reorganization under Grau; guest season by Damrosch-Ellis Company)*
1898–1903	Maurice Grau
1903–1908	Heinrich Conried
1908–1910	Giulio Gatti-Casazza Andreas Dippel
1910–1935	Giulio Gatti-Casazza
1935–1950	Herbert Witherspoon *(died 5/10/35)* Edward Johnson
1950–1972	Rudolf Bing
1972–1973	Goeran Gentele *(died 7/18/72)* Schuyler G. Chapin *(Acting General Manager)*
1973–1975	Schuyler G. Chapin
1975–	Anthony A. Bliss, *Executive Director* James Levine, *Music Director* John Dexter, *Director of Production*

THE REPERTORY

OPERA	COMPOSER	METROPOLITAN PREMIERE DATE
Adriana Lecouvreur	Francesco Cilèa	11/18/07
L'Africaine	Giacomo Meyerbeer	12/7/88 (in German)
Die Ägyptische Helena	Richard Strauss	11/6/28 (U.S. premiere)
Aida	Giuseppe Verdi	11/12/86 (in German)
Alceste	Christoph Willibald von Gluck	1/24/41
Alessandro Stradella	Friedrich von Flotow	2/4/10
Amelia al Ballo	Gian Carlo Menotti	3/3/38 (in English)
L'Amico Fritz	Pietro Mascagni	1/10/94
L'Amore dei Tre Re	Italo Montemezzi	1/2/14 (U.S. premiere)
L'Amore Medico	Ermanno Wolf-Ferrari	3/25/14 (U.S. premiere)
Andrea Chénier	Umberto Giordano	3/7/21
Anima Allegra	Franco Vittadini	2/14/23 (U.S. premiere)
Antony and Cleopatra	Samuel Barber	9/16/66 (world premiere)
Arabella	Richard Strauss	2/10/55 (U.S. premiere)
Ariadne auf Naxos	Richard Strauss	12/29/62 (Prologue in English)
Ariane et Barbe-Bleue	Paul Dukas	3/29/11 (U.S. premiere)
Armide	Christoph Willibald von Gluck	11/14/10 (U.S. premiere)
Asrael	Alberto Franchetti	11/26/90 (in German) (U.S. premiere)
L'Assedio di Corinto	Gioacchino Rossini	4/7/75 (U.S. premiere)
Aufstieg und Fall der Stadt Mahagonny	Kurt Weill	11/16/79 (in English)
Un Ballo in Maschera	Giuseppe Verdi	12/11/89 (in German)
Der Barbier von Bagdad	Peter Cornelius	1/3/90 (U.S. premiere)
Il Barbiere di Siviglia	Gioacchino Rossini	11/23/83
Billy Budd	Benjamin Britten	9/19/78
Boccaccio	Franz von Suppé	1/2/31
La Bohème	Giacomo Puccini	12/26/00
Boris Godunov	Modest Mussorgsky	3/19/13 (in Italian) (U.S. premiere)
La Campana Sommersa	Ottorino Respighi	11/24/28 (U.S. premiere)
The Canterbury Pilgrims	Reginald De Koven	3/8/17 (world premiere)
Caponsacchi	Richard Hageman	2/4/37 (U.S. premiere)
Carmen	Georges Bizet	1/9/84 (in Italian)
Cavalleria Rusticana	Pietro Mascagni	12/30/91
La Cena delle Beffe	Umberto Giordano	1/2/26 (U.S. premiere)
Le Cid	Jules Massenet	2/12/97
Cleopatra's Night	Henry Hadley	1/31/20 (world premiere)
I Compagnacci	Primo Riccitelli	1/2/24 (U.S. premiere)
Les Contes d'Hoffmann	Jacques Offenbach	1/11/13
Le Coq d'Or	Nikolai Rimsky-Korsakov	3/6/18 (in French) (U.S. premiere)
Così Fan Tutte	Wolfgang Amadeus Mozart	3/24/22 (U.S. premiere)
Crispino e la Comare	Luigi and Federico Ricci	1/18/19
Cyrano de Bergerac	Walter Damrosch	2/27/13 (world premiere)
La Dame Blanche	François Boieldieu	2/13/04 (in German)
La Damnation de Faust	Hector Berlioz	12/7/06
Death in Venice	Benjamin Britten	10/18/74 (U.S. premiere)
Dialogues des Carmélites	Francis Poulenc	2/5/77 (in English)
Diana von Solange	Ernst II, Duke of Saxe-Coburg Gotha	1/9/91 (U.S. premiere)
Dinorah	Giacomo Meyerbeer	1/29/92
Don Carlos	Giuseppe Verdi	12/23/20 (in Italian)
Don Giovanni	Wolfgang Amadeus Mozart	11/28/83
Don Pasquale	Gaetano Donizetti	1/8/00
Don Quichotte	Jules Massenet	4/3/26
Donna Juanita	Franz von Suppé	1/2/32
Le Donne Curiose	Ermanno Wolf-Ferrari	1/3/12 (U.S. premiere)
Duke Bluebeard's Castle	Béla Bartók	6/10/74 (in English)
Elaine	Herman Bemberg	12/17/94 (U.S. premiere)
Elektra	Richard Strauss	12/3/32
L'Elisir d'Amore	Gaetano Donizetti	1/23/04
The Emperor Jones	Louis Gruenberg	1/7/33 (world premiere)
Die Entführung aus dem Serail	Wolfgang Amadeus Mozart	11/29/46 (in English)
Ernani	Giuseppe Verdi	1/28/03
Ero e Leandro	Luigi Mancinelli	3/10/99 (U.S. premiere)
Esclarmonde	Jules Massenet	11/19/76
Eugene Onegin	Peter Ilich Tchaikovsky	3/24/20 (in Italian) (U.S. premiere)
Euryanthe	Carl Maria von Weber	12/23/87 (U.S. premiere)

OPERA	COMPOSER	METROPOLITAN PREMIERE DATE
The Fair at Sorochintsy	Modest Mussorgsky	11/29/30 (in Italian) (U.S. premiere)
Falstaff	Giuseppe Verdi	2/4/95 (U.S. premiere)
La Fanciulla del West	Giacomo Puccini	12/10/10 (world premiere)
Faust	Charles Gounod	10/22/83 (in Italian)
La Favorite	Gaetano Donizetti	11/29/95 (in Italian)
Fedora	Umberto Giordano	12/5/06 (U.S. premiere)
Fernand Cortez	Gasparo Spontini	1/6/88 (in German) (U.S. premiere)
Fidelio	Ludwig van Beethoven	11/19/84
La Fille du Régiment	Gaetano Donizetti	1/6/02
Die Fledermaus	Johann Strauss	2/16/05
Der Fliegende Holländer	Richard Wagner	11/27/89
La Forza del Destino	Giuseppe Verdi	11/15/18
Fra Diavolo	Daniel François Auber	2/5/10
Fra Gherardo	Ildebrando Pizzetti	3/21/29 (U.S. premiere)
Francesca da Rimini	Riccardo Zandonai	12/22/16 (U.S. premiere)
Die Frau ohne Schatten	Richard Strauss	10/2/66
Der Freischütz	Carl Maria von Weber	11/24/84
Germania	Alberto Franchetti	1/22/10 (U.S. premiere)
Gianni Schicchi	Giacomo Puccini	12/14/18 (world premiere)
La Gioconda	Amilcare Ponchielli	12/20/83 (U.S. premiere)
I Gioielli della Madonna	Ermanno Wolf-Ferrari	12/12/25
Giovanni Gallurese	Italo Montemezzi	2/19/25 (U.S. premiere)
Das Goldene Kreutz	Ignaz Brüll	11/19/86 (U.S. premiere)
Götterdämmerung	Richard Wagner	1/25/88 (U.S. premiere)
Goyescas	Enrique Granados	1/28/16 (world premiere)
Guillaume Tell	Gioacchino Rossini	11/28/84 (in German)
La Habanera	Raoul Laparra	1/2/24
Hamlet	Ambroise Thomas	3/10/84 (in Italian)
Hänsel und Gretel	Engelbert Humperdinck	11/25/05
L'Heure Espagnole	Maurice Ravel	11/7/25
Les Huguenots	Giacomo Meyerbeer	3/19/84 (in Italian)
In the Pasha's Garden	John Laurence Seymour	1/24/35 (world premiere)
Iphigénie en Tauride	Christoph Willibald von Gluck	11/25/16 (in German) (U.S. premiere)
Iris	Pietro Mascagni	12/6/07
The Island God	Gian Carlo Menotti	2/20/42 (world premiere)
L'Italiana in Algeri	Gioacchino Rossini	12/5/19
Jenufa	Leoš Janáček	12/6/24 (in German) (U.S. premiere)
Jonny Spielt Auf	Ernst Křenek	1/19/29 (U.S. premiere)
La Juive	Fromental Halévy	1/16/85 (in German)
Julien	Gustave Charpentier	2/26/14 (U.S. premiere)
Khovanshchina	Modest Mussorgsky	2/16/50 (in English)
The King's Henchman	Deems Taylor	2/17/27 (world premiere)
Die Königin von Saba	Karl Goldmark	12/2/85 (U.S. premiere)
Königskinder	Engelbert Humperdinck	12/28/10 (world premiere)
Lakmé	Léo Delibes	2/22/92
The Last Savage	Gian Carlo Menotti	1/23/64 (U.S. premiere)
The Legend	Joseph Breil	3/12/19 (world premiere)
Linda di Chamounix	Gaetano Donizetti	3/1/34
Lobetanz	Ludwig Thuille	11/18/11 (U.S. premiere)
Lodoletta	Pietro Mascagni	1/12/18 (U.S. premiere)
Lohengrin	Richard Wagner	11/7/83 (in Italian)
Loreley	Alfredo Catalani	3/4/22
Louise	Gustave Charpentier	1/15/21
Lucia di Lammermoor	Gaetano Donizetti	10/24/83
Lucrezia Borgia	Gaetano Donizetti	12/5/04
Luisa Miller	Giuseppe Verdi	12/21/29
Lulu	Alban Berg	3/18/77
Die Lustigen Weiber von Windsor	Otto Nicolai	3/9/00
Macbeth	Giuseppe Verdi	2/5/59
Madama Butterfly	Giacomo Puccini	2/11/07
Madame Sans-Gêne	Umberto Giordano	1/25/15 (world premiere)

OPERA	COMPOSER	METROPOLITAN PREMIERE DATE
Madeleine	Victor Herbert	1/24/14 (world premiere)
Madonna Imperia	Franco Alfano	2/8/28 (U.S. premiere)
The Man Without a Country	Walter Damrosch	5/12/37 (world premiere)
Manon	Jules Massenet	1/16/95
Manon Lescaut	Giacomo Puccini	1/18/07
Manru	Ignace Jan Paderewski	2/14/02 (U.S. premiere)
Marouf	Henri Rabaud	12/19/17 (U.S. premiere)
Martha	Friedrich von Flotow	3/14/84 (in Italian)
Il Matrimonio Segreto	Domenico Cimarosa	2/25/37 (in English)
Mefistofele	Arrigo Boito	12/5/83
Die Meistersinger von Nürnberg	Richard Wagner	1/4/86 (U.S. premiere)
Merlin	Karl Goldmark	1/3/87 (U.S. premiere)
Merry Mount	Howard Hanson	2/10/34 (world premiere)
Messa da Requiem	Giuseppe Verdi	2/17/01
Messaline	Isidore de Lara	1/22/02 (U.S. premiere)
Mignon	Ambroise Thomas	10/31/83 (in Italian)
Mireille	Charles Gounod	2/28/19
Mona	Horatio Parker	3/14/12 (world premiere)
Mona Lisa	Max von Schillings	3/1/23 (U.S. premiere)
Mourning Becomes Electra	Marvin David Levy	3/17/67 (world premiere)
La Muette de Portici	Daniel François Auber	12/29/84 (in German)
Nabucco	Giuseppe Verdi	10/24/60
La Navarraise	Jules Massener	12/11/95 (U.S. premiere)
Norma	Vincenzo Bellini	2/27/90 (in German)
La Notte di Zoraima	Italo Montemezzi	12/2/31 (U.S. premiere)
Le Nozze di Figaro	Wolfgang Amadeus Mozart	1/31/94
Oberon	Carl Maria von Weber	12/28/18
L'Oiseau Bleu	Albert Wolff	12/27/19 (world premiere)
L'Oracolo	Franco Leoni	2/4/15 (U.S. premiere)
Orfeo ed Euridice	Christoph Willibald von Gluck	12/30/91
Otello	Giuseppe Verdi	1/11/92
Pagliacci	Ruggiero Leoncavallo	12/11/93
Parsifal	Richard Wagner	12/24/03 (U.S. premiere)
Les Pêcheurs de Perles	Georges Bizet	1/11/96
Pelléas et Mélisande	Claude Debussy	3/21/25
La Perichole	Jacques Offenbach	12/21/56 (in English)
Peter Grimes	Benjamin Britten	2/12/48
Peter Ibbetson	Deems Taylor	2/7/31 (world premiere)
Philémon et Baucis	Charles Gounod	11/29/93
Phoebus and Pan	Johann Sebastian Bach	1/15/42 (in English)
The Pipe of Desire	Frederick S. Converse	3/18/10
Pique-Dame	Peter Ilich Tchaikovsky	3/5/10 (in German)
Der Polnische Jude	Karel Weiss	3/9/21 (in English) (U.S. premiere)
Le Preziose Ridicole	Felice Lattuada	12/10/30 (U.S. premiere)
Prodaná Nevěsta	Bedřich Smetana	2/19/09 (in German)
Prince Igor	Alexander Borodin	12/30/15 (in Italian) (U.S. premiere)
Le Prophète	Giacomo Meyerbeer	3/21/84 (in Italian)
I Puritani	Vincenzo Bellini	10/29/83
The Rake's Progress	Igor Stravinsky	2/14/53 (U.S. premiere)
La Reine Fiammette	Xavier Leroux	1/24/19 (U.S. premiere)
Das Rheingold	Richard Wagner	1/4/89 (U.S. premiere)
Rienzi	Richard Wagner	2/5/86 (U.S. premiere)
Rigoletto	Giuseppe Verdi	11/16/83
Robert le Diable	Giacomo Meyerbeer	11/19/83 (in Italian)
Le Roi de Lahore	Jules Massenet	2/29/24
Le Roi d'Ys	Edouard Lalo	1/5/22
Roméo et Juliette	Charles Gounod	12/14/91
La Rondine	Giacomo Puccini	3/10/28 (U.S. premiere)
Der Rosenkavalier	Richard Strauss	12/9/13 (U.S. premiere)
Le Rossignol	Igor Stravinsky	3/6/26 (in French) (U.S. premiere)
Sadko	Nikolai Rimsky-Korsakov	1/25/30 (in French) (U.S. premiere)
Saint Elizabeth	Franz Liszt	1/3/18 (in English) (U.S. premiere)
Salammbô	Ernest Reyer	3/20/01

OPERA	COMPOSER	METROPOLITAN PREMIERE DATE
Salome	Richard Strauss	1/22/07 (U.S. premiere)
Samson et Dalila	Camille Saint-Saëns	2/8/95
Il Segreto di Susanna	Ermanno Wolf-Ferrari	12/13/12
Semiramide	Gioacchino Rossini	1/12/94
La Serva Padrona	Giovanni Battista Pergolesi	2/23/35
Shanewis	Charles Wakefield Cadman	3/23/18 (world premiere)
Siegfried	Richard Wagner	11/9/87 (U.S. premiere)
Il Signor Bruschino	Gioacchino Rossini	12/9/32 (U.S. premiere)
Simon Boccanegra	Giuseppe Verdi	1/28/32 (U.S. premiere)
Snegurochka	Nikolai Rimsky-Korsakov	1/23/22 (in French) (U.S. premiere)
La Sonnambula	Vincenzo Bellini	11/14/83
Suor Angelica	Giacomo Puccini	12/14/18 (world premiere)
Svanda Dudák	Jaromir Weinberger	11/7/31 (in German) (U.S. premiere)
Il Tabarro	Giacomo Puccini	12/14/18 (world premiere)
Tannhäuser	Richard Wagner	11/17/84
The Temple Dancer	John Adam Hugo	3/12/19 (world premiere)
Thaïs	Jules Massenet	2/16/17
Tiefland	Eugen d'Albert	11/23/08 (U.S. premiere)
Tosca	Giacomo Puccini	2/4/01 (U.S. premiere)
Die Tote Stadt	Erich Wolfgang Korngold	11/19/21 (U.S. premiere)
La Traviata	Giuseppe Verdi	11/5/83
Tristan und Isolde	Richard Wagner	12/1/86 (U.S. premiere)
Der Trompeter von Säkkingen	Viktor Ernst Nessler	11/23/87 (U.S. premiere)
Il Trovatore	Giuseppe Verdi	10/26/83
Les Troyens	Hector Berlioz	10/22/73
Turandot	Giacomo Puccini	11/16/26 (U.S. premiere)
Vanessa	Samuel Barber	1/15/58 (world premiere)
Il Vassallo di Szigeth	Antonio Smareglia	12/12/90 (in German) (U.S. premiere)
Les Vêpres Siciliennes	Giuseppe Verdi	1/31/74 (in Italian)
Versiegelt	Leo Blech	1/20/12 (U.S. premiere)
La Vestale	Gasparo Spontini	11/12/25 (in Italian)
La Vida Breve	Manuel de Falla	3/6/26 (U.S. premiere)
Le Villi	Giacomo Puccini	12/17/08 (U.S. premiere)
Violanta	Erich Wolfgang Korngold	11/5/27 (U.S. premiere)
Der Wald	Ethel Smyth	3/11/03 (U.S. premiere)
Die Walküre	Richard Wagner	1/30/85
La Wally	Alfredo Catalani	1/6/09 (U.S. premiere)
The Warrior	Bernard Rogers	1/11/47 (world premiere)
Werther	Jules Massenet	4/19/94
Der Widerspenstigen Zähmung	Hermann Götz	3/15/16
Wozzeck	Alban Berg	3/5/59 (in English)
Die Zauberflöte	Wolfgang Amadeus Mozart	3/30/00 (in Italian)
Zazà	Ruggiero Leoncavallo	1/16/20
Der Zigeunerbaron	Johann Strauss	2/15/06

All operas are listed under their original titles, with the exception of works originally in Russian or Hungarian. The language of the performance is given only if it was not sung in the original tongue.

PICTURE CREDITS

COLOR

© Beth Bergman 1979: *Tannhäuser* top left; *The Bartered Bride*
Frank Dunand: *Otello; La Bohème* far left, top center and bottom right; *Il Trittico; Tristan und Isolde; Der Rosenkavalier; Die Frau ohne Schatten; Orfeo ed Euridice; Die Zauberflöte; Le Nozze di Figaro; Fidelio; Hansel and Gretel; Carmen; Les Troyens; Boris Godunov; La Bohème* on dust jacket
Burt Glinn: view of auditorium from stage; *Carmen* rehearsals; ballet rehearsals top; lighting booth; onstage control board; auditorium on dust jacket
Henry Grossman: Sills costume fitting
James Heffernan: exterior of Opera House by day; view of auditorium facing stage; chandeliers; *Rigoletto; Aida; La Bohème* top right and bottom center; *Lohengrin; Tannhäuser* top right; *Aida* on dust jacket
Terry Hourigan: dust jacket; exterior of Opera House by night
© 1966 Donald A. Mackay/New York TIMES: cross-section drawing of backstage area of Opera House
Karl Roodman: box adjoining proscenium; costume shop
Henry Schneider: ballet rehearsal bottom; wig shop; wardrobe department
Wist Thorpe: *Tannhäuser* bottom left, top center and bottom right; Levine rehearsing; *Billy Budd*

BLACK AND WHITE

© Beth Bergman 1979: 40 bottom, 64 right, 65, 72 bottom, 73–75, 77 top, 78–79 far left, far right and bottom, 80 bottom, 83–85, 86 bottom, 87 top, 88–89, 92–93, 94–95 center top and bottom, 97, 99, 172, 176–77, 256–57, 263 top
Charles Biasiny: 217 top
Dean Brown: 185 top, 192, 253 top left and right, 254–55
The Cleveland Press: 238–39
M. A. Como: 147
Eugene Cook: 119 top, 120, 125, 149 bottom, 260 top
Culver Pictures, Inc.: 48 top right, 231 top
© Erika Davidson 1979: 59 top, 67, 81, 90, 94 top and bottom left, 95 top and bottom right, 96, 168 top, 170 top left, 171 bottom right, 173, 182 bottom, 211 top, 215 top right, 244–45, 247 top
Frank Dunand: 58 top left, 60 top, 64 left, 66 top, 68 bottom, 72 top, 76 top, 77 bottom, 82 top, 87 bottom, 128 top, 129, 130 top left, 133 bottom right, 134 left, 135 bottom left, 136, 140 bottom left, 141 top, 142 top right, 203 bottom, 259 top, 266
Ellinger: 122–23
Maurey Englander: 261
Sam Falk: 159 bottom
Fayer: 171 top right
Stan Fellerman: 41
Gerald Fitzgerald: 26 bottom, 35, 59 bottom, 116–17, 170–71 center top and bottom, 179 top and bottom, 180–81, 182 top, 183, 186, 193, 196–97, 200 bottom, 202 bottom, 204, 207 top, 212, 214 bottom left, center and right, 216, 223 top, 224–25, 246, 247 bottom, 251 top, 253 bottom, 263 bottom
John W. Freeman: 170 bottom left
Beverley Gallegos: 248 top, 249
Michael Geiger: 222, 223 bottom
Alexandre Georges: 16 bottom
Burt Glinn: 153 bottom
Michael Gold: 26 top, 28–29, 58 right, 126 bottom, 128 bottom, 138, 139 top, 143 bottom, 205, 213, 259 bottom
Irwin Goldstein: 16 top, 163
Joel Grill: 57 bottom
Henry Grossman: 124 bottom
Harvard Theatre Collection: 12, 14 bottom left, 42, 43 top, 45 top, bottom left and bottom right, 46–47, 48 bottom, 51 top, 100 top
James Heffernan: 78–79 top center, 82 bottom, 91, 98, 127, 188–89, 242–43, 250 bottom
Terry Hourigan: 130 top right and bottom right, 131, 133 left and top right, 134 bottom right, 135 top left and far right, 137, 139 bottom, 140 top left, top right, bottom right, 142 top left, 142 top
Carolyn Mason Jones: 86 top
Sedge LeBlang: 146 bottom, 150–51, 152 bottom, 153 top, 154 bottom
Paulus Leeser: 159 top right
Frank Lerner: 156 bottom
The Library of Congress: 15, 48 top left, 100 bottom, 101, 105 bottom right
© Lincoln Center for the Performing Arts, Inc.: 20 top, 21 top, 218
Harvey Lloyd: 13, 27, 31 top, 37, 39, 61, 121 top, 165 bottom, 265, 270
Alen MacWeeney: 155
Louis Mélançon: 31 bottom, 56, 76 bottom, 114, 119 bottom, 148, 158, 160–61, 164, 165 top, 166 bottom, 240 bottom
Metropolitan Opera Archives: 43 bottom, 44, 50, 51 bottom, 102 top, 103 top and bottom left, 104 bottom, 105 top, 110, 112 top, 113, 144, 146 top right, 152 top, 159 top left, 166 top, 229 top, 262 top
Metropolitan Opera Guild/*Opera News:* 14 top and bottom right, 16 center, 17, 24 bottom, 45 center right, 49, 52 top, 53, 57 top, 102 bottom, 103 bottom right, 104 top, 105 bottom left, 106–9, 111, 112 bottom, 115, 118 bottom, 130 bottom left, 134 top right, 137 top, 141 bottom, 146 top left, 157, 229 bottom, 230, 231 bottom, 234–35, 237 bottom, 240 top, 258
Duane Michals: 168 bottom, 169
Gjon Mili: 154 top, 174 bottom
© Jack Mitchell 1979: 126 top
Courtesy of Mrs. Frances Moore: 38 top, 56
Museum of the City of New York: 228
© Arnold Newman 1979: 18–19
The New York Times, Inc.: 201, 207 bottom, 250 top
Louis Péres: 248 bottom
Frank Reed: 238–39
Günter R. Reitz: 206
Gary Renaud: 34 bottom, 54 bottom, 55, 60 bottom, 69, 124 top, 162, 167, 195, 198–99, 210, 219 bottom, 269
Courtesy of Francis Robinson: 52 bottom, 156 top, 232–33, 237 top, 252
Karl Roodman: 34 top, 219 top
Ed Rooney: 54 top
Arnold Rosenberg: 175, 178 top and bottom, 184, 185 bottom, 187, 190–91, 194, 202 top, 203 top, 208–9, 211 bottom, 214 top left and center, 220–21, 226 bottom
Henry Schneider: 58 bottom left, 174 top, 200 top, 260 bottom
Paul Seligman: 226 top, 241
Bob Serating: 22 bottom, 23 top, 25, 30, 36 top, 218
E. Fred Sher: 36 bottom, 66 bottom, 68 top, 262 bottom
Adrian Siegel: 118 top
Vernon L. Smith: 38 bottom, 62–63, 70–71
Christian Steiner: 20 bottom
© Susanne Faulkner Stevens 1979: 21 top and center, 32, 264, 268
Ezra Stoller Associates: 20 top, 24 top right
William Stuart: 23 bottom
Martha Swope: 149 top, 251 bottom
Barney Taxel: 121 bottom
Katrina Thomas: 24 top left
Courtesy of Wally Toscanini: 145
United States Information Service: 33
Vogel: 22 top

INDEX

NOTE: *italicized numbers indicate photographs. Page numbers followed by c direct the reader to the color inserts.*

Abbado, Claudio, 127
Abbey, Henry E., 43, *43,* 44, 46–47, 258
Abramovitz, Max, 23
Academy of Music, 12, *12,* 48
Adler, Kurt, 185, *260*
Adriana Lecouvreur, 67, 99, 117, 162, 192
Aeschylus, 174
Aida, 43, 51, *64c,* 80, 83, 107, 112, 117, *120,* 121, 124, 131, 137, 141, 147, 148, 162, 181, 182, 186, 189, 211, 224, 229, 252, 253, 258, 263, 266
Ailey, Alvin, 193, *193c*
Albanese, Licia, 107, 115, 183
Alceste (Alcestis), 137
Alda, Frances, 51, 132
Alice Tully Hall, 19, 23
Allen, Ivan, 192, *192, 193c*
Allen, Reginald, 20, 21, *21,* 54, 56
Alliance Studios, 196
Alonso, Alicia, 248, *249*
Alten, Bella, *230*
Alva, Luigi, 167, 168
Alvary, Max, 44, *45,* 46, 103
Amahl and the Night Visitors, 118
Amara, Lucine, *20,* 21, *242,* 243
Amato, Pasquale, 138, *144*
Amberson Productions, 58
Ambrose Monell Foundation, 263
Amelia al Ballo, 158
American Ballet Theatre, 57, 163, 176, 192, 193, 202, 248
American Conductors Project, 43
American Export Company, 253
American Federation of Musicians, 181
American Institute of Musical Studies, 212
Amore dei Tre Re, L', 52, 107, 132
Amparán, Belén, 60, 61
Anderson, Judith, 86
Anderson, Marian, 54, 137, *138,* 252
André, Georges, 176, *177,* 243
Andrea Chénier, 117, 137, 142, 182, 257
Andrew H. Mellon Foundation, 263
Andrey, Pauline, *188,* 189
Anni, Anna, 72
Anouilh, Jean, 34
Anthony, Charles, 118
Antony and Cleopatra, 38, 60, *61,* 68, 118, 128, 131, 167, 207, 211, 223
Aoyama, Yoshio, 158, 164
Apres-midi d'un Faune, L' (ballet), 193
Arabella, 56, 118, 121
Aragall, Giacomo, 86, *86*
Arditi, Luigi, *44*
Ariadne auf Naxos, 121, 138, 147, 158, 162
Ariane et Barbe-Bleue, 107
Armistead, Horace, 154
Aronson, Boris, 62, 168, *169,* 241
Arroyo, Martina, 72–76, 263
Arts Appreciation, 241
Art Students League, 196
Ashenden, Arthur, 224, *225*
Assedio di Corinto, L', 76, *78–79,* 80, 83, 121, 168, 173, 224
Atherton, James, *172,* 173
Atlanta Ballet, 189
Atlantida, 124
Auchincloss, Louis, 46
"Auditions of the Air," 111
Aufstieg und Fall der Stadt Mahagonny, 99
Australian Opera, 127
Avery Fisher Hall, 19, *23,* 25, *26, 32c,* 38, 124
Azuma, Atsuko, 258, 259

Babes in Toyland, 44
Baccaloni, Salvatore, 112
Bach, Johann Sebastian, 25, 32, 37, 112
Bachianas Brasileiras No. 5 (Villa-Lobos), 137
Bacquier, Gabriel, *65, 92*
Baer, Joseph, *204*
Bakst, Harry, 202, *203*
Bakst, Léon, 173
Balanchine, George, 23, 176
Baldani, Ruza, *240c*
Baldwin, Billy, 37
Baldwin, Marcia, *65c,* 258, 259
Ballet Nacional de Cuba, 248
Ballet News, 258
Ballet Russe de Monte Carlo, 193, 248
Ballo in Maschera, Un, 43, 58, 112, 137, 138, 158, 211, 252
Bamboschek, Giuseppe, *232,* 235
Bampton, Rose, 111
Bancroft, Anne, 92
Barber, Samuel, 38, *39,* 60, 118, 128, 131, 158
Barbiere di Siviglia, Il, 131, 157, 181, 240, 252
Barbieri, Fedora, 112, *113*
Barnard College, 251
Baronova, Irina, 193
Barrault, Jean-Louis, 168, *168*
Barrymore, Ethel, 86
Bartered Bride, The, 43, 104, 112, 211, 223, *257c,* 271
Baryshnikov, Mikhail, 192, 248, 249
Baum, Kurt, 112
Bavarian State Opera, 162
Bayreuth Festival, 15, 48, 92, 99, 104, 115, 121, 143, 168, 173
Beaton, Cecil, 62, 64, 158, 164, *164*
Beau Danube, Le (ballet), 193
Beaumarchais, Pierre Augustin Caron de, 240
Bedford, Steuart, 80
Beecham, Sir Thomas, 53, 112, *113,* 115
Beethoven, Ludwig van, 32, 58, 108, 112, 121, 137, 143, 241
Belasco, David, 144, 145, 204
Bellini, Vincenzo, 12, 68, 80, 83
Bell Laboratories, 38
Belluschi, Pietro, 23
Belmont, Eleanor Robson (Mrs. August), ix, 31, 37, 52, 258, *258,* 260; Room, *34,* 37, 143
Belong (ballet), 189
Bennington College, 251
Benois, Alexander, 173
Benois, Nicola, 173
Benvenuto Cellini, 43
Bérard, Christian, 148
Berg, Alban, 37, 83, 158
Berger, Erna, 251
Bergman, Ingmar, 158
Berini, Mario, *234,* 235
Berlin, Irving, 137
Berlin Opera, 158
Berlin Philharmonic, 115
Berlioz, Louis Hector, 43, 58, 76, 141, 168, 256
Berman, Eugene, 121, *146,* 147, 157, 202
Bernheimer, Martin, 253, *254*
Bernstein, Leonard, 20, 21, *21, 33,* 58, 76, 103, 124, *124,* 127, 164, 167, *192c,* 252, 268, 271
Berry, Walter, 62, *97c,* 168, *170–71*
Billy Budd, 43, 99, 179, 201, 202, *257c*
Bing, Lady, *38*
Bing, Rudolf, *20,* 21, 25, 31, 32, *38,* 53–54, *55,* 56, 60, 72, 111, 112, 115, 116, 117, 118, 124, 127, 132, 138, 141, 147, 148, 154, *156,* 157, 158, 164, *164,* 176, 212, 224, 241, 251, 252, 253, 256, 257, 258, 260, 268
Bizet, Georges, 21, 121, 243, 256
Bjoerling, Jussi, 112, *113,* 137, 154
Blass, Robert, *230*
Blayman, Herbert, 176, *177*
Blegen, Judith, 62, 72, *73,* 83, *180,* 181, *240c, 241c*
Blein, Sylvia, 142
Bliss, Anthony A., ix, 19, *19,* 40, *41,* 54, 56, 57, 244, 264
Bliss, Cornelius N., 40, 137, 258
Bliss, Lillie, 40
Bluejackets Choir, 185
Bodanzky, Artur, 51, 108–11, *108,* 143
Bohème, La, 47, 59, 60, *65c,* 91, 107, 116, 118, 127, 132, 143, 243, 252, 253, 257, 263, 271
Böhm, Karl, 62, 67, 68, 72, 121, *122–23,* 224
Boky, Colette, *257c*
Bolshoi Ballet, 248
Bolshoi Opera, 80, 248
Bonynge, Richard, 76, 86, *126,* 127
Book-of-the-Month-Club, 253
Bori, Lucrezia, ix, 37, 108, 131, 132, 143, *143,* 198, *232–33,* 235, 240, 258
Boris Godunov, 43, 56, 60, 62, 80, 107, 115, 118, 127, 132, 173, 185, 196, 211, 226 *256c*
Borkh, Inge, 263
Boston Symphony Orchestra, 111, 124, 141
Boucher, Gene, *65*
Brahms, Johannes, 108, 268
Brandt, Marianne, 44
Branzell, Karin, 52, *108,* 141
Brendl, Wolfgang, *240c*
Britten, Benjamin, 58, 60, 80, 257
Broiles, Melvyn, 176, *177*
Bronson, Michael, *58,* 59
Brook, Peter, 111, 154, 157
Brooklyn College, 54
Brooks (costumer), 211
Brownlee, John, 132, 152, *153,* 236, *237*
Brubaker, E. Scott, 176, *177*
Bruhn, Erik, *248*
Buchter, Jacob, 217
Buffalo Symphony Orchestra, 124
Bugler, Marcus, *188,* 189, *190–91*
Bumbry, Grace, 68, *69,* 72, 76, *96c,* 99, *240c*
Burghauser, Hugo, 117–18
Burg Theater (Vienna), 48
Busch, Fritz, 53, 115, *115*
Butler, Henry, 163, 168, *169*
Byrd-Hoffman Foundation, 251

Caballé, Montserrat, 59, 62, *68,* 72, *74–75*
Cacoyannis, Michael, 62, 168, *169*

Caine, Charles, 207, *211, 224c*
Calamari, Christina, 212, *212,* 217
Calamari, Rose, 212, *224c*
Caldwell, Sarah, 83, 127, *127*
Callas, Maria, 44, 54–55, *56,* 57, 67–68, 72, 112, 158
Callegari, Arthur, 212
Callegari, Victor, 212, *214–15*
Calvé, Emma, *46,* 132, 141
Cammarota, Paul, 176, *177*
Campana Sommersa, La, 111
Campanini, Cleafonte, 43, 100, *101,* 102
Campanini, Italo, *42,* 43, 102
Campione, Eugene, *180,* 181–82
Campione, Mrs. Eugene, 181
Canadian Opera Company, 86
Capobianco, Tito, 99
Capoul, Victor, *228,* 229
Cappiello, Stanley, 196, *197*
Carl Rosa Opera Company, 212
Carlson, Lenus, 86
Carmen, 21, 33, 43, 57, 58, 60, 76, 102, 107, 111, 112, 116, 124, 127, 137, 152, *154,* 181, *192c,* 193, 229, 230, 235, 243, 252, *256c,* 263
Carnegie, Andrew, 103
Carnegie Hall, 19, 103
Carnegie Tech, 189
Carreras, José, 212, *215*
Carson, Margaret, 53
Carter, Jimmy, 264
Carter, John, 236, *237*
Caruso, Enrico, 40, 47–48, *49,* 51, 62, 99, 104, 107, 108, 128, 131, 132, 137, 138, *142,* 143, *144,* 217, 230, *230, 231,* 240
Caruso, Mrs. Enrico, 137, 141
Casamassa, Angelo, 217
Casamassa, John, 217, *224c,* 236, *237*
Casei, Nedda, *242,* 243
Cassidy, Claudia, 54, 112, 168
Castle Garden, 143
Catalani, Alfredo, 107
Cavalleria Rusticana, 21, 68, *69,* 124, 167, 185, 263, 271
Cehanovsky, George, 52, 132, 158, 173
Cene delle Beffe, La, 111
Cenerentola, La, 158, 162–63
Central Opera Service (COS), 260
Century Lighting Company, 173
Cervini, Jennie, 212, 236, *237*
Cesbron, Jacques, *188,* 189
Cézanne, Paul, 40
Chagall, Marc, 26, *30,* 31–33, 34, 62, 198, 240; murals, *32c*
Chaliapin, Fedor, 62, 132, *141*
Chamber Music Society of Lincoln Center, 23, 268
Chapin, Schuyler G., 57–59
Charles E. Culpeper Foundation, 271
Charlottenburg Opera (Berlin), 56
Charpentier, Gustave, 112, 132
Cheek, John, *257c*
Chekhov, Anton, 158
Cherubini, Luigi, 56
Chicago, *see* Lyric Opera (Chicago)
Chicago Auditorium, 100, 102
Chicago *Daily News,* 236
Chicago Symphony Orchestra, 43, 115
Chicago *Tribune,* 54
Chookasian, Lili, *65c*
Chramer, Fred, 198
Christians, Mady, 48
Christians, Rudolf, 48
Christina, Princess, 137
Chubu Nippon network (Japan), 243
Churchill, Winston, 52
Cilèa, Francesco, 192
Cimara, Pietro, 183
Cincinnati College-Conservatory of Music, 181
Cincinnati May Festival, 43
Cincinnati Opera, 127
Cincinnati Symphony Orchestra, 43, 56, 118, 181
City Auditorium (Houston), 236
City Center (New York), 224
Clavell, Richard J., 59, 260, 263, *263*
Cleva, Fausto, 43, *116–17,* 117–18, 142, 185
Cleva, Mrs. Fausto, *116–17,* 117–18
Cleveland Institute of Music, 268
Cleveland Orchestra, 43, 111, 115, 121, 268
Cluytens, André, 121
Coleman, Emily, 53
Colonnello, Attilio, 62, 64, 68, 168
Columbia Artists Management, 58
Columbia Concerts Symphonietta, 181
Columbia Literary Columns (publication), 104
Columbia Records, 58, 252–53
Columbia University, 38, 59, 83, 247, 263
Colzani, Anselmo, 167
Combat, The (ballet), 192
Comédie Française, 168
Conlon, James, 118, 127
Connolly, James, 204, *205*
Conreid, Heinrich, 47, 48–51, *48,* 142
Conried, Richard G., 142
Conservatoire (ballet), 248
Consul, The, 118
Contes d'Hoffmann, Les, 76, *76,* 111, 127, 157
Coq d'Or, Le, 111, 112
Coquelin, 168
Corelli, Franco, *56,* 57, 62, *63,* 68, *69,* 72, *72,* 118, 138, *164,* 168
Corena, Fernando, 72, *73,* 76, *77,* 121, 252
Cornell, Katharine, 80, 121, 148
Così Fan Tutte, 148–52, *152, 153,* 181
Cossotto, Fiorenza, 68
Costa, Ricardo, 189, *190–91*
Cotrubas, Ileana, *64c,* 92
Court Opera (Vienna), 108
Covent Garden, *see* Royal Opera House (Covent Garden)
Coward, Noël, 164
Crapster, Thaddeus, *19*
Creation, The (Haydn), 111
Crespin, Régine, 82, 86, 121
Crofoot, Alan, *257c*
Cross, Milton, *252,* 253, 258
Cruz-Romo, Gilda, *65c,* 263
Curtis Institute of Music, 56, 138, 181
Cushing, Mary Watkins, 107
Cuvilliés Theater (Munich), 33

Dali, Salvador, 154, 157
Dalis, Irene, *65c,* 162, *162–63*
Daly, Ray C., *19*
Damrosch, Frank, 102, 111
Damrosch, Leopold, 44, *45,* 46, 102, 103, 111
Damrosch, Walter, 44–46, 102–3, *102,* 111
Damrosch Park, *23, 32c,* 103
Danilova, Alexandra, 248
Danise, Giuseppe, 137, *232–33,* 235
Daphne, 121
Darmstadt, 56, 158
Da Vinci, Leonardo, 271
Davis, Colin, 62, 127
Davis, Ivan, 253, *254–55*
Davis, Peter G., 92
Dayton Opera, 189
Death in Venice, 58, 80, *80*
De Basil, Colonel W., 193, 248
Debussy, Claude, 99, 100, 124
Defrère, Désiré, *112,* 113, *115,* 147, *234,* 235
Deiber, Paul-Emile, 68, 168, 173
Della Casa, Lisa, 121
Dell'Orefice, Antonio, *234,* 235
Del Monaco, Mario, 252
De los Angeles, Victoria, 141, 154, 251
De Luca, Giuseppe, 60, *130,* 131, 137
De Mille, Agnes, 193
De Paolis, Alessio, 118, 164, *165, 234,* 235, 252
De Paul, Judith, *97c*
De Reszke, Édouard, 47, *228,* 229
De Reszke, Jean, *46,* 47, 104, *228,* 229
De Santis, Thomas, 202, *203*
Destinn, Emmy, 51, *144*
Dexter, John, 40, *40,* 43, 58–59, 64, 80, 83, 86, 91, 92, 99, 147, *172,* 173, 257
Diaghilev, Serge, 173, 193
Diaghilev Ballet, 111, 124, 176
Dialogues des Carmélites, 43, *82,* 83, 86, 91, 99, 257
Diana von Solange, 46
Diaz, Edward, 224, *225*
Díaz, Justino, 59, 76, *78–79,* 83, 92, 168, *170–71, 240c, 260*
Diaz, Stephen, 224, *225*
Dietz, Howard, 148, 154
Diffen, Ray, 92, *211*
Di Franco, Loretta, *242,* 243, 258, *259*
Dinesen, Isak, 158
Dinkaloo, John, 23
Di Nunzio, Guido, *224*
Dippel, Andreas, *51*
D-minor Piano Concerto (Mendelssohn), 43
Dobriansky, Andrij, *257c*
Doe, Doris, 112, *113*
Doherty, Grace Raroin, 32
Doherty Charitable Foundation, 32, 263
Domingo, Placido, 59, 62, *64, 64c,* 68, 76, *76,* 92, 176, *177*
Don Carlo, 72, 76, 80, 92, *94–95,* 112, 115, 127, 132, 147, 148, 150–51, 192, 211, 251, 256
Dönch, Karl, *241c*
Don Giovanni, 20, 38, 47, 105, 112, 121, 131, 137, 147, 263, 271
Donizetti, Gaetano, 91, 168, 266
Don Pasquale, 43, 92, *93,* 107, 121, 148, 168, 173, 211, 266
Dooley, William, 97
Douglas, Mrs. Lewis E., *260*
Downes, Edward, 253
Dresden Opera, 115, 211
Dresser, Carey, 189, *190–91*
Dreyer, Leslie, *180,* 181
Dudley, William, 257
Dufy, Raoul, 34, 196, 219
Dukas, Paul, 107

Dunn, Mignon, 72, 80, *82,* 86, 91, *96, 212,* 263
Duplessis, Joseph Sifrede, 138
Dupont, Jacques, 168
Duse, Eleonora, 68
Dusenberry, Sigurd, 131
Dvořák, Antonin, 104

Eames, Emma, *47,* 132, *133*
Eastern Airlines, 67, 253
Eaves, 211
Ebert, Carl, 57, 158, *159*
Ecuitorial (dance), 251
Eddy, Nelson, 118
Edinburgh Festival, 53–54, 58, 112
Edward John Noble Foundation, 263
Edwards, Carlo, *232–33,* 235
Eglevsky Ballet, 189
Einstein on the Beach, 250, 251
Eisenhower, Dwight D., 19, 264
Eleanor Belmont Room, *34,* 37, 143
Elektra, 97c, 168
Elias, Rosalind, 60, *61,* 62, *97c,* 158, 167, *240c, 241c*
Eliot, T. S., 193
Elisir d'Amore, L', 62, 127, 162, 163, 181, 212
Elizabeth II, Queen, 54, 127
Elster, Reinhardt, *179*
Emmy Awards, 58
Emperor Jones, The, 132
Ernster, Dezso, *234,* 235
Ernst II, Duke, 46
Errolle, Ralph, 185
Esclarmonde, 86, 127, 158, 186, 257
Escoffier, Marcel, 72
Esquivel, Jorge, 248, *249*
Esterházy family, 147
Eugene Onegin, 60, 108, 118, 132, 157, 186
Evans, Maurice, 147
Everding, August, 72, 80, 91, 96, 173, *173,* 256
Ewing, Maria, 86

Fair Park Auditorium (Dallas), 236
Falla, Manuel de, 124
Falstaff, 124, 164–68, *166,* 181, 229
Fanciulla del West, La, 38, 117, 144, *144,* 168
Fancy Free (ballet), 193
Farbman Quartet, 181
Farley, Carole, *83, 84–85*
Farrar, Geraldine, 48, *48,* 104, *105,* 107–8, 132, 137, 141, 142–43, 204, 258
Faust, 12, 43, 44, 62, 102, 111, 121, 131, 147, 148, 154, 168, 189, 229, 263
Favorita, La, 90, 91, *91,* 99, 257
Feld, Eliot, 248
Fenn, Jean, *240c*
Festival of Two Worlds (Spoleto), 118, 127, 185
Fidelio, 31, 32, 68, 72, 105, 112, 127, 137, 168, 235, *241c,* 263
Fiedler, Johanna, 59
Fille du Regiment, La, 72, *73,* 173
Firebird, The (ballet), *248*
Firebird, The (Stravinsky), 31, 32
Fischer, Emil, 44, *45,* 103
Fisera, Vicki, 189, *190–91*
Fisher, J. William, 256
Fitzgerald, F. Scott, 131
Flagello, Ezio, 62, 148, *149*
Flagstad, Kirsten, 52, 54, 108, *109,* 112, 116, 128, 131, *137,* 141, 212
Fledermaus, Die, 132, 148, 154, 263
Fledermaus Variations (ballet), 189
Fliegende Holländer, Der, 98, 99, 116, 173, 257
Flotow, Friedrich von, 229
Flute of Pan (dance), 251
Foldi, Andrew, *240c, 257c*
Fontanne, Lynn, 157
Fonteyn, Margot, 162, 173, 193
Ford, Edward B., *194,* 196
Ford, Gerald, 264
Ford Foundation, 43, 263, 268
Fordham University, 19
Forrestal, James V., 59
Forza del Destino, La, 43, 112, 141, 142, *146,* 147, 183
Founders Hall, 34, 37, 128, 131, 138, *139,* 142, 143
Fox Theater, 226, *227*
Franko, Nahan, *230*
Franz Joseph, Emperor, 51
Frau ohne Schatten, Die, 60, 62, 68, *97c,* 121, 138, 162, 179, 196, 202, 212, 218, 224
Freischütz, Der, 168
Fremstad, Olive, 48, *48,* 51, 104, 107, *107,* 132, *134,* 137, 230
Freni, Mirella, 62, *62*
Friedman, Erick, 40
Frohman, Mae, *234,* 235
From the House of the Dead, 43
From the New World (Dvořák), 104

Gadski, Johanna, 47, 103, 131
Gaîté Parisienne, 157
Galli, Rosina, 51, 176
Galli-Curci, Amelita, 100, *130,* 131
Garden, Mary, *100,* 132, 143
Gatti-Casazza, Giulio, 16–19, 43, *50,* 51, 52, 53, 54, 107, 117, 131, 142, 143, 176
Gedda, Nicolai, 59, 72, *92,* 158, *240c, 257c*
Gemito, 131
Genovese, Alfred, 176, *177*
Gentele, Goeran, 57, *58,* 59, 76, 252, 256
Gentele, Marit, 57
Gérard, Rolf, 111, 148, *149,* 152, 154, 196, 240
German Dance Congress (1930), 168
German Theater (Prague), 56
Gesellschaft der Musikfreunde, 108
Ghazal, Edward, 185–86, *185*
Ghiaurov, Nicolai, 92, *94–95*
Giacomini, Giuseppe, 92, *94–95*
Giaiotti, Bonaldo, *64c,* 80, 91, *96c,* 99
Gianni Schicchi, 65c, 83, 92, 131, 201
Gibbs, Raymond, *65,* 99
Gibbs, Mrs. William Francis, *116–17*
Gigli, Beniamino, 142
Gilman, Lawrence, 99, 141–42
Gioconda, La, 43, *62, 63,* 86, 117, 158, 168, 189, 224
Giordano, Umberto, 111, 142
Giselle (ballet), 248, *249*
Gish, Dorothy, 196
Gish, Lillian, 196
Glass, Philip, 251
Glaz, Hertha, *234,* 235
Gleason, Michael, 189, *190–91*
Glossop, Peter, 72, *257c*
Gluck, Alma, 131
Gluck, Christoph Willibald von, 127, 131, 137, 138, 141, 168, 240
Glyndebourne Festival, 53, 148, 158, 212
Gniewek, Raymond, 99, *180,* 181
Goelet, Francis, 256
Goelet, Robert Walton, 256
Goerlitz, Ernest, *230*
Goethe, Johann Wolfgang von, 48, 111, 158
Gogorza, Emilio de, 132, 141
Golczewski, Magdalena, 176, *177*
Goldberg, Arthur J., 256
Goldmark, Karl, 230
Goldovsky, Boris, *253*
Goodloe, Robert, *172,* 173, *257c*
Goodman, Saul, 182
Goranson, Paul, *201*
Gordon, Ruth, 86
Götterdämmerung, 51, 67, *67,* 107, 116
Gounod, Charles François, 12, 43, 46, 62, 111, 148
Graf, Herbert, 97, 121, *146,* 147, 158
Graf, Max, 147
Graham, Colin, 80
Graham, Martha, *20,* 21, 118, 248, 251, 267, 268; Dance Company, 251
Graham, Richard, 207
Gramm, Donald, *83,* 86, 124
Gramma Fisher Foundation, 256
Grande, John, 183, *183*
Grand Tier Restaurant, 34
Grau, Maurice, 46–47, *47, 228,* 229
Graves, Kimberly, 189, *190–91*
Greater Miami International Opera, 57
Greenway, Lauder, *37*
Greer, Frances, *234,* 235
Grisi, Giulia, 12, 80
Grist, Reri, *97c*
Grove's Dictionary, 44, 132
Guarrera, Frank, *65c,* 118, 152, *153,* 252
Guggenheim, Daniel, 23
Guggenheim, Florence, 23
Gustav III, King, 58
Guthrie, Tyrone, 62, 152, 154, *155,* 252
Gutman, John, 56, *57,* 111, 148, *260*
Guys, Constantin, 34
Gypsy Baron, The, 157

Hacker, Sander, 224–25
Hadley, William, *116–17*
Hagegard, Haken, *92, 93*
Hagen, Walter, 183
Halévy, Fromental, 142
Hall, Peter J., 64, 72, 80, 86, 96, 207, *211,* 256
Halmi, Arthur, 132, 141, 143
Hamburg Opera, 43, 58, 162, 173
Hamlet, 46
Hamlet (Shakespeare), 147, 268
Hammerstein, Oscar, 100
Hammerstein, Oscar, II, 196
Hansel and Gretel, 62, 67, 162, 211, *241c,* 252
Hardwicke, Cedric, 148
Harkness Ballet, 173

Harper, Elinor, 186, *187*
Harris, Cyril M., 23, 37–38
Harris, Julie, 20–21, *21*
Harrison, Wallace K., *24,* 25, 33, 37, 38, 57, 217
Hauser, Caroline, 202
Hauser, Christine, 202
Hauser, Judy, 202
Hauser, Lauren, 202
Hauser, Richard, 202, *202*
Hauser, Susan, 202
Haydn, Josef, 111
Haynes, Edward, *201, 207*
Hebert, Richard, 181
Heeley, Desmond, 68, 92, 168, *170,* 173
Heifetz, Jascha, 40, 58
Heinrich, Rudolf, 65, 67, 97, 168
Hempel, Frieda, *104*
Henahan, Donal, 268
Hepburn, Katharine, 92
Herbert, Jocelyn, 83
Herbert, Victor, 44, 143
Herbert-Förster, Therese, 44
Herman, Robert, 54, *54,* 57, *260*
Hermann, Jane, *251*
Hermann, Dr. John S., 251
Hertz, Alfred, 104, *105,* 108
Hertzog, Jack, *188,* 189, *190–91*
Heyes, Patricia, 189, *190–91*
Hicks, David, 37
Hill, Orrin, 189
Hines, Jerome, 80, *240c, 241,* 252
Hitler, Adolf, 112
Hoeflin, Eugenia, *174, 188,* 189, *190–91*
Hoffman, Malvina, 37, 143
Hofmann, Josef, 181
Hofmannsthal, Hugo von, 34
Holtzman, Elizabeth, 263
Homer, Louise, 51, 131, *131*
Honegger, Arthur, 111
Horne, Marilyn, 60, *64c,* 68, *70,* 76, *77,* 80, 91, 92, 95, *192c,* 212, *215,* 252, *256, 256c*
Horowitz, Richard, *179*
Horowitz, Vladimir, *250,* 251
Howard, Howard T., 176, *177*
Hubay, Alfred A., 247
Huguenots, Les, 47, 137
Humperdinck, Engelbert, 104, 241
Huneker, James Gibbons, 53
Hurok, Sol, 72, 248
Hyndman, Elihu M., 260, *261*

Indiana University, 53
Ingpen, Joan, 59
Instrumentalist, The (magazine), 181
Insull, Samuel, 117, 236
International Music Camp, 181
Irving Place Theater, 48
Isbrandtsen Lines, 253
Island of God, The, 158
Italiana in Algeri, L', 76, *77,* 173, 212
Ives, Charles, 38

Jacobsen, Edmund, 181
Janáček, Leoš, 76
Janks, Hal, *181*
Jenufa, 76, *77,* 127, 158
Jepson, Helen, 99
Jeritza, Maria, 54, *116–17,* 132, *135,* 138, 147
Jersey City State College, 204
Jessner, Irene, *234,* 235
Jeux d'Enfants (ballet), 193
Joardan, Vilhelm L., 37
Joffrey Ballet, 248
Joffrey II Ballet, 189
Johnson, Edward, ix, 52–53, *52, 53,* 54, 56, 112, 115, 118, 137, 138, 143, 176, 201, *234,* 235, *235,* 241, 258
Johnson, Lyndon B., 264
Johnson, Mrs. Lyndon B., *37*
Johnson, Philip, 23
Jones, Isola, *64c, 224*
Jones, Junetta, *260*
Jonny Spielt Auf, 132
Josefstadt Theatre (Vienna), 34
Journet, Marcel, 47, *230*
Jouvet, Louis, 148
Judd, George, 20, *21,* 141
Judson, Arthur, 118
Juilliard, A. D., 52
Juilliard School, The, 19, 20, *22,* 23, 43, 102, 138, 141, 182; Orchestra, 118; Theater, 23
Juive, La, 142, 143, 217
June Festival, 68, 72

Kahn, Otto H., 19, 51, 62, 147, 256, 258
Kane, Trudy, 176, *177*
Kanin, Garson, 148
Karajan, Herbert von, 67, 124–27, *124,* 196, 219
Karinska, 211
Katerina Ismailova, 92
Katzman, Bruce, 204, *204*
Kay, Richard, 176, *177*
Kaye, Danny, 57, 252, 253, 258, *259*
Keane, Audrey, 189, 192, *193, 193c*
Keane, Lorraine, 185, *185,* 186
Keene, Christopher, 127
Keilholz, Heinrich, 23
Keleman, Zoltán, *66,* 67
Kelley, Norman, 143
Kempe, Rudolf, 118
Kennedy, John F., 19, 116, 256; Center for Performing Arts, 21, 38, 248
Kennedy, Mrs. John F., 19
Kessler, Ingrid, 193
Khovanshchina, 173
Killam, Mrs. Izaak Walton, 256
King, James, 62, *97c*
King's Henchman, The, 111
Kirkland, Gelsey, 248, 249
Kirov Ballet, 248
Kirsten, Dorothy, 53, 127, 148, *234,* 235, *242,* 243, 263
Klein, Maureen Ting, *210,* 211 *224c*
Kliegl Brothers, 217
Klippstatter, Kurt, *212*
Knoll, Rudolf, *97c*
Kollo, René, 86, *96c*
Kolodin, Irving, 142
Königskinder, 104, *105*
Kónya, Sándor, 263
Kook, Eddie, 173
Korbel, Mario, 143
Kord, Kazimierz, 127
Koussevitsky, Serge, 127, 181
Kraft, Jean, *224, 240c*
Krause, Tom, 252
Krauss, Clemens, 67
Krawitz, Herman E., 34, 54, *54,* 57, 173, 217
Krehbiel, Henry E., 43, 104
Krips, Josef, 124
Krupa, Gene, 182
Kubelik, Rafael, *58,* 59, 67, 76
Kubiak, Teresa, *65c,* 76, *77*
Kuntner, Rudolph, *216,* 217

Lablache, Luigi, 80
La Forge, Frank, 137
La Guardia, Fiorello, 19
Lake George Opera, 268
Langlitz, David, *181*
La Scala, *see* Teatro alla Scala
Lasker, Mrs. Albert, 256
Lassen, Helen Lee Doherty, 32
Last Savage, The, 86, 158
Lauckner, Harold, *194,* 196
Laurence, Suzanne, *174, 188,* 189, *190–91*
Lauri-Volpi, Giacomo, 62, 137–38, 142
Lawrence, Marjorie, 52, 112, 142
Lawson, Nina, 211–12, *213, 215*
Lear, Evelyn, 60, 83, *240c,* 263
Lee, Gypsy Rose, 48
Lee, Ming Cho, 80, 83, 86, 96, 99, *173,* 256
Lehmann, Lilli, 43, 44, *45,* 103, 132, *140,* 141, 142
Lehmann, Lotte, 52, 54, 108, 121, 128, *129,* 132, 138
Lehmann, Peter, 168
Lehmbruck, Otto, 26
Lehnhoff, Nikolaus, 162, *162–63*
Leider, Frida, 108
Leinsdorf, Erich, 67, 72, 111, 158, *159,* 183
Leoncavallo, Ruggiero, 48, 68
Leoni, Franco, 138
Leonore Overture No. 3 (Beethoven), 68
Lerner, Edward R., 104
Leroux, Xavier, 111
Lessing, Gotthold Ephraim, 48
Levine, James, 40, *40,* 43, 59, 72, 80, 83, 91, 99, 108, 118, 127, 176, 181, 185, *192c*
Levine, Marks, *234,* 235
Levy, Diana, 189, *190–91,* 192, *193*
Levy, Marvin David, 60, 62, 168, *169*
Lewis, Earle R., 40, 53
Lewis, Mrs. Earle R., 40
Lewis, Henry, *126,* 127
Lewis, John L., 235
Lewis, William, *76,* 83, *84–85, 99*
Library and Museum of the Performing Arts, 19
Licameli, Mark Antonio, *194,* 196
Lichine, David, 193
Life (magazine), 31, 212
Lilac Garden (ballet), 193
Lillie, Beatrice, 148
Lincoln Center Festival, 57, 173
Lincoln Center for the Performing Arts, 12, *18, 19–26,* 32, 54, 56, 58–59, 103, 118, 124, 219, 226, 251, 260
Lincoln Center Plaza, 34, *36,* 37, 247
Lind, Jenny, 128, 132, *133,* 137, 143
Lindsay, John V., 263
Lipton, Martha, *234,* 235

List, Emanuel, 132, *134*
List Hall, 37, 176, 185, 218, 219, 253, *254–55*
Liszt, Franz, 44
Literary Digest, 112
Little Orchestra Society, 181
"Live from the Met," 167, 267, 271
Lloyd, David, 268
Lobmeyr, J. & L. (Vienna), 33, 34
Lohengrin, 44, 86, 91, *96c,* 115, 121, 141, 168, 173, 202, 211
London Festival Ballet, 248
London Symphony Orchestra, 43
Long, Huey, 138
"Look-ins," 252, 253, 258
López-Cobos, Jesús, 99, 127
Lorengar, Pilar, 86, *96, 96c*
Los Angeles Philharmonic, 127
Louis Calder Foundation, 263
Louise, 112, 132, 147, 189
Louis XIV, King, 51
Louisiana State University, 138
Love, Shirley, *64c, 224, 242,* 243
Lucia di Lammermoor, 127, 131, 132, 138, 141, 168, 263, 271
Ludwig, Christa, 62, *72,* 76, *97c,* 168
Ludwig, King, 92
Luisa Miller, 62, *68,* 162, 211, 271
Lulu, 43, 83–86, *83, 84–85,* 99, 179
Lunt, Alfred, 62, 64, 115, 148, 152, *152, 153,* 157, 225
Lutheran Church of the Good Shepherd, 186
Lynchburg College, 196
Lyric Opera of Chicago, 51, 52, 53, 91, 100, 108, 117, 173, 185, 236, 257

Maazel, Lorin, 121–24, *121*
Macbeth, 54, 158, 207, 252
McClintic, Guthrie, 80
McCormack, John, 143
McCracken, James, 60, *64c,* 72, 76, 80, 86, *87,* 91, *96c,* 99, 121, *192c, 242,* 243, 252, *256, 256c*
McIntyre, Donald, 91, *96, 96c*
Mackay, Donald A., 224
MacNeil, Cornell, *64c, 65c,* 80, 92, 212, *214–15,* 263
Macurdy, John, 72, *96c,* 99
Madama Butterfly, 48, 100, 118, 144, 158, 217, 263
Madeira, Jean, 252
Mlle, Modiste, 44
Magyar, Sarolta, 212, *213*
Mahler, Gustav, 51, 104, *105,* 107, 108, 111, 118, 138
Maillol, Aristide, 26, 244, 251
Mainsheet Eye (ship), *236–37*
Maison, René, 112, *113*
Makarova, Natalia, *248*
Maliponte, Adriana, 252, *256c*
Manchester *Guardian,* 83
Manhattan Opera, 100
Mankiewiecz, Joseph, 154
Manley, Jack, 236
Mann, Thomas, 80
Mannes College of Music, 141
Manon, 107, 111, 137, 158, 189
Manon Lescaut, 48, 51, 108, 112, 132, 143, 181, 198
Mansouri, Lotfi, 86
Manuel, Michael, 56
Man Without a Country, The, 103
Mapelson, Mrs. Lionel, *230*
Marcos, Ferdinand, *37*
Marcos, Mrs. Ferdinand, *37*
Marcus, Abraham, 176, 182, *182*
Marek, George R., 267
Mario, Giovanni, 12
Markevitch, Igor, 127
Markova, Alicia, *20,* 21, 148, *149,* 192
Marouf, 111
Marritt, Naomi, 189, *190–91, 193c*
Martha, 158, 162
Martinelli, Giovanni, 60, 131, 132, *135,* 137, 138, 142, 176, *232–33,* 235, 258
Martini, Nino, *234,* 235
Mary Flagler Cary Foundation, 263
Mascagni, Pietro, 21, 68, 185
Masefield, John, 193
Mason, Edith, 108
Masonic Funeral Music (Mozart), 108
Mass (Bernstein), 21
Massenet, Jules Émile, 86, 100, 127, 168
Materna, Amalia, 44, *44*
Matta, Elizabeth, 198, *199*
Matzenauer, Margarete, 91, *140,* 141
Mauceri, John, 127
Maurel, Victor, *47*
Meader, George, 111
Mechanic's Hall (Boston), 241
Medea, 56
Mehta, Zubin, 124, *125,* 168, *169*
Meistersinger von Nürnberg, Die, 44, 56, 103, 115, 141, 147, 162, 163–64, 181, 258
Melano, Fabrizio, 65, 83, 91
Melba, Nellie, 47, *136,* 137, 141
Melchior, Lauritz, 52, 54, 68, 108, *109,* 131, 132
Mendelssohn, Felix, 43
Menotti, Gian Carlo, 118, 158, 159
Mérimée, Prosper, 76
Merlin, 276
Merrill, Nathaniel, 60, 62, 64, 67, 68, 76, 97, 162, *162–63,* 163, 164, *164,* 241, 256
Merrill, Robert, 25, 53, 72, 111, 112, *113,* 118, *119,* 147, 152, 154, 252, 253
Merry Widow, The (ballet), 173
Messa da Requiem (Verdi), 112
Messel, Oliver, 121, 157, 162
Met Marathon, The, 251
Metropolitan Museum of Art, 268
Metropolitan Opera: audience and future of, 264–71; background of, 12–39; backstage (the "unseen army"), 194–225; ballet, 176, 189–93, *193c;* chorus, 176, 184–87; conductors, 100–27; directors and designers, 144–73; economics of, 244–63; first opening night (1883), ix; first performance (new house), 38; general managers of, 279; management of, 40–59; new house, Lincoln Center, *32c, 33c;* number of performances, 60; orchestra, 51, 100, 121, 176–83, 217; product of, 60–99; repertory, 274–77; singers, 128–43; televised performances, 59, 91, 115, 117, 167, 244, 251–52, 257, 267–68, 271; on tour, 226–43
Metropolitan Opera Association, 141, 258, 268
Metropolitan Opera Guild, 37, 52, 115, 143, 157, 217, 241, 251, 256, 258, 266, 267
Metropolitan Opera National Company, 56, 141, 158, 162
Metropolitan Opera Studio, 56, 59
Met T-shirts, 251
Meyer, Kerstin, 121
Meyerbeer, Giacomo, 86
Mielziner, Jo, 23, 80
Mignon, 112, 143
Milanov, Zinka, *19,* 53, 72, 112, *116–17,* 142, 252, 253
Miller, Gilbert, 34
Miller, Mildred, 185
Milnes, Sherrill, 62, *64c,* 68, *69,* 72, 80, 83, 86, *88–89,* 91, 92, *94–95,* 99
Mini-Met, 57
Minnelli, Liza, *251*
Minnesota Orchestra, 38
Mitropoulos, Dimitri, 118, *119,* 141
Mitzi D. Newhouse Theater, 23, 57
Moffo, Anna, *64,* 118, 263
Moiseiwitsch, Benno, 152
Moiseiwitsch, Tanya, 62, 64, 91, 152, 154
Molière, Jean Baptiste, 147
Monk, Allan, 91
Montemezzi, Italo, 107, 132
Monteux, Pierre, 111, *111,* 124, 154, 175
Monteverdi, Claudio, 174, 176
Montresor, Beni, 62, 86, 158, *159,* 163, 168
Moody, Michaux, 38
Moore, George S., 43–44
Moore, Grace, 51, 112, 131, 132, *133,* 137
Moore, Henry, 23
Moore, Richard L., 137
Morel, Jean, 43, 118, *118,* 121
Morgan, J. P., 48
Morgana, Nina, 132
Moroney, Clare, 247
Morris, James, *64c, 80,* 83, *257,* 258, *259*
Moscona, Nicola, 148, *149*
Moscow Conservatory, 181
Moser, Edda, *240c*
Moses and Aaron, 99
Mourning Becomes Electra, 60, 124, 168
Mozart, Wolfgang Amadeus, 25, 31, 108, 115, 121, 131, 138, 152, 163, 240, 268
Muck, Karl, 121
Munich Opera, 173
Munsel, Patrice, 148, 152, *153,* 156, 157
"Music Appreciation Hour," 103
Mussorgsky, Modest, 80, 107, 115, 118, 256
Muzio, Claudia, 60

Nabucco, 158, 162
Nagasaka, Motohiro, 158
Nagy, Robert, 118, *257c*
National Ballet of Canada, 248
National Broadcasting Company (NBC), 103, 258; Symphony Orchestra, 51
National Committee on United States-China Relations, 248
National Council of the Metropolitan, 256, 258, 260; Central Opera Service (COS), 260
National Endowment for the Arts, 263, 271
Natoma, 143

Naughty Marietta, 44
Neblett, Carol, *98,* 99
Neher, Caspar, 158, *159*
Nelson, John, 127
Netzer, Dick, 268
New England Conservatory of Music, 185, 212
New Philharmonia Orchestra, 43
Newsweek (magazine), 53, 92
New World Records, 57
New York City Ballet, 19, 23, 25, 92, 202
New York City Opera, 19, 23, 25, 56, 80, 92, 99, 186, 264
New Yorker, The (magazine), 258
New York Philharmonic, 19, 20, 25, 51, 111, 118, 124, 132, 182
New York State Council on the Arts, 263
New York State Theater, 19, *22,* 23, 25, *32c*
New York Symphony Orchestra, 102, 111
New York Symphony Society, 103
New York *Times,* 80, 91–92, 99, 104, 176, 224, 253, 263, 268
New York *Tribune,* 104
New York University, 173, 212, 268
New York *World,* 218
New York *World Telegram,* 112
Niemann, Albert, 44, *45*
Nijinsky, Vaslav, 193
Nikolaidi, Elena, 112
Nilsson, Birgit, *65, 66,* 67, *67, 96c, 97,* 118, 121, 164, 165
Nilsson, Christine, *42,* 43
Niska, Maralin, *65c,* 91
Noces, Les (ballet), 92
Norden, Betsy, *65c,* 86, *224, 256c*
Nordica, Lillian, 47, 143, 241
Norma, 12, 68, *70–71, 72,* 112, 137, 173, 223
Northwestern University, 185
Novara, Franco, *42,* 43
Novotná, Jarmila, 143
Nozze di Figaro, Le, 83, 112, 132, 137, 143, 147, 157, 158, 163, 185, 240
Nureyev, Rudolf, *248*
Nutcracker, The (ballet), 248, 249

Ober, Margarete, *104*
Odeon Théâtre (Paris), 240
Odinokov, Vladimir, 198, 199, *201*
Oedipus (Stravinsky), 141
Oenslager, Donald, 173, 251
Offenbach, Jacques, 121, 127
Offenkrantz, Paul, *256c*
O'Hearn, Robert, 60, 62, 67, 68, 97, 162, 163, *163,* 240, 241
Olivier, Laurence, 43
Once for the Birth of. . . (ballet), 189
O'Neill, Eugene, 62
Opera Arts Association (Atlanta), 185
Opera Café, 34
Opera Club, 34, 137
Opera Company of Boston, 127
Opera News (magazine), 176, 217, 218, 235, 258
"*Opera News* on the Air," 253
Opera Orchestra of New York, 248
Opera Week (Cleveland), 241
Oratorio Society, 102, 103
Orfeo, 174, 176
Orfeo ed Euridice, 111, 124, 131, 168, *240c*
Ormandy, Eugene, 54, 118, *118*
Ortiz, Joseph, *183*
Osborne, John, 43
Otello (Rossini), 173
Otello (Verdi), *64c,* 72, 83, 91, 112, 115, 121, 138, 147, *147,* 167, 173, 174, *175,* 186, 202, 207, 211, 212, 251, 271
Othello (Shakespeare), 43
Owl and the Pussycat, The (dance), 251

Paderewski, Ignace Jan, 38, 192
Pagliacci, 48, 62, 68, *69,* 117, 167, 251, 263, 271
Palmer, Lilli, 148
Panizza, Ettore, *112*
Papi, Gennaro, *232–33,* 235, 241
Paris Conservatory, 112
Paris Opera, 15, 31, 59, 62, 86, 219, 248
Park Theatre (New York), 12
Parsifal, 44, 48, 52, 68, 104, *104,* 108, 111, 115, 121, 147, 148, 162, 258
Patané, Giuseppe, 127
Patineurs, Les (ballet), 91, 192
Patrons of the Metropolitan Opera, 263
Patti, Adelina, *229*
Paul, St., 236
Paul Recital Hall, 23
Pavarotti, Luciano, *65c,* 68, 72, *73,* 80, *81,* 83, *90,* 91, 99, 173, *242,* 243, 252
Pavilion (Cleveland), 241
Pavlova, Anna, 37
Pears, Peter, 80, 99, *257, 257c*
Pearson-Smith, Virgil, 189, *190–91*
Pêcheurs de Perles, Les, 83
Pechner, Gerhard, *234,* 235
Peerce, Jan, 53, 107, 112, *234,* 235, 236, *237,* 263
Pelléas et Mélisande, 67, 72, *73,* 100, 108, 124, 127, 147, 173
Pelletier, Wilfred, 111, *232,* 235
Peloso, Antoinette, *188,* 189, *190–91*
Peltz, Mrs. John DeWitt, *216,* 217, 218
Performing Arts Company of the People's Republic of China, 248
Peri, Jacopo, 174
Perichole, La, 118, 121, *156,* 157
Perry, Commodore Matthew, 243
Perry, Seborn, 266
Perry, Virginia, 266
Peter Fellers Company, 225
Peter Grimes, 60, 62, 91, 127, 152, 154
Peter Ibbetson, 52, 111
Peters, Roberta, 121, 251, 263
Petina, Irra, 112, 148, *234,* 235
Petrouchka (ballet), 173, 176
Petrouchka (Stravinsky), 111
Philadelphia Opera, 147
Philadelphia Orchestra, 56, 112, 118
Philharmonic Hall, *see* Avery Fisher Hall
Philharmonic Society, 104
Phoebus and Pan, 112
Piccone, Jack, 207, *207*
Piccone, Ralph, 207, *207*
Pillar of Fire (ballet), 193
Pinza, Ezio, 92, 112, *130,* 131, 132, *234,* 235, 258
Piper, John, 80
Pique-Dame, 104, 158, 163, 168
Pirandello, Luigi, 225
Pittsburgh Symphony Orchestra, 115, 124
Pixley, Dorothy, *20*
Pizzi, Peter Luigi, 65, 91
Plançon, Paul, *228,* 229
Plasson, Michel, 86
Plishka, Paul, *65c,* 91, *256c*
Polacco, Giorgio, 108, 112
Ponchielli, Amilcare, 43, 62, 168
Ponnelle, Jean-Pierre, 99, 168, *171,* 173
Pons, Lily, 40, 131, 132, *135,* 138, 148, 236, *237*
Ponselle, Rosa, 40, 51, 52, 62, 80, 112, 128, 131, 132, 137, 176, *232–33,* 235
Poulenc, Francis, 83, 86
Powell, Thomas, *186*
Praetorius, Emil, 67
Pratt Institute, 196
Prêtre, Georges, *121*
Prey, Hermann, 124, *240c*
Price, Leontyne, 25, 60, *61, 64c, 68,* 80, 128, 168
Prideaux, Tom, 212
Prilik, Edith, *232–33,* 235
Prophète, Le, 43, 60, 86, *87,* 91, 127, 131, 257
Public Auditorium (Cleveland), 112, 236, *238–39,* 241
Public Broadcasting System (PBS), 65, 167, 257, 267–68, 271
Puccini, Giacomo, 48, 65, 67, 83, 91, 107, 111, 118, 128, 131, 132, 144, 145, 158, 164, 198, 268
Puritani, I, 80, 81, 83, 173, 211

Rabaud, Henri, 11
Rachmaninoff, Serge, 189
Radio City Music Hall, 181, 186, 225
Radio Corporation of America (RCA), 267
Raisa, Rosa, 107
Raitzin, Misha, *96c*
Rake's Progress, The, 154
Randall, Tony, 202
Rank, J. Arthur, 56
Rape of Lucretia, The, 80, 212
Raskin, Judith, 167
Rath, Hans Harald, *33,* 34
Ravinia Festival, 43
Reardon, John, 62, *63, 242,* 243
Reclining Figure (Moore), *23*
Ree, Jean van, 99
Regional Auditions Program, 260
Reine Fiammette, La, 111
Reiner, Fritz, 53, *114,* 115–16, 121, 127, 147, 154, 251, 252
Reinhardt, Max, 34, 86, 91, 147
Rennert, Günther, 158, *159,* 162–63, 240
Rensselaer, Kenneth van, 143
Reppa, David, 64, 65, 80, 83, 86, 92, *200,* 201, 202, 257
Reppa, Mary Ann, 198, *199, 200,* 201, *201,* 202
Resnik, Regina, 53, *97c,* 115, 158, 167, 263
Respighi, Ottorino, *110,* 111
Rethberg, Elisabeth, 52, 111, 115, *130,* 131, 132, 137, 258, 266
Reuben, David M., 59
Revere, Paul, 258
Rheingold, Das, 66, 67, 80, 121, 124, 176, 217
Riabouchinska, Tatiana, 193

Ricci, Luigi, 185
Ricciarelli, Katia, 212, *214*
Rich, Buddy, 182
Rich, Maria F., 260
Richard, Betti, 138
Richter, Karl, 121
Riecker, Charles, *58,* 59, 117, 212
Riecker, Wally Cleva, *116–17*
Rievman, Ellen, 189, *190–91*
Rigal, Delia, 112, *113,* 132
Rigoletto, 43, *64c,* 68, 91–92, 131, 147, 173, 186, 196, 263, 268, 271
Rimsky-Korsakov, Nikolai, 111
Rinehart, Jonathan, 67
Ring des Nibelungen, Der, 44, *66,* 67, *67,* 115, 121, 124, 253
Ritchard, Cyril, *156,* 157
Robert, Debby, *260*
Robin Hood Dell, 226
Robinson, Francis, *58, 116–17, 226, 234,* 235, 271
Rochester Symphony Orchestra, 111
Rockefeller, Mrs. John D., Jr., 256, 260
Rockefeller, John D., 3rd, 19, *37*
Rockefeller Brothers Fund, 263
Rockefeller Foundation, 57
Rodgers, Richard, 196
Roeger, Dave, *188,* 189, *190–91*
Rogers, Patricia, *180,* 181
Roi David, Le, 111
Romeo and Juliet (ballet), 248
Romeo and Juliet (Shakespeare), 80
Roméo et Juliette, 32, 62, 127, 173, 229
Rome Opera, 173
Roosevelt, Franklin D., 142
Roosevelt, Theodore, 230
Rosenkavalier, Der, 67, *97c,* 104, *104,* 121, 128, 132, 147, 162, 181, 251
Rosko, 137
Ross, Elinor, 263
Rossi-Lemeni, Nicola, 154
Rossini, Gioacchino, 76, 80, 143, *143,* 168, 173, 240
Rothier, Léon, 232–33, 235
Rougier, Michael, 31
Royal Academy of Dramatic Arts (Sweden), 57
Royal Ballet (England), 91, 162, 212, 248
Royal Court Theatre (London), 43
Royal Opera (Sweden), 57
Royal Opera House (Covent Garden), 43, 59, 72, 76, 80, 100, 116, 127, 154, 173
Royal Shakespeare Theatre, 59
Rubini, Giovanni-Battista, 80
Rudel, Julius, 253, *254–55,* 264
Rudolf, Max, 43, 53, 56–57, *57*
Rullman, Fred, *228,* 229
Ryan, Mrs. John Barry, 256
Rysanek, Leonie, 62, 68, *96c, 97c,* 99, 121, 158, 168, *170–71, 241c,* 252

Saarinen, Eero, 23
Sacre du Printemps, Le (ballet), 111, 118
Sadler's Wells Ballet. *See* Royal Ballet (England)
St. Denis, Ruth, 243
St. Leger, Frank, 53, 116, 141, *234,* 235
St. Louis Symphony, 38, 181
Salome, 48, 115, 118, 158, 168, 181
Salvatini, Mafalda, 148
Salzburg Festival, 43, 67, 111, 124, 147
Samson et Dalila, 62, 111, 121, 147, 162, 189, 224, 263
San Diego Opera Company, 99
San Francisco Opera, 43, 99, 173, 189, 257
San Francisco Symphony ,104, 111
Santiago, Anthony, 91
Sardou, Victorien, 67
Sargent, John Singer, 132
Saunderson, Mr. and Mrs. Alexander, 260, *261*
Sayão, Bidù, 132, 137, 185, 258
Scalchi, Sofia, *42,* 43
Schaffer, Peter, 43
Scheff, Fritzi, 47
Scheherazade (ballet), 173, 248
Schenk, Otto, 65, 67, 68, 92, 96, 168, *170–71,* 241
Schick, George, *260*
Schildkraut, Joseph, 68
Schiller, Johann Christoph Friedrich von, 48
Schippers, Thomas, 38, *39,* 62, 91, 118
Schneider-Siemssen, Günther, 67, 72, 92, 96, 168, *171*
Schoeffel, John B., 46–47
Schoenberg, Arnold, 99
Schoen-René, Anna Eugenie, 141
Schonberg, Harold C., 138, 268
Schorr, Dr. Eugene, 142
Schorr, Friedrich, 52, 108, 111, 142
Schuman, William, *20*
Schumann-Heink, Ernestine, 47, 91, 137, *141*
Schumer, Harry G., 183
Schütz, Willy, *228,* 229
Sciorsci, Lucia, 189, *190–91*
Scotti, Antonio, 47, 51, 131, 138, *138, 232–33,* 235, 241
Scotto, Renata, 59, 60, *65c,* 83, 91, 92, *94–95,* 252, 263
Sebastian, Stuart, 91
Seetoo, Dennis, 99
Seidl, Anton, *44,* 103–4, *103,* 137
Seidl-Kraus, Auguste, 103, *103*
Seligman, Vincent, 194
Sembrich, Marcella, 138, *140,* 141, *230*
Sequi, Sandro, 72, 80, 168, *170–71,* 173
Serafin, Tullio, 67, *110,* 111, 112, 243
Sereni, Mario, 167, 212, *214*
Setti, Giulio, 117, 176
Seventh Army Orchestra, 127
Shakespeare, William, ix, 38, 48, 60, 124, 147, 148, 164
Shapiro, Marilyn, 263, *263*
Shaw, Brian, 91
Shaw, George Bernard, 67, 148
Shawn, Ted, 168
Sheen, Archbishop Fulton, 86, 138
Sheridan, Margherita, 68
Shicoff, Neil, 92
Shindhelm, George, 212
Shouse, Jouett, 62
Siegfried, 46, 67, *67,* 111, 141
Siepi, Cesare, 72, *72,* 121, 142
Silberstein, Jascha, *180,* 181
Sills, Beverly, 76, *78–79,* 80, 83, *88–89,* 92, *93,* 99, 168, *170–71,* 173, *224c*
Simon Boccanegra, 112, 118, 131, 138, 141, 147, 148
Simonson, Lee, 115
Sixth Symphony (Mahler), 118
Skalicky, Jan, 257
Slavenska, Mia, 189
Sleeping Beauty, The (ballet), 162
Slezak, Leo, 137, 138, *140,* 141
Slezak, Walter, 137
Smetana, Bedřich, 257
Smith, Alma Jean, *224*
Smith, Mr. and Mrs. Dayton, 241
Society of the Friends of Music, 111
Sodero, Cesare, 117
Sodero, Edgardo, *182*
Solti, Sir George, 121
Sonnambula, La, 168
Sources of Music, The (Chagall), *32c*
Souvaine, Geraldine, *253*
Sparemblek, Milko, 240
Spectre de la Rose (ballet), 248
Spofford, Charles M., 19
Stade, Frederica von, 83, *240c*
Stanton, Edmund C., 46, *46*
Starr, Cornelius V., 158
Steber, Eleanor, 53, 111, 121, 152, *152,* 153, 158, 251
Steinberg, William, 124
Stella, Antonietta, *158*
Stevens, Risë, 53, 56, 132, 141, 148, 152, *154, 234,* 235, 251, 252
Stevens, Scott, *180,* 181
Stewart, Thomas, *66,* 67, 72, *73,* 263
Stiedry, Fritz, 53, 112, *113,* 148, 152, 260
Stilwell, Richard, 99, *257c*
Stivender, David, *124, 184,* 185, 186
Stocker, Christopher, 189, *190–91*
Stokowski, Leopold, 56, 118, *119, 164*
Story, Julian, 132
Stoss, Veit, 163
Stratas, Teresa, 62, 68, *69, 167, 241c, 257c,* 263
Stratford, Ontario, Festival, 173, 212
Strauss, Johann, 118, 189
Strauss, Josef, 189
Strauss, Richard, 34, 48, 60, 97, 108, 115, 116, 121, 128, *129,* 132, 137, 138, 168, 211, 268
Stravinsky, Igor, 111, 141, 182
Stuttgart Ballet, 248
Summer (Maillol), 26, *29, 245*
Sundelius, Marie, 185
Suor Angelica, 65c, 257
Surovy, Walter, 141
Sussman, Arthur, *181*
Sutherland, Joan, 68, *71,* 72, *73,* 76, *76,* 80, *81,* 83, 86, *86, 126,* 127, 137, 173, 243
Svanholm, Set, 115
Svoboda, Josef, 59, 76, 173, 256, 257
Swan Lake (ballet), 192
Swarthout, Gladys, 141
Sweeney, James, Sr., *204*
Sylphide, La (ballet), 163
Sylphides, Les (ballet), 148, 192
Szayer, Magda, 212, *213, 224c*
Szell, George, 43, 53, 112, 115, *115,* 121, 124

Tabarro, Il, 65c, 83
Talvela, Martti, 80, *256c, 257c*
Tamburini, Antonio, 80
Tanglewood, 183
Tannhäuser, 33, 91, 92, *96c,* 99, 115, 121, 131, 142, 185, 189, 235

Taplin, Frank E., *268*
Taubman, Howard, 176
Taussig, Walter, *224*
Tavernia, Patrick, 99
Taylor, Deems, 52, 111, 218
Taylor, Elizabeth, 154
Tchaikovsky, Peter Ilich, 163, 186
Teatro alla Scala, 15, 51, 76, 80, 100, 107, 118, 127, 173
Tebaldi, Renata, *62,* 67–68, 152
Tedlow, Mr. and Mrs. Samuel L., 256
Te Kanawa, Kiri, 83
Telva, Marion, 132, 137
Ternina, Milka, 104, *104*
Texaco, Inc., 247, 252, 253, 271
"Texaco Opera Quiz," 253, *254–55*
Thaïs, 86, *88–89,* 91, 99, 100, 257
Theatre, Television and Film Lighting Symposium, 217
Theatre Guild, 111
Theatre Network Television, 251–52
Thebom, Blanche, 152, *153,* 252
Theyard, Harry, 76, *78*
Third Symphony (Mahler), 118
Thomas, Ambroise, 46
Thomas, Jess, 67, *67,* 72, *96c,* 121
Thomas, Theodore, 104
Thorborg, Kerstin, 52, 108, 112
Tibbett, Lawrence, 51, 112, 131, 132, *134,* 258
Tobin, Mrs. Edgar, 256
Toffler, Alvin, 263
Tokatyan, Armand, 258
Toledo Opera Company, 189
Tolstoy, Leo, 100
Tomlinson, Nadine, 189, *190–91*
Tommy, the Who, 251
Toms, Carl, 99
Top of the Met, 34, 196
Tosca, 53, 56, 57, *65,* 67, 72, 118, 127, 138, 168, 176, 201, 263, 271
Toscanini, Arturo, 51, 106, 107–8, 112, 117, 127, 131, 137, 144, 145, 147, 173, 176, 185, 240
Toumanova, Tamara, 193
Tozzi, Giorgio, 62, 118, *119,* 121, 158, 168, *170–71, 241c,* 263
Traub, Dorothy, 243
Traub, Harold, 243
Traubel, Helen, 260
Traviata, La, 56, 62, *64,* 83, 117, 121, 127, 137, 173, 189, 204, 207, 236, 243, 260, 263
Traxler, Vieri, *116–17*
Trimble, Michael, *260*
Tristan und Isolde, 32, 44, 47, 51, 72, *96c,* 103, 104, 107, 108, *109,* 115, 116, 121, 147, 173, 260
Trittico, Il, 65, 83
Triumph of Music, The (Chagall), *30,* 31, 32
Trovatore, Il, 64, 68, 117, 121, 124, 162, 176, 186, 212
Troyanos, Tatiana, 83, *83*
Troyens, Les, 58, 76, 127, 162, 168, 179, 207, 211, *256c*
Tucci, Gabriella, 167, *240c*
Tucker, Richard, 53, 62, 68, *69, 116–17,* 142, *142,* 143, 152, *153, 154,* 168, 251, 252, *253,* 263
Tucker, Mrs. Richard, *116–17*
Tudor, Anthony, 176
Turandot, 40, 108, 111, 118, 124, 147, 162, 164, *165,* 263
Twentieth Century Fund, 268

University of Miami, 26
University of Minnesota, 212
Uppman, Theodor, 121, 124, 157, *157, 240c*
Urban, Joseph, *146,* 147, 217
Urbont, Charles, *181*

Vaghi, Giacomo, *234,* 235
Valency, Maurice, 157
Valletti, Cesare, 121, 251
Van Dam, Jose, *99*
Van Dyck, Sir Anthony, 132
Vanessa, 118, 131, 158, 252
Vanity Fair (publication), 37
Varnay, Astrid, *76, 77*
Veitch, Patrick L., *247,* 248
Velis, Andrea, *65c, 97c, 240c*
Verdi, Giuseppe, 12, 13, 32, 53, 54, 58, 64, 68, 72, 92, 112, 115, 124, 131–32, 147, 148, 158, 164, 167, 186, 268
Verrett, Shirley, 76, *78,* 80, 86, *90, 91,* 99, *256c*
Vesak, Norbert, 99, 189, *189, 193c*
Vespri Siciliani, I, 43, 58–59, 72, *74–75*
Vianesi, Auguste, 100, *100*
Viardot, Pauline, 141
Vickers, Jon, *60,* 62, *72,* 76, *241c, 256c, 257c*
Victor Book of the Opera, 186
Victoria, Queen, 47, 51
Vienna Conservatory, 108
Vienna Opera, 15, 26, 67, 105, 108, 117, 129, 173
Vienna Philharmonic, 112, 117, 132
Villa-Lobos, Heitor, 137
Villi, Le, 107
Vinay, Ramon, 115
Vivian Beaumont Theater, 19, 21, *23, 32c,* 57
Volpe, Joseph, *223,* 225
Votipka, Thelma, 236, *237*

Wagner, Dick, 207, 211, *211*
Wagner, Gisela, 207, 211, *211, 224c*
Wagner, Richard, 32, 44, 48, 67, 72, 86, 96, 99, 102, 103, 104, 107, 108, 111, 115, 118, 121, 128, 131, 138, 141–42, 168, 176, 268
Wagner, Wieland, 168
Wakhevitch, George, 67
Walker, David, 256
Walker, Edyth, *230*
Walküre, Die, 66, 67, 105, 121, 124, 127, 132, 137, 196, 219
Wallace, Mrs. DeWitt, 256
Wallenstein, Alfred, 43
Wallmann, Margherita, 168, *168*
Wally, La, 107
Walter, Bruno, 53, 54, 62, 112, *112,* 132, 137, 142, 260
Ward, David, *257c*
Wardwell, Allen, 258
Warner Brothers, 38
Warren, Leonard, 53, 54, 111, 112, 115, 138, *139,* 141, 142, 147, 152, 158, 185, 251, 252
Watermill (ballet), 92
Weaver, William, 253, *254–55*
Webster, Ben, 147
Webster, David, 157
Webster, Margaret, 147, 148, *149,* 251
Wechsler, Gil, *172,* 201
Weidinger, Christine, 76, *77*
Weikl, Bernd, *96c,* 99
Weill, Kurt, 99
Weintraub, Albert, *176*
Wekselblatt, Herbert, *176*
Welitsch, Ljuba, 53, *114,* 115, 148, 154, 157
Werfel, Franz, 12, 167, 264
Werther, 72, 127, 168
Wesker, Arnold, 43
West Berlin Opera, 121
Westermann, David, 115
Western Opera Theatre, 127
Wexler, Peter, 76, 86, 91, 168, *170,* 256, 257
Wharton, Edith, 12
"What Makes Opera Grand?," 271
Whitehead, Robert, *21*
Whitty, Dame May, 147
Wilhousky, Peter, 185
Williamson, John Finley, 185
Wilson, Robert, 251
Winkler, Robert, *196,* 198, *199*
Witherspoon, Blanche, 52
Witherspoon, Herbert, 52
Wixell, Ingvar, *65c,* 91
Woitach, Richard, 127
Wolf-Ferrari, Ermanno, 107
Wolf Trap, 62, 226, 264
Woollcott, Alexander, 86, 217
Wozzeck, 118, 127, 158, *160–61,* 193
WQXR (radio station), 251
Wymetal, Wilhelm von, *146,* 147

Yarborough, Dr. John M., Jr., 142
Yomiuri Shimbun (newspaper), 243

Zauberflöte, Die, 31, 32, 62, 118, 124, 158, 198, *240c*
Zeffirelli, Franco, 38, *39,* 60, 64, 68, 72, 124, 147, 164, 167–68, *167,* 207
Ziegfeld, Florenz, 147, 217
Ziegler, Edward, 53, *53,* 103, *232–33,* 235
Zimbalist, Efrem, 181
Zipprodt, Patricia, 92, 96
Zirato, Bruno, *116–17,* 132
Zylis-Gara, Teresa, *64c,* 72